A

PRACTICAL

ARABIC GRAMMAR.

BY

DUNCAN STEWART, Esq.

DARF PUBLISHERS – LONDON
1994

First Edition 1841
(John W. Parker)
New Impression 1994

British Library Cataloguing-in-Publication Data
A catalogue record for this book
is available from the British Library

ISBN 1 85077 168 5

*Printed and bound in Great Britain
by BPCC Wheatons Ltd., Exeter*

TO

THE BARON VON HAMMER AND PURGSTALL,

WHOSE

PROFOUND LEARNING AND VARIED TALENTS

. HAVE BEEN

SO LONG AND SO EARNESTLY DEVOTED TO THE SERVICE

OF

ORIENTAL LITERATURE.

THIS ATTEMPT

TO FACILITATE THE ʟSTUDY OF THE ARABIC LANGUAGE IN ENGLAND,

IS WITH GREAT RESPECT

DEDICATED

BY

THE AUTHOR.

PREFACE.

In composing the following Grammar, my intention has been, to supply the English student with a work calculated for the use of those, who not making the study of languages the chief pursuit of life, learn Arabic, less for the purpose of reading the many valuable books which it contains, than for its importance as the language of the Religion and Law of the Muhammadan world, and of absolute necessity to every one, who wishes to become a complete and accurate master of either Persian or Turkish.

In seeking to attain this end, I hope however the work will be found not unworthy the notice of those, desirous of obtaining a deeper and more minute knowledge of one of the finest of languages.

No Grammar that has yet appeared, combines, I think, these advantages; those compiled by the early Italian orientalists, Martellotto, Guadagnoli, and others, are abstruse and difficult, and, besides, are of such rare occurrence as to be almost confined to public libraries.

The Grammar of Erpenius is indeed an excellent performance, and comprises the rudiments of the language, arranged with great skill; yet how much it leaves to be supplied, may be readily supposed, when it is

known, that the Syntax occupies but nine small quarto
pages of large print.

Mr Richardson's Grammar, chiefly taken from that
of Erpenius, is the work of an acute and intelligent
mind; but it is very brief, and the erroneous system
upon which it is written, and by which the vowel points,
and rules of permutation, are considered to be of little
or no consequence, wholly disqualify it for the use of
those who wish to become accurate Arabic scholars.

The *Grammaire Arabe* of M. de Sacy, on the contrary, may be considered as wholly unfit for the use of
the beginner; it fills two volumes of six hundred large
octavo pages each, closely printed; nor does the mark
of the paragraphs, distinguishing those adapted for the
use of the young student, from those which are only fit
for the perusal of the advanced scholar, completely answer, it is conceived, the design of the learned author.
The eye becomes confused in looking over the pages,
and the attention is distracted by separating one para-
graph from another. It may even be doubted whether
the selection is always judicious: of the merits of this
great work, however, it is wholly unnecessary to speak
here, or to enlarge upon the services rendered to Arabic
literature by that amiable and learned man; no eulo-
gium of mine can equal the beautiful tribute paid to his
memory, by his friend M. Freytag, a gentleman to whom
oriental learning already owes such immense benefits.

The mantle of his prophet-master has indeed fallen upon him*.

The *Grammatica Critica* of M. Ewald, is unquestionably a work of great merit and research: but the plan of the author was to consider the Arabic, as in connection with its sister dialects of the Semitic family, and to investigate the causes of the language; and thus its execution qualifies it more for the study of the professed philologist, than for that of him who is engaged in active life.

I do not speak of the Arabic Grammar of Mr Lumsden, or of the very ingenious and learned, though somewhat whimsical work of Major A. Lockett. They will be found of great value to those who are already proficient in the language; but the first is incomplete, and the second contains only the translation of a treatise upon one part of Arabic Grammar; neither of them were intended to answer the purpose for which the present Grammar has been compiled.

---

* Viri illius de litteris Orientalibus merita plures verbis describere conati sunt; sed ut nemo vicem eius explere potest, sic nemo satis digno modo laudare eum mihi posse videtur. Quantis ego ei obstrictus eram beneficiis, tantas ei gratias persolvere nunquam valui. Eheu! praeceptore privatus sum, cuius sciendi fons nunquam exhauriebatur, fautore et amico in beneficiis apud me collocandis non fatigando, qui usque ad extremum vitae halitum benevolentiam mihi suam semper conservavit. Terra ei sit super ossa levis! *Arabum Proverbia*, Praef. iv.

By the exertions of eminent and accomplished scholars, during the last twenty years, many valuable Arabic works, which had hitherto been confined to four or five of the national libraries of Europe, have been printed, and are accessible to every student. To M. de Sacy we are indebted for the *Kalilah wa Dimnah*, and the *Makamát of Hariri*, with an excellent commentary.

M. Freytag has just published a beautiful and correct edition of all the proverbs of *Maidáni*; the same gentleman had before edited the *Fákihat ul Khuláfá*, and that precious collection of ancient Arabian poetry, the *Hamása*. His *Lexicon Arabicum* would have quite superseded that of Golius, had it appeared in one folio volume; four quartos are less adapted however for frequent use, although the inconvenience is in some degree remedied by the smaller Dictionary which M. Freytag has published in one volume. In India, Mr W. H. Macnaghten is publishing a correct edition of the 1001 *Nights*, in the original Arabic; and the liberal patronage of the Asiatic Society has enabled M. Flügel to give us in Arabic and Latin a fine edition of the great bibliographical work of Hajji Khalfa.

To our countrymen in India we are indebted for many works of the Arabian Grammarians, and for an edition of the *Kamús*; the orientalists of the continent have also printed several pieces of Arabic Grammar, including the *Ajrumia*, by M. Vaucelle, and the *Alfiyya*, by M. de Sacy, whose *Anthologie Grammaticale Arabe* would alone have entitled him to our gratitude.

This very slight view of the progress that has been lately made in publishing Arabic works, may suffice to shew that the scholar has now ample materials for study, and will be no longer deterred from devoting his time to this noble language, by reflecting, that when he has made himself a master of its Grammar, there is but little to reward him for his toil.

How far the present Grammar may assist the beginner it becomes not me to say; my endeavour has been, as I before observed, to avoid the extremes of brevity or prolixity. If the Syntax of Erpenius in nine pages be too short, the beginner will find that of M. de Sacy, which occupies five hundred pages, as much too long. Syntax, it seems to me, is that part of Grammar upon which the greatest labor is bestowed with the least fruit. I repeat, that to the advanced scholar, M. de Sacy's Grammar is of incalculable value, and will be found an excellent introduction to the study of the Arabian Grammarians and Commentators, but to him who has no intention of examining those authors, or who is beginning the study of Arabic, I consider it as less useful than even the old work of Erpenius; defective as that book may be, it has hitherto been the only one well adapted for the use of a beginner desirous of acquiring a correct knowledge of the language. Imperfect as my own experience may be considered, I may presume to speak of it, having in early youth been guided by the advice of Sir W. Jones, who, in his discourse upon the Arabs, recommends the student, after having made himself a master of the Grammar of Erpenius, to proceed with the assistance of the Lexicon of Golius, to read through that author's edition of the *History of Tímúr*, by Ibnu Arabsháh. This course of study I rigorously followed, substituting only the more portable Lexicon of Willmet, to the accuracy of which I can bear full witness; and taking occasionally the assistance of the edition of Arabsháh by Manger. That I often erred, and that much more grammatical knowledge than Erpenius affords, is desirable, and even requisite, for him who wishes to properly understand and appreciate the life of Tímúr, is unquestionable: but the advice of Sir W. Jones is not to be treated lightly, or his authority to be considered of little weight, because in the course of his vast and varied reading he may sometimes err.

The student is however now provided, as I have observed before, with every assistance he can require; and I should recommend him first to read the *Fákihat ul Khulafá* of Arabsháh, published by M. Freytag. I do not recommend the Korán, the enigmatical and abrupt style of which renders it unfit for the learner, whom it will, besides, supply with a very small stock of words.

I have not thought it necessary to expatiate upon minute orthographical points, belonging almost wholly to manuscripts of the Korán, or to enter into long details upon the divisions and subdivisions *ad infinitum*, of the Arabian Grammarians. However ingenious the writings of those authors, it is much to be regretted that their attention was so extensively directed to such learned trifles; there can, I think, be no doubt that their waste of time and talent upon the metaphysical subtleties of Grammar, had a most unhappy effect in diverting them from the more important and useful pursuits of science, in the cultivation of which, although they did much, we should have owed still more to them, had they not forgotten that Grammar is to be considered as a means, and not as an end.

It will be observed, that in the Paradigmata of the verbs, I have given, conformably with the plan of Erpenius, the verbal adjective as a participle, and the noun of action in the accusative, as an infinitive. There has, I presume to think, been much needless discussion upon this subject; Erpenius, though exhibiting them as participles and infinitives, in consequence of their verbal origin, confesses they must be regarded, strictly speaking, as the verbal adjective and noun of action; and M. Ewald, very properly, I think, considers that M. de Sacy has gone too far in separating them entirely from the verb, although they do not wholly answer to the ideas attached to the words participle and infinitive in the Latin Grammar. I have more particularly enlarged upon their nature and qualities under the heads of verbal adjective, and noun of action.

I have not, however, employed myself in discussing subjects of this, as it seems to me, unprofitable nature. I am wholly of Major Lockett's opinion, "Theoretical disquisitions are good in their proper place, but they are not in their proper place in an elementary treatise, which should aim rather at the illustration of specific rules, than the discovery or examination of abstract principles." *The Miut Amil*, by A. Lockett.

CONTENTS.

CORRIGENDA AND ADDENDA.

PAGE 23, note, line 2, *for* final *read* initial, and add—M. de Sacy probably specifies only the initial and medial letters, because the final ف and ق are often written without any point whatever.

Page 30, line	18	*for*	اِتِّسام	*read*	اِتّسام
62	9, 11	...	صيغةٌ	...	صيغة
73	7	...	أنَّى	...	أنَّى
75	11	...	لِنَقتُلَن	...	لِنَقتُلَن
96	10	...	تاكُل	...	تاكُل
111	3	...	Hamzah's	...	Hamzahs
133	19	...	graize	...	graze
145	16	...	اَلْ اِسْم	...	الاسم

164, last line *after* "servile letters"—*add* sometimes

175, line	6	*for*	غُلَاميةٌ	*read*	غُلَاميه
179	3	...	الأيلَّ	...	الليل
188	13	...	لَا	...	ال
208	20	...	here	...	there
218	7	...	ينفِح	...	ينفِخ
224	16	...	ثلاثة	...	وثلاثة and
...	... ...	...	سِت	...	سِت
226	14	...	Wednesday	...	Tuesday

A PRACTICAL GRAMMAR

OF THE

ARABIC LANGUAGE.

———

The Arabic Alphabet consists of twenty-eight letters, differently shaped, according to their position at the beginning, middle, or end of words; the names and powers, the order and figure of which may be seen in the following Table.

				Final.		Medial. Connec.	Initial.	Numerical value.	Hebrew.	Syriac.
				Connec.	Uncon.					
1	A	اَلِف	Alif	ا	ا	ا	ا	1	א	ا
2	B	بَاء	Ba	ب	ب	بـ	بـ	2	ב	ܒ
3	T	تَاء	Ta	ت	ت	تـ	تـ	400	ת	ܬ
4	Th	ثَاء	Tha	ث	ث	ثـ	ثـ	500	תּ	ܬ
5	J	جِيم	Jim	ج	ج	جـ	جـ	3	ג	ܓ
6	H	حَاء	Hha	ح	ح	حـ	حـ	8	ה	ܚ
7	Kh	خَاء	Kha	خ	خ	خـ	خـ	600	כ ך	ܟܚ
8	D	دَال	Dal	د	د	د	د	4	ד	ܕ
9	Dz	ذَال	Dzal	ذ	ذ	ذ	ذ	700	דּ	ܕ
10	R	رَاء	Ra	ر	ر	ر	ر	200	ר	ܪ
11	Z	زَاء	Za	ز	ز	ز	ز	7	ז	ܙ
12	S	سِين	Sin	س	س	سـ	سـ	60	ס	ܣ
13	Sh	شِين	Shin	ش	ش	شـ	شـ	300	שׁ	ܫ
14	S	صَاد	Sad	ص	ص	صـ	صـ	90	צ	ܨ
15	D	ضَاد	Dad	ض	ض	ضـ	ضـ	800	צּ	ܨ
16	T	طَاء	Ta	ط	ط	طـ	طـ	9	ט	ܛ
17	D	ظَاء	Da	ظ	ظ	ظـ	ظـ	900	טּ	ܛ
18	Â	عِين	Ain	ع	ع	عـ	عـ	70	ע	ܥ
19	Gh	غِين	Ghain	غ	غ	غـ	غـ	1000	ג	ܓ
20	F	فَاء	Fa	ف	ف	فـ	فـ	80	פ ף	ܦ

TABLE.

			Final.		Medial. Connec.	Initial.	Numerical value.	Hebrew.	Syriac.
			Connec.	Uncon.					
21	K	قَاف Kaf	ق	ق	ﻗ	ق	100	ק	ܩ
22	K	كَاف Kef	ک	ک	ک	ک	20	ך כ	ܟ ܟ
					ک	ک			
23	L	لَم Lam	ل	ل	ﻟ	ل	30	ל	ܠ
24	M	مِيم Mim	م	م	ﻤ	ﻣ	40	ם מ	ܡ
25	N	نون Nun	ن	ن	ﻨ	ﻧ	50	ן נ	ܢ
26	W	وَاو Waw	و	و	و	و	6	ו	ܘ
27	H	هَاء Heh	ه	ه	ﻬ	ﻫ	5	ה	ܗ
					ﻪ	ﻫ			
28	Y	يَاء Ya	ي	ي	ﻴ	ﻳ	10	י	ܝ
	Lá	لَم اَلِف	لا	لا					
				ﻼ					

Short Vowels a ◌َ   i ◌ِ   u ◌ُ

Long Vowels a ا ◌َ   i (ee) ◌ِ ي   u و ◌ُ

1	2	3	4	5	6	7	8	9	0	1840
١	٢	٣	٤	٥	٦	٧	٨	٩	٠	١٨٤٠

These figures, which are called رقم هَنْدِي or Indian ciphers, are used in preference to the inconvenient mode of the letters of the Alphabet. They are written from left to right, as may be seen by the date 1840. This is a sufficient indication of their foreign origin.

OBSERVATIONS ON THE ALPHABET.

THE Arabic Alphabet, like those of the other Semitic nations, is composed of consonants alone. The letters ا, و, and ي, often indeed appear to perform the part of vowels ; but that term is really correct, only when applied to the three points, which will be described hereafter.

The character here used, is that which is named *Naskhi* نَسخِى, the only one employed in printed Arabic, and of which all others are but variations, chiefly made for the purpose of ornament.

Among these the *Shulsí*, شُلسى, is peculiar to Inscriptions, the titles of books, &c., and is distinguished by the greater size and thickness of the letters, and by the elegance of its flourishes.

The *Taâlik* تَعلِيق, is the beautiful flowing character used in Persian poetry, and the *Shakastah* شَكَستَه or broken, is a careless scrawl, also used in Persian, and in which the diacritical points distinguishing the various letters, are almost wholly neglected. These two last are employed in writing Persian only. The Arabs being great admirers of Calligraphy, have however other variations, but as these are confined to manuscripts, and easily to be distinguished, as formed from the *Naskhi* it is not deemed necessary to dwell upon them here.

The order in which the letters are placed in this Alphabet, is not that which has always prevailed; a more ancient one is known by the technical term *Abujad*, which is the first of the following eight unmeaning and imaginary words, اَبَجَدٍ هَوَز حَطِّى كَلَمَن سَعَفَص قَرَشَت ثَخَذ ضَظَغ. According to this arrangement it is that the letters are used as numerals.

The African Arabs have an *Abujad* somewhat different from that which belongs to Asia, but it may be here observed that by the term of Arabs of Africa, not those of Egypt, but of Western Africa (Maghrib) are always to be understood. The *Lám-Alif* is added to the Alphabet, merely to shew the peculiar mode in which the *Alif* is included in, or added to the *Lám*.

The various columns in which the Alphabet appears, shew, 1st, their order; 2nd, their names; 3rd, 4th, 5th and 6th the different forms which each letter assumes, as being 1st, wholly isolated; 2nd, joined to the preceding letter; 3rd, joined to the preceding and following; 4th, joined only to the following one. Some letters, it will be seen, are never joined to their succeeding one, though when ز ر ن د and و are followed by ه at the end of a word they may be joined together.

Several letters are distinguished from others of the same shape by the addition of one or more points; these, which the Arabians denominate نقطة, *noktah*, we call diacritical, or distinctive. As these points are frequently omitted by the carelessness of transcribers, proper names are often minutely described by Arabian authors; every letter being carefully enumerated, and the vowel points ascertained; in such cases, as an additional precaution, those letters which resemble others in form are distinguished by the epithets مُهْمَلَة, *without points*, (diacritical,) and مُعْجَمَة *pointed**.

To avoid the mistakes which may arise from the similarity of different letters, other means are also used; the letters د ر س are marked thus نْ رّ سّ; and ح ص ط ع are repeated in smaller characters underneath. This sometimes distinguishes س also, or three points are written below it پس; these precautions are however only to be found in the most accurate manuscripts, but it is not to be supposed that the want of them, leaves any great difficulty to be surmounted; he who is well acquainted with but a few of the many books now printed, will find little difficulty in reading manuscripts, which are, after all, seldom so badly written as to offer much obstacle to the Student.

The African character differs little from that of Asia, but in the former, the letter ف initial or medial, has the diacritical point below ڡ ڢ; ق in the same places has only one point above ڧ ڧ†. The Africans sometimes use the three letters ج ق and

---

* Thus in the History of Tímúr,

اِسْمُهُ تِيمُور بِتَاءٍ مَكْسُورَةٍ مُثَنَّاةٍ فَوْقًا و يَاءٍ سَاكِنَةٍ مُثَنَّاةٍ تَحْتًا

و وَاوٍ سَاكِنَةٍ بَيْنَ مِيمٍ مَضْمُومَةٍ و رَاءٍ مُهْمَلَةٍ.

His name was Tímúr, with *Tá* having *Kasrah,* and two points above; and *Yá* quiescent, with two points below; and *Wáw* quiescent, between *Mím* bearing *Dammah,* and *Rá* without any points.

† I give this upon the authority of M. de Sacy, not having had myself the opportunity of examining African manuscripts. Erpenius

ت with three points above, or beneath; they then have the pronunciation of our g in *get*, or *guard*; by the addition of these points below they also give to the letter ش, the sound of our *ch* in *chip*, *charm*, &c. ڜ

The Arabic, like the Hebrew, and many other Eastern languages, is written from right to left.

No combination of letters, or directions for using the organs of speech, can convey all the sounds of the Arabic Alphabet correctly; nor, were it possible, would it be easy to decide what standard of pronunciation was to be preferred to all others. The Arabic language is that of the religion and law of Muhammadan states, from the Ganges to the Straits of Gibraltar and the banks of the Danube; from Cape Comorin to Chinese Tartary; it is not only pronounced in various ways by these various people, but even near its native deserts, great differences exist in the sounds given to many of its letters. In the towns the pronunciation is far from being as correct as among the Bedouins. Baghdád discriminates د, ن, ض and ظ, while Aleppo makes ذ, ظ and ز nearly the same, but ض like د. Egypt sounds ج hard, like *g* in *go*, and ل in some parts of Syria is pronounced like ش, *Markab*, or *Marshab*.

These variations however are of no great consequence; he who uses the mode prevailing at Delhi, will find no difficulty whatever in conversing with a native of Fez or Morocco*.

---

makes no such distinction as to this taking place, only in medial, or final ف and ق; both he and M. Ewald give it as a general rule, whether those letters be initial, medial, or final.

* Mr Lumsden notices the difficulty which a native of India has to understand an Arab; it is within my own knowledge, however,

The-most harmonious pronunciation indeed is that of the learned of Turkey and Persia, who soften down those hard and guttural letters, to which they find it so difficult to give the genuine Arabic sounds.

Alif, when attended by *Hamzah* ء (see p. 32), is the soft breathing of the Greeks, or English *h* not aspirated, and is a species of consonant always accompanying the vowels which are preceded by no other consonant. When unaccompanied by *Hamzah*, *Alif* is employed to lengthen the vowel *Fathah*, or *A*, which goes before it.

ب and ت are precisely our *b* and *t*.

ث this letter, though said to have the power of our *th* in *thing*, is, among the Arabs themselves, almost always pronounced like ت ; some even consider the first sound as vicious. The Turks and Persians pronounce it like *S*.

ج answers to our *j* in *jest*, &c. In Egypt, as has been before said, it is pronounced like hard *g* in *get*, *give*, &c. This prevails also at Maskat, and some other places.

ح is our *h* strongly aspirated or slightly guttural.

خ this is the German *ch*, as in the words *Nacht*, *Buch*. Among the Turks and Persians, it is however much softened and reduced to almost the simple *h*. خط is by them pronounced حط ; we express it by the letters *kh*, as in خليفة *Khalif*.

---

that the native Professor at Haileybury, some years back, conversed fluently with a merchant of Algiers, and the latter being asked if they understood each other easily, replied with great signs of astonishment, "Understand each other! pourquoi non?"

د is our *d*.

ذ this generally corresponds, like the preceding, with our *d*; some, however, as the Arabs of Maskat, give it the sound of our *z*, which is also done by the Turks and Persians.

ر is exactly our *r*, and ز our *z*.

س is our *s* and ش *sh*.

ص is the letter *s*, with a stronger articulation than س, which however it so much resembles, as to be often confounded with it.

ض answers among the Arabs to our *d*, uttered with a kind of emphasis; the Turks and Persians use it as another *z*.

ط is a strong *t*.

ظ differs nothing from ض, for which it is often written. In Egypt, as always among the Turks, it becomes *z*.

ع the articulation of this letter is given up by all our grammarians, as impossible to be conveyed to European ears; it is a stronger kind of *Hamzah* or guttural *a*; by the operation of the vowel points it often takes the sound of *i*, *o*, or *u*.

غ this is best represented by the letters *gh*, though in some countries rather taking the sound of *rh*.

ف is our *f*.

ق is nearly our *k*, receiving, however, among many of the Arabs, a guttural emphasis, which it would be as difficult as it is useless to attempt to imitate. Those of Maskat, Morocco, and other places, confound it with غ.

ك is our *k*; many of the Arabs soften it into the French *q*, in *queue*, *qui*; and this is the practice among the Turks, who insert, as it were, a short *i* after it when it comes before ا or و:

as كاغد *Kiághit, paper* ; ملوكانه *Mulúkiánah, royal* ; at Maskat, it becomes a hard *g*, so as to be by those Arabs confounded with ج and ق.

ل *l* ; م *m*.

ن before ا ح خ ع غ ء , sounds like the English *n*, which is its natural articulation, or what the Arabian grammarians call إظهار or *manifestation*. When followed by ب it becomes *m*, and when it precedes any of the letters forming the technical word لومير it takes the sound of the following letter, as من بَيتٍ *mim baitin* ; منمّحس *mir rabbin* ; مِن رَبٍّ *mil lailin* ; مِن لَيلٍ *mummahisun* ; أن يتقدم *ayyatakaddama* ; منوّال *mauwalun*. Before all the other letters it sounds like *ng* in the word *bring* ; as مِن طينٍ *ming tinin*.

و is among the Arabs pronounced like our *w* ; with the Turks and Persians it is *v* ; when quiescent, and following *Dammah*, it becomes a long *u*.

ء is *h* with a very slight aspiration ; when at the end of words and surmounted by two points, it generally marks the feminine gender, and is pronounced like ت , *t* ; being generally changed to that letter by the Persians and Turks, when they borrow such words from the Arabic.

ى is our *y*, as in *yelp, yonder*. When quiescent and following *Kasrah* it coalesces with that vowel, and is pronounced like *ee*.

On the Different Classes of Letters.

The Alphabet may be divided under the heads of pronunciation, strength, affinity, office, and society.

1st. Six letters are called *Gutturals* ه غ ع خ ح ا; four, *Labials* و م ف ب; four, *Palatials* ى ل ق ج; eight, *Dentals* ش ص ض ر ز س; and six, *Linguals* ت ث د ذ ط ظ ل ن. The *Dentals* and *Linguals* are called solar letters, the rest lunar.

2nd. *Strength*. The three letters ا و ى are called *infirm letters*, حَرُوفُ ٱلْعِلَّةِ being considered as having no sound but what they receive from the vowel points, either attending themselves or the preceding letters. All the others are stiled robust.

3rd. *Affinity*. Some letters are permutable, being such in general as are formed by the same organs, as ص with س, د with ت, but particularly ا و ى; which are often substituted one for another.

4th. *Office*. Some are denominated Radical, others servile; the Radicals are sixteen, ق غ ع ظ ط ض ص ز ش ر ث ج ح خ د ذ, and are so called, because they are never found excepting in the roots of Arabic words. The rest are called serviles, being employed in forming the derivatives, and other inflexions from the roots. The servile letters, however, are often Radicals, particularly in the imperfect verbs, but the Radicals are never serviles, excepting ط and د, which are sometimes substituted for ت.

5th. *Society*. Some are compatible, which may follow one another in the same word; the others cannot, and are therefore called incompatible. These consist of the *Gutturals* ه غ ع

خ ح (though ه is sometimes subjoined to ع) together with the following :

ب with ف and م.

ث   ظ and ط ض ص س ت.

ج   غ ق and ل.

خ   ظ ق and ل.

د   ن.

ذ   ظ and ط ض ص.

ر   ل.

ز   ظ and ض ص.

س   ض and ص.

ش   ض.

ص   ظ and ط ض.

ض   ظ and ط.

ط   ل and ظ.

ظ   ق and غ.

غ   ل and ق.

ق   ل.

ل   ن { except لَنْ *by no means.*
           and عَلَنَ *he manifested.*

The servile letters in the above list, are only included as incompatibles when they constitute part of the root of any word ; for when acting as serviles, they may be joined with any letter, as بِفِضَّةٍ *in silver :* كَقَوْلِكَ *as you say.* These observations may be of some use in manuscripts, where the diacritical points are either neglected, or irregularly placed ; as also in fixing ambiguous meanings and distinguishing the pure from the corrupted Arabic.

Of Vowels.

The Arabians have only three characters for vowels, which they call *Fathah* فَتْح or فَتْحَة, *Kasrah* كَسْر or كَسْرَة, and *Dammah* ضَم or ضَمَّة. The first represented by a small oblique line over the letter, the second by a similar stroke under the letter, and the third by a small curve like a comma.

Fathah	sounding as ă	تَ
Kasrah	ĭ	بِ
Dammah	ŭ	بُ

These are sometimes doubled in the final letters, which is called تَنْوِين *Tanwín*, or *nunnation*, because pronounced as if terminated by ن; as رَجُلٌ Rajulun, *a man*, رَجُلٍ Rajulin, *of a man*, رَجُلًا Rajulan, *a man*; the first marks the nominative case of substantives, adjectives, or participles; the second the genitive, and the third the accusative, as also infinitives and nouns placed adverbially.

Although it be impossible to fix precisely the circumstances in which the Arabian vowels represent a sound more or less open, it may be observed in general that *Fathah* is pronounced somewhat like *a* in the word *all*, and *Dammah* like *oo* in *moon*: when these two vowels are placed over a guttural or hard consonant, or immediately precede such an one, the letters which produce this effect are the following: ظ ع غ ق ح خ ص ض ط. In other places *Fathah* frequently takes a sound resembling *e* in *scene* or *ai* in *gain*; and *Dammah* is pronounced like *u* in *but*, *o* in *above*, or *ou* in *rough*. These distinctions however are seldom observed; *Fathah* usually receives the sound of our English short *a* in *rap* or *bat*, and *Dammah* is pronounced almost always like *u* in *but*.

Kasrah has the short sound of *i* in *thin*, but never that of the English *i* in *thine*.

When those vowels are placed over any letter preceding ا و ى quiescent, that is, without vowels, they coalesce with them, their respective sounds being lengthened; as قَار *kār*; قُور *koor*; قير *keer*.

ا و ى are said to possess their homogeneous or natural vowels when *Fathah* is placed over or precedes ا; *Kasrah* ى; and *Dammah* و; if otherwise, they are called heterogeneous or dissimilar; when the dissimilar vowels *precede* those letters quiescent, they either form diphthongs with them, as لَيْل *night*; جوهر *a jewel*; or remain silent, as مَتَى *when*; but when they have vowels placed *over* them, they assume, like other consonants, the sound of such superscribed vowels, whether natural or dissimilar; as اتْسام Ittisámun, *the assuming a badge*, or *marking one's self*; انصر Unsur, *assist thou*; وزراء Wuzará, *Vazirs*; وبر Wabara, *he delayed*; يَمين Yamín, *the right hand*; يضرب Yadrubu, *he strikes*.

It must be observed that و and ى, preceded by *Fathah*, often take the place of long *Alif*, as صلوة *prayer*; رَمَية *he threw him*; for صلاة and رَمَاه. In such cases these letters do not bear *Jazmah*, a mark which will be spoken of in the next article.

The long *Alif* is sometimes omitted in the middle of words,

such omission being indicated by the *Fathah* being placed perpendicularly, as هدا ,هاذا ,زمن ,رَصَان. These three letters
of prolongation perform that office, and are then called
حروف آلمَدّ letters of extension, chiefly in the beginning and
middle of words; when belonging to the last syllable, as in
قَلْبِى ,تَفْزُو ,دَعا their effect is not very perceptible. They
however, in all cases, compose long syllables in poetry.

Of Syllables and Orthographical Signs.

Syllables are divided into pure and mixed, the pure consisting of only one consonant and one vowel, as بَ بِ بُ; the
mixed of two consonants, joined by one vowel, as لَنْ *lan*;
مِنْ *min*; هُمْ *hum*; no syllable in this language either beginning with a vowel, or consisting of one simply. Over the second
letter of every mixed syllable is placed the following character
(ْ) called

Jazmah جَزْم or *amputation*, so named, because it sepa-
rates the artificial syllable at the end of which it is found,
from the syllable following; it is also called سكون *sukún* or
rest. The second letter of the mixed syllable is not expressed
when followed by another of the same kind, but is represented
by a character named

Tashdíd تَشْدِيد (ّ) signifying *corroboration*, which doubles
the letter over which it is placed, as نَزَّل, where the two ز

coalesce, instead of being written نَزْزَل . This character may be
put over any letter but ا, and is used, first, in the coalition
of two similar letters as above. Secondly, when ت follows د;
in order to avoid a harshness of sound, as وجَدْتَّ Wajattu.
Thirdly, when any of the solar letters follow the article أَلْ,
as اَلدِّينِ Addínu, *the faith*; اَلشَّمْسُ Ashshamsu, *the sun*; and
fourthly, when ن Jazmated or the nunnation points, precede
any of the letters in the technical word لَوْمَير, as مِن لِسانِ
millisani, &c. In all which cases the preceding letter loses its
own, and takes the sound of that over which *Tashdíd* is placed.

Hamzah هَمْزَة (ء) is only another name and form for ا,
and is made subservient to it in a variety of respects; it always
accompanies the vowel which attends ا, as أَضْرِبُ ,أَبيضَ.

When و and ى take the place of *Alif* moveable, *Hamzah*
is placed above those letters; as, جِئْت ,مُوٴِس . In such cases
it is more regular to suppress the points of the ى thus قائِل and
not قائِل .

It often occurs that instead of writing either ا or the و
or ى with *Hamzah* substituted for it, as has been just said,
the *Hamzah* only is written, and the letter which should ac-
company it is suppressed.

This happens, (1) often in the middle, and always at the
end of words, after a letter of prolongation, or a letter jazmated,
as مَقروٴَة ,مَوٴباتِ ,توٴَم ,رِدٴ ,شىٴ ,ضوٴ ,جِى ,سوٴ ,جاٴ

(2) In the middle of words, after an *Alif* of prolongation, every time that *Hamzah* has *Fathah* for its vowel, as أَعداءَكم, تفاءَلوا, يتَساءَلون.

(3) In the middle, and at the end of words, when two و or two ى meet, of which the second would be quiescent if the letter bearing *Hamzah* were not suppressed خاسِيِّين for خاسِئِين, بدوُّا for بدوُؤا, رووس for رؤوس.

(4) In the middle of words, when *Hamzah* has *Fathah* for its vowel, and is immediately preceded by a letter bearing *Jazmah*, to which the vowel of the *Hamzah* is carried, the articulation of *Hamzah* being quite suppressed

سواقَ for سوءَة, مسالة for مسألة.

The suppression of و and ى in the cases noticed under (3) is not constantly observed, and such words are often written رووس &c.

Wasla (ﺻ) وَصل, implies conjunction, and is only inscribed over *Alif* at the beginning of a word, to mark an union with the preceding one, *Alif* being then silent, as بَيت المَال. *Alif* is superscribed with *Wasla*, first in the imperative of the first conjugation. Secondly, in the preterite active, imperative, and infinitive, of the derivative conjugations of the second and third classes. Thirdly, in the following ten nouns: إمرَا امرَأ *a man*; *a woman*; إبن *a son*; إبنة *a daughter*; إبنم *a son*; اثنَان *two*, (masc.), اثنَتان *two*, (fem.) إسم *a name*; إست *the buttocks*;

3

ايمَن *an oath;* and lastly in the article اَلّ; in all which cases, unless beginning a sentence, or following the article, the initial ١, is not pronounced, the subsequent letter being always jazmated and united in pronunciation to the vowel with which the preceding word ends, as يد أمرأة *the hand of a woman,* ١ being sometimes even altogether omitted, as حدَّث ٱلحرث بن همَّام. *Harith, the son of Hammám, related.* It is also dropped when the subsequent letter has a vowel; as مدَّ for أمدَّ, *extend thou.* If any word, whose final letter is naturally jazmated, precedes *Alif* of union, that *Alif* does not, in pronunciation, take the vowel which belongs to it, but the jazmated letter preceding it takes either *Fathah, Kasrah,* or *Dammah;* but the choice is not arbitrary.

Fathah is used, first after مَن ,مَع ,مِن followed by the article اَلّ or the word ايمَن.

2nd. After the affixes of the first person ى or ني, when they are followed by the article اَلّ, as أهدنى الصَّراطَ.

Kasrah is employed, first after مَن ,مَع ,مِن followed by any other *Alif* of union, than that of the article اَلّ or the word ايمَن.

2nd. After any other monosyllable ending in a jazmated letter, as هَل ,قَد ,بَل ,إن, &c. excepting مذ; and also after the word لكن.

3rd. After the third person singular feminine, of the preterite, and in the future or indefinite tense bearing apocope, after the third person masculine and feminine of the singular;

the second person masculine of the same number; and the first person common both of singular and plural, تَكْتُبْ, يَكْتُبْ, and after the second person singular masculine of the imperative اُكْتُبْ.

4th. After genitives of duals in construction, as

مَدِينَتَيِ ٱلْحِجَازِ.

5th. After the second person feminine of the indefinite tense bearing apocope, and of the imperative of defective verbs whose final ى is preceded by *Fathah*, as تَفْزَى by apocope for تَفْزِين; أَرْضِى by apocope for تَرْضِين; and أَرْضَى by contraction for تَرْضَى.

Dammah is employed, first after the pronoun اَنْتُمْ and the affixed pronouns كُمْ and هُمْ.

2nd. After the second person plural masculine of the preterite نَصَرْتُمْ.

3rd. After مُذْ.

4th. In those persons of the plural of defective verbs, where, in consequence of a contraction, the و, characteristic of the plural, instead of being quiescent after *Dammah*, as in يَكْتُبُوا, كَتَبُوا, اُكْتُبُوا is preceded by *Fathah*, as يَتَمَنَّوْا, ٱشْتَرَوْا, رَمَوْا. In these cases, if an *Alif* of union follows, *Dammah* is added, and such words are written thus, يَتَمَنَّوُا, ٱشْتَرَوُا, رَمَوُا.

The affixed pronoun هُمْ, changing its *Dammah* in certain cases into *Kasrah*, the م takes, according to some, for its casual

3—2

vowel, *Kasrah*; and according to others *Dammah*, حَقَّ عَلَيْهِمُ ٱلْقَوْلُ,

or حَقَّ عَلَيْهِمُ ٱلْقَوْلُ. When the word preceding the *Alif* of union

ends in a nunnation, *Kasrah* is supplied though not written, as

رَسُولٌ ٱسْمُهُ مُوسَى, *Rasúlun-i-Smuhu Músa*.

Sometimes the *Alif* of union is wholly suppressed; this takes

place first in the formula بِسْمِ ٱللّٰهِ ٱلرَّحْمٰنِ ٱلرَّحِيمِ where the

Alif of the word ٱسْمُ is dropped.

2nd. In the word ٱبْن when between two correlative proper

names, as زَيْدُ بْنُ عَمْرٍو *Zaid, son of Amru*; but not when it

is not between two proper names, as زَيْدٌ ٱبْنُ عَمِّى *Zaid, son*

of my uncle; or when these two names form two different parts

of the proposition, as in زَيْدٌ ٱبْنُ مُحَمَّدٌ *Zaid* (*is*) *the son of*

Muhammad.

3rd. In the article أَلْ preceded by the prefix لِ, or the

adverb of affirmation لَ, لِلرَّجُلِ and لَلْحَقُّ for لِلْرَّجُلِ and لَالْحَقُّ.

4th. In verbs and nouns when it is preceded by the inter-

rogative adverb أَ, as ٱبْنُكَ and ٱصْطَفَى for أَٱبْنُكَ and أَٱصْطَفَى.

5th. In the article أَلْ preceded by the interrogative adverb أَ,

as ٱلْمَاءُ for أَٱلْمَاءُ; in this case however the *Alif* of union

may also be preserved.

Madda (ـٓ) مَدّ, or extension. When the *Alif* of pro-

longation is immediately followed by ا moved, either by a simple

vowel or a nunnation, in place of the last of these two *Alifs*, the *Hamzah* with its proper vowel is written only, and *Madda* is put over the *Alif* of prolongation, as سَمَآءٌ *heaven*. This sign is particularly used when the *Hamzah*, which follows the *Alif* of prolongation, terminates a word.

The *Madda* is also placed over *Alif* at the commencement of a word or syllable, when that *Alif* is radical, moved by *Fathah*, and ought to be followed either by *Alif-hamzah* with *Jazmah*, or by an *Alif* of prolongation, as اٰمَنَا for وَالمٰنَا, and اٰكلُون for اَكْلُون. In general the *Madda* points out the absence of *Alif*, and when the *Madda* is used, the *Hamzah*, if it be an *Alif-Hamzah*, is usually suppressed, as well as the vowel, which is always *Fathah*.

It is also inscribed over arithmetical signs, and likewise over abbreviations. A single word is represented by the first letter, as صۤ for صَدِيقٌ *just*; if there are two words, the initial letter of the first, and the final of the second are used, عۤ مۤ for عَلَيهِ الّسَلٰمُ *peace be upon him!* if three, the initial of the first, a medial of the second, and the final of the third, are generally taken, as مۤ لۤ اۤ for اَنَا اللّٰه اَعلَمُ *I am the most wise God.* But when there are many words, their initials are most commonly made use of.

Of the Pause.

The pause وَقْفٌ, which takes place after a word, being the last of a period, of a phrase, or even of a proposition, makes in the manner of reading or pronouncing that word, some alterations necessary to be noticed.

In general, when a pause occurs, the vowel or nunnation of the last letter is suppressed; thus, instead of saying ضَرَبَنِي زَيْدٌ *Zaid has struck me*, and جَاءَنِي عَبْدُ ٱلْحَمِيدِ *Abd ul Hamid has come to me*, pronouncing in the first example the nunnation of زَيْدٌ, and in the second the final *Kasrah* of ٱلْحَمِيدِ, we say only زَيْد *Zaid*, and ٱلْحَمِيد *al Hamid*.

If however the nunnation is ـً as in this example لَمْ نَرَ مُحَمَّدًا *we have not seen Muhammad*, the ن of the nunnation is only dropped, and the *Fathah* followed by ا is preserved, thus مُحَمَّدا.

Analagous to this, in those forms of the indefinite and imperative, which, under the influence of certain particles, as will be shewn hereafter, terminate in ن jazmated, the ن is withdrawn in pronunciation, and the word is pronounced as if the vowel immediately preceding the ن were followed by its homogeneous letter of prolongation, thus تَكْتُبِى for تَكْتُبِنْ, يَكْتُبَا for يَكْتُبَانِّ, تَكْتُبِينَ for تَكْتُبِينِّ, اكْتُبَا for اكْتُبَانّ, اكْتُبِى for اكْتُبِنّ, يَكْتُبُوا for يَكْتُبُنّ, اكْتُبِينَ for اكْتُبِينّ.

It is the same with the word إِنَّنْ, which in a case of pause is pronounced إِنَّا.

The general rule applies equally to the inflections of verbs, when they end in a simple vowel, thus ضَرَبْ for ضَرَبَ, ضَرَبْتَ for ضَرَبْتِ, ضَرَبْتُ. The ة at the end of nouns feminine and others, loses, in case of وَقْف, its vowel or nunnation, and changes into ة quiescent, as مَدِينهْ for مَدِينَةٌ, مَدِينَةٍ, مَدِينَةَ.

The affixed pronouns كَ كِ كُ هُ and هِ, lose their vowels in cases of pause, and become quiescent, اِبْنَكْ for اِبْنَكِ اِبْنَكَ.

Nouns, which according to the rules of permutation, which will be hereafter explained, having for third radical و or ى, lose that third radical by contraction, and throw the ن of the nunnation on the vowel preceding, as قَاضٍ for قَاضِىٌ, and قَاضِىٍ, in cases of pause lose the final vowel, as قَاضْ; final ى may however be used قَاضِى.

The cutting off of the vowels or nunnation, in cases of pause, is applicable also to words terminating verses, or the periods of rhymed prose, سَجْع. In this case, the nunnation may be taken away entirely, or only the ن which it contains be dropped, and the vowel preserved. Thus سَبَبْ for سَبَبٌ and سَبَبْ; or else سَبَبُ for سَبَبٌ and سَبَبَ for سَبَبً.

RULES OF PERMUTATION OF THE LETTERS
ی و ا.

1. THE letters ی و ا, are often used for each other; these permutations being considered as an imperfection, the Arabian Grammarians denominate them infirm letters حروف العلَّة. In the beginning of a word, however, they usually remain, except when, by the influence of some prefixed inseparable particles, they cease to be initial.

2. When, being themselves without vowels, and following those which are dissimilar, they become analogous to them. *Alif* is considered as analogous to *Fathah. Waw* to *Dammah*, and *Ya* to *Kasrah.* Thus

نوی	for ناي	*a trench.*
بِیر	بار	*a well.*
نار	نور	*fire.*
میعاد	موعاد	*the said place or time.*
دار	دیر	*a house.*
موقن	میقن	*certifying.*

و and ي sometimes remain after *Fathah*; in this case, if bearing *Jazmah*, they form a diphthong with the preceding *Fathah*; as in لیل یوم; or not having *Jazmah*, they are pronounced as a long *Alif*, as رمیة ,رماہ like صلوت like صلاة.

3. The letters ی و ا when quiescent, and followed by *Jazmah* are omitted, as يَخَفْ for يَخَافْ, يَقُمْ for يَقُومْ, ويَسِرْ for يَسِيرْ.

4. The *Alif* of union is not subjected to this rule, as فَانْصُرْ.

SPECIAL RULES.

Alif.

1. *Alif-hamzah*, in the middle of a word, when moved by *Dammah* is changed into و, when by *Kasrah* into ی, whether preceded by a vowel or letter jazmated;

	for	
روف	for	رَأْف
وِف		وَأْف
أبمة		أُمَة
أنوب		أذْأب
يِس		يَأْس
رِی		رَأْی

2. *Alif-hamzah*, in the middle of a word, when moved by *Fathah*, after *Dammah* is changed into و, after *Kasrah* into ی, as

	for	
دوب	for	دَأْب
فِیة		فَأْة

3. *Hamzah* or *Alif-hamzah*, quiescent in the middle of a word, is changeable into ا و or ی quiescent; agreeably to the

vowel preceding; the articulation of the *Hamzah* being wholly
suppressed, as

راسْ for رَأْسْ

اسْتاجَر   اسْتَأْجَر

بوسْ   بُؤْسْ

ذِيبْ   ذِئْبْ.

4.   *Hamzah*, preceded by و or ى quiescent, acting as servile
letters, is changeable after و into وّ, and into يّ after ي,
uniting with the preceding letter by *Tashdíd*, and losing all
articulation of the *Hamzah*. Thus

مَقْروّة for مَقْروءَة

خَطِيّة   خَطِيئَة

هَنِيّ   هَنِيّ.

5.   In the middle of a word, *Hamzah*, being preceded by a
quiescent letter, other than و or ى, the *Hamzah* may be suppressed, and the vowel belonging to it transferred to the preceding
letter, as

مَسَلة for مَسْئَلة

مَسول   مَسْئُول

تَسَل   تَسْئَل.

6.   *Alif-hamzah*, at the end of a word, is changed, after
Dammah into وّ, after *Kasrah* into ى;

دَنْو for دَنَأ

خاطا   خاطِى.

7. *Alif-hamzah*, at the end of a word after *Fathah*, when moved by *Dammah*, is changed into و, when by *Kasrah* into ي, as

تَفْتَأُ for تَفْتَؤُ

سَنَأ.‏ سَنَئِ

But it is equally correct to write تَفْتَأُ or تَفْتَؤُ, and it is thus that grammarians usually write المُبْتَدَأُ or المُبْتَدَؤُ.

8. *Alif-hamzah*, at the end of a word, and preceded by *Jazmah*, is written as *Hamzah* only, but the vowel may be transferred to the jazmated letter, and *Hamzah* then becomes ا و or ى, according to the vowel preceding. Thus

الجُزْءُ for الجُزُو

الجُزْءِ الجُزِى

الجُزْءَ.‏ الجُزَا

9. Should two *Alif-hamzahs* meet together in the same word, and the first be moved by a vowel, and the second be jazmated, the latter loses its *Hamzah*, and becomes merely long, changed, if need be, into و or ى;

ءَامَنَ for أَمَنَ or أَأْمَنَ

أُوسِنَ for أُؤْسِنَ.‏ and إِيمَان for إِأْمَان

10. *Alif*, quiescent, preceded by another *Alif* moved by *Fathah*, is dropped; this is pointed out by the position of the *Fathah*, which is written perpendicularly, or by *Maddah*;

أَامَرَ or أَمَرَ for أَامَرَ

آكَلَة   أَكَلَة   أَاكَلَة

مَاَل   مَاَل   مَاَل.

This suppression takes place in some words of very frequent recurrence, when quiescent *Alif* is not preceded by another ا, as in

رَحمَان for رَحمَن

.قِيَامَة   قِيَامَة

11.   When two *Alifs* meet in the middle of a word, the first being *Hamzah* moved by *Fathah*, and the second quiescent, the first is often changed into و without *Hamzah*, as

تَآمَرُوا or تَأَامَرُوا for تَوَامَرُوا

ذَآئِب   ذَأَائِب   ذَوَائِب

.الأَاخَر   أَوَاخِر

12.   The inseparable particles بَ فَ لَ لِ and وَ which are used at the beginning of words, alter nothing in the nature of *Alif*, which is still considered to be the first letter of the word, though those particles may be prefixed, as لِأَبِ كَأَمِ, and not .كَوِمِ لَيَبِ

Some compound words must be excepted, in which custom has established the change, as لَءَلَا for لَأَلَا, and لَئَن for .لَإِن

13. When the interrogative particle أَ is followed by *Alif-hamzah*, if the second be moved by *Fathah*, one of them, with its vowel, is dropped, or an *Hamzah* is placed first, and then an *Alif* with *Maddah*. Thus

أَنتَ or ءَانتَ for الأَنتَ

أنذرتهم ءانذرتهم الأنذرتهم

أَلان ءَ لان ءَالان

ألَّد ءَآلَّد .الأَلَّد

14. If the second *Hamzah* have *Dammah* for its vowel, the *Alif* becomes و, or the second ا is suppressed and its *Hamzah* only retained;

اونبيكم or اَنبيكم for .الاُنبيكم

15. If the second *Hamzah* have *Kasrah*, the *Alif* is changed into ى;

اين for أَان

اذا .الاَذا

Waw.

1. *Waw* in the beginning of a word, when followed by another moved by a vowel, is changed into *Alif-hamzah*, to avoid the meeting of two و;

أَواصِل for وواصِل pl. of واصِلة

أَواضِح وواضِح واضِحة

أَواقى وواقى .واقِية

2. If there be two و at the beginning of a word and the first be moved by *Dammah*, it may be changed into *Hamzah*;

أُورِىَ for وُورِىَ.

3. When in the middle of a word there are two وو, the first moved by *Dammah*, and the second quiescent, if the letter preceding the first is neither jazmated nor quiescent, and the first is not doubled by *Tashdíd*, the first و is often changed into *Hamzah*, preserving the figure of و. Thus

خُوولَة for خُوولَة

نُورَة نُوورَة.

In this case one of the two و is sometimes dropped; this occurs particularly when the first و is preceded by long *Alif*;

دَاوُد for دَاوُد

طَاوُس طَاوُوس.

If they meet only in consequence of a contraction, this rule is not observed;

يَستوِيُون for يَستوُون.

4. و in the middle of a word, moved by *Fathah*, and preceded by *Kasrah*, is often changed into ي;

ثِوَاب for ثِيَاب.

This however does not always take place,

طُولٌ طِوَالٌ سِوًّ جِوَارٌ سِوَارٌ شِوَاءٌ.

5. Sometimes in the middle of a word, after a letter bearing *Jazmah*, و moved by *Dammah* assumes *Hamzah* or is changed into *Alif-hamzah*, as

ادور for ادور or ادار .

6. In words derived from roots having و for second radical, it often happens when the second radical is doubled, that و is changed into ى;

قيم قيام قيوم from قام for قوم

صيب صياب صاب صوب

صيت صات صوت

صيم صام صوم.

This occurs even when the second radical is jazmated and not doubled, as مميت قيل, &c.

7. Final و, when immediately preceded by *Fathah*, admits of no vowel, but becomes quiescent, and is changed into ا, if the word have but three letters, or into ى if it have more than three;

غزا for غزو *he assaulted*.

يغزى يغزو *he is assaulted*.

The same takes place when after و there is ة final;

مرقاة for مرقوة .

If the final و bear a nunnated vowel, the nunnation is thrown back on the preceding *Fathah*;

عَصَا for عَصْوٌ عِصْوٌ عَصَوٌ *a staff*.

مُعْطًى for مُعْطَوٌ مُعْطِوٌ مُعْطَوٌ *given*.

8. In defective verbs, final و when immediately preceded by *Dammah*, and subject to be moved by *Dammah*, loses that vowel, as

يَغْزُو for يَغْزُوُ.

9. In nouns derived from defective roots, when the final و is immediately preceded by *Dammah*, it changes itself into ى, and converts into *Kasrah* the *Dammah* preceding. Should, in this case, the ى have *Fathah* for its vowel, it remains; if it be *Kasrah* or *Dammah* it is dropped, and ى remains quiescent. If there be a nunnated vowel, the ى disappears, unless the vowel be *Fathah*.

Thus جَرْوٌ دَلْوٌ عَصًا, of which the plurals would otherwise be اَجْرُوٌ اَدْلُوٌ اَعْصُوٌ, make اَجْرٍ اَدْلٍ اَعْصٍ.

Thus in the Nom. and Gen. it is اَدْلٍ for اَدْلُوٌ and اَدْلٍ; and in the Accus. اَدْلِيًا for اَدْلُوًا.

When there is no nunnation, it is اَدْلِى for اَدْلُوُ and اَدْلُوُ and اَدْلِى for اَدْلُوُ.

10. When, at the end of a word, two و meet, of which the first is quiescent after *Dammah*, they unite by *Tashdíd*. Thus

عَسُوٌّ for عَسُوْوٌ, عَدُوٌّ for عَدُوْوٌ.

This is equally the case with ة at the end فُتُوَّة.

11. In plurals however of the form فَعُولٌ, and in nouns of action of the forms فَعُولٌ and فَعُولٌ, the two و are often changed into ى, and the *Dammah* of the second into *Kasrah*;

. عِصوٌ for عِصِىٌّ دَلوٌ for دَلِىٌّ

12. When و quiescent after *Dammah* is followed by ى final, the *Dammah* becomes *Kasrah*, and the و is changed into ى, which coalesces with the ى final by *Tashdíd*,

. بَغوٌ for بَغِىٌّ

13. In nouns of the form فَعِيلٌ, the last letter being و, it is changed into ى, and the two ى unite by *Tashdíd*,

. رَضِيوٌ for رَضِىٌّ , صَبِيوٌ for صَبِىٌّ

14. Final و, immediately preceded by *Kasrah*, is changed into ى,

. رَضِوَ for رَضِىَ

15. Servile و at the end of a word always has after it an *Alif* mute,

. أُولُوا , رَمَوْا , كَتَبُوا

Ya.

1. In the middle of a word ى moved by *Fathah* and immediately preceded by *Dammah*, is sometimes changed into و;

. شِيِيَة for شُوِيَة

This is however of rare occurrence.

4

2. When two ى meet in the middle of a word, the first moved by *Kasrah*, and the second quiescent, the second is often dropped; this is only when the first is in the place of *Alif-hamzah*,

. رِئِيس for رِئْس

In every other case, the two ى coalesce by *Tashdíd*;

. طَيِّبٌ طَيِّبٌ

3. Final ى immediately preceded by *Fathah*, bears no vowel, but becomes quiescent, throwing the nunnation, if there be one, on the *Fathah* preceding;

أُولَى for أُولَى , أُولَى and أُولَى

. فَتَّى فَتَّى , فَتَّى فَتًى

This takes place also when ة follows ى,

. مَرْمِيَّة for مَرْمَاة

4. If the final ى is preceded by another ى, the last is changed into a short *Alif*,

. هَدَايَا for هَدَايَى

Except the two proper names, يَحْيَى and رَيَّى .

5. Final ى preceded immediately by *Kasrah*, bears neither *Dammah* nor *Kasrah*, but losing them becomes quiescent,

. ٱلْجَافِى for ٱلْجَافِىٌ and ٱلْجَافِى

If in this case there be a nunnation in the nominative, or genitive, it is thrown back on the preceding vowel, and ى is dropped;

. رَامِي for رَامِىٌ and رَامٍ

6. Final ى preceded by *Dammah* changes it to *Kasrah*, remaining itself unchanged, but following the preceding Rule, becoming quiescent when moved by *Dammah* or *Kasrah*, and being dropped when it bears a nunnation in the nominative or genitive;

تَمَنِّي for تَمَنَّى and تَمَنِّي

أَيْدٍ أَيْدِى أَيْدٍ.

If in these cases final ى has *Fathah* for its vowel with or without nunnation, it remains and preserves its vowel, ٱلْحَافِى,

ٱلْأَيْدِى, تَمَنِّيًا, رَامِيًا.

7. ى in the middle of a word bearing *Jazmah*, and following *Dammah*, often changes that *Dammah* into *Kasrah*, instead of being itself changed into و, (2nd gen.) becoming quiescent, بِيضٌ for بُيضٌ , حِيكَى for حُيكَى , and ضِيزَى for ضُيزَى.

8. When two ى meet at the end of a word, the first being quiescent after *Kasrah*, they unite by *Tashdíd*;

مَرِىٌّ for مَرِىٌ.

Rules common to و and ى.

1. و and ى preceded by, and also bearing vowels, are dropped when immediately followed by و or ى quiescent, their vowels in this case are also lost, if *Fathah* goes before; the و or ى quiescent forming a diphthong with that *Fathah*.

4—2

رَمَيُوا for رَمَوْا

.تَغْزِوِينَ تَغْزِينَ

2. If in this case the vowel preceding be *Dammah* or
Kasrah, it is suppressed, and replaced by the vowel belonging
to the و or ى which has been dropped;

.غَازِيُونَ for غَازُونَ ,اَغْزِوِی for اَغْزِی .

3. When و and ى meet, so that the first bears *Jazmah*,
و is changed into ى, and the two ى unite by *Tashdíd*;

اَيْوَامٌ for اَيَّامٌ

كَوْیٌ كَیّ

.اَسْيِوِدُّ اَسِیدُّ

4. At the end of a word, after *Alif* quiescent, و and ى
are changed into *Hamzah*;

رِدَایٌ for رِدَآءٌ

.سَمَاوٌ سَمَآءٌ

5. و and ى bearing vowels, and immediately following
Fathah, are often changed into ا quiescent;

قَوَمَ for قَامَ

طَوَلَ طَالَ

سَيَرَ سَارَ

.خَوِفَ خَافَ

6. If after this *Alif* quiescent, a letter bearing *Jazmah*
follow, the *Alif* is dropped, and *Dammah* or *Kasrah* substituted for the *Fathah* preceding. *Dammah*, when the و whose
place is taken by *Alif*, would bear *Dammah* or *Fathah*, as
طَلَّتُ for طَالَتْ, of which the regular form would be طَوُلَتْ,
and so قُمْتُ for قَامَتْ, regularly قَوَمَتْ.

When the *Alif* quiescent is in the place of ى or of و,
moved by *Kasrah*, *Kasrah* is used instead of *Dammah*, سِرْتُ
for سَارَتْ, reg. سَيَرْتُ, خِفْتُ for خَافَتْ, reg. خَوِفْتُ.

7. When و and ى in the middle of a word are moved
by *Kasrah*, and preceded by *Alif* quiescent, they are replaced
by ى with *Hamzah*;

مَايِلٌ for مَائِلٌ, قَاوِلٌ for قَائِلٌ.

8. When و and ى in the middle of a word bearing
vowels, and being preceded by *Jazmah*, are followed by a letter
bearing a vowel also, they often transfer their own vowel to the
letter having *Jazmah*, and become quiescent. In this case, if
the vowel is *Fathah*, the و or ى changes into ا; if *Kasrah*,
the و changes into ى, according to the second general Rule;

يَطُولُ for يَطُوُلُ

يَسِيرُ　　يَسْيِرُ

يَخَافُ　　يَخْوَفُ

يَهَابُ　　يَهْيَبُ

مستقيم   مستقوم

مسيرة   مسيرة

مقامة   مقومة

مقال   مقول

مقالة   مقولة.

9. This change does not however take place in nouns of the forms مِفْعَل and مِفْعَلَة, nor in those where the و or the ى is followed by *Alif* quiescent, as in the forms مِفْعَال and مِفْعَالَة, nor finally in adjectives of the form أَفْعَل. Thus

مقود   from   قَادَ   for   قود

مزواد   زَادَ   زود

مكيلة   كَالَ   كيل

أسود   سَادَ   سود

أسوأ   سَاءَ   سوأ.

10. If by this change the quiescent letter falls before a letter bearing *Jazmah*, the former one is wholly suppressed; أقامت for أقومت.

11. When و and ى are moved by *Kasrah*, and preceded by *Dammah*, the *Kasrah* generally takes the place of the *Dammah*, which itself disappears; و then changes into ى quiescent.

قَوْلَ   قِيلَ

سِيرَ   سَيَّرَ

General Observations.

1. When the letters ا و ى are said to be preceded by a vowel, it must be understood that they are so preceded immediately, and without the interposition of *Jazmah*, or a quiescent letter. It must not be forgotten that there is a latent *Jazmah* in *Tashdíd*. Thus, in مَدَّ the *Fathah* which is over the د is not immediately preceded by the *Dammah* of the م, because مَدَّ is the same as if it were written مَدْدَ.

2. *Alif* final ceases to be so considered, and is regarded as being in the middle of a word, when an affixed pronoun is added to the end of that word. Thus, in مَاوُهُ *Alif-hamzah* is changed into و, as being in the middle of a word, though this is not always strictly observed.

3. On the contrary, و and ى terminating a word, are not affected by such an affix, and are still looked upon as final letters, as in غَزَاهُ and رَمَاهُ, where the addition of هُ does not prevent the و of غَزْوُ, and the ى of رَمْىُ from becoming quiescent, as if at the end of a word. The only change made by the affixed pronoun is that of ى into ا; the ى may here however be preserved, provided that *Jazmah* is not used, as رَمْيَهُ.

_____

VERB.

Of the Verb in General.

1.   THE original or primitive verb, is by the Arabians denominated مجرد (*naked*), because composed of only those letters
which constitute the root.   The root أصل, is always the third
person singular masculine of the preterite tense, and active voice.
The letters constituting the root are called أصليّة, or radicals.
The seven letters of the word يتسمنوا (*they fatten*) are called
زوائد augments, or serviles.

The primitive verb contains either three letters ثلاثي (triliteral) or four رباعي (quadriliteral).

In triliterals, the first letter is called فآء *fa*, the second عين
âain, and the third لام *lám*, because the verb فعل (*he made*)
is usually taken as the paradigm of the regular triliteral verb.
In the quadriliteral roots, the paradigm being فعلل, the first
letter is named *fa*, the second *âain*, the third *lám the first*,
and the fourth *lám the second*.

From the primitive triliteral verb are derived twelve other
forms, making altogether thirteen conjugations or forms of one
root.   Quadriliterals have but four forms.

Derivative verbs (of triliterals) are divided into three classes.
The first contains those formed by the addition of one letter,
the second those made by adding two letters, and the third
comprehends those receiving an addition of three letters.

Derivatives.

Primitive.	First Class.	Second Class.	Third Class.
		5 تَفَعَّلَ	10 اِسْتَفْعَلَ
	2 فَعَّلَ	6 تَفَاعَلَ	11 اِفْعَالَّ
1 فَعَلَ	3 فَاعَلَ	7 اِنْفَعَلَ	12 اِفْعَوْعَلَ
	4 أَفْعَلَ	8 اِفْتَعَلَ	13 اِفْعَوَّلَ
		9 اِفْعَلَّ	

Quadriliterals.

Derivatives.			
1 فَعْلَلَ	2 تَفَعْلَلَ	3 اِفْعَنْلَلَ	4 اِفْعَلَلَّ

From the root فَعَل the Arabian grammarians make the technical words, which become the names of all the various grammatical forms. The fifth form, for instance, of a triliteral verb, is called تَفَعَّل; the second of a quadriliteral is called تَفَعْلَل, and so with all others. It is thus with every inflection of a verb, with the nouns and adjectives derived from it, and even with the rules of prosody, and the various feet employed in verse.

Of these thirteen forms of the triliteral verb, the twelfth and thirteenth are of very rare occurrence. Some grammarians give a fourteenth and a fifteenth form; thus, 14 اِعْلَنْكَكَ *he had clustering hair;* 15 اِعْلَنْدَى *he was corpulent and strong,* (a camel), but the few verbs which exist of these forms may be considered as in the third form of the quadriliteral verb, اِفْعَنْلَل.

It is to be observed that in the eighth form اِفْتَعَل, the place of ت is sometimes supplied by ط or د.

When the first letter of the root is one of these, ض, ص, ط or ظ, the ت is changed into ط, as اِصْطَبَغ it was dyed, for اِصْتَبَغ; اِطَّبَع it was printed, for اِطْتَبَع; اِظَّلَم he was unjustly treated, for اِظْتَلَم, in which instance the ط is also changed into ظ, and is joined to the first by Tashdíd.

When the first letter of the root is د ن or ز, in the eighth form, ت is changed into د, thus for اِدْتَرَأ he was repelled, is written اِدَّرَأ; for اِدْتَكَر it was recorded اِدَّكَر, where the radical ن is changed into د, or اِذَّكَر, where the د becomes ذ, or اِدْدَكَر, where both remain.

When the first radical is ث, و or ى, in the eighth conjugation, it is changed into ت, and the two ت unite by Tashdíd, as اِتَّسَر for اِتْتَسَر, اِتَّجَر for اِوْتَجَر, اِتَّبَت for اِتْتَبَت.

In the first form or conjugation, the original and simple signification is to be found, whether that be a transitive or intransitive one, as كَتَب he wrote, حَزِن he was sorrowful.

The second and fourth conjugations form transitive verbs from intransitives, as from عَظُم he was great, عَظَّم, and أَعْظَم he rendered great, he honored. From verbs transitive in the first form, the second and fourth make others, which may be called double transitives, as from كَتَبَ *he wrote,* كَتَّبَ and اكْتَبَ *he made another person write.*

Verbs in the second form are frequently however mere synonyms of the first, or only distinguished by being understood as a species of intensitives, كَسَرَ and كَسَّرَ *he broke,* فرق and فَرَّق *he separated or dispersed,* &c.

The third form has usually the signification of the first, with this difference, however, that the indirect complement of the verb, which in the first form demanded the intervention of a preposition, becomes here a direct complement, and meets the verb immediately. Thus كَتَبَ and رسل have in the first form the preposition إِلَى before the indirect complement of the preceding verb, كَتَبْتُ إِلَى ٱلْمَلِكِ رِسَالَةً *I wrote a letter to the king;* رِسَلْنَا أَخَانَا إِلَيْكَ *we sent our brother to you.* If the third form is used, the person to whom we write or whom we send, becomes the direct complement, and meets the verb without the preposition إِلَى. Thus رَاسَلْتُ and كَاتَبْتُ ٱلْمَلِكَ and ٱلْوَزِير *I wrote to the king—I sent to the Vazír.* So with intransitive verbs also, جلس *he sat down,* in the third form signifies, to sit down with or near one, جَالَسَ ٱلسُّلْطَان *he sat down near the Sultán.* In the first form this would be جَلَسَ عِنْدَ ٱلسُّلْطَانِ.

This form indicates also a reciprocal or mutual acting. Thus قَاتَل *he sought to kill another,* (*that other seeking to kill him*).

The fifth form almost always has a passive signification, derived from the second. Thus from عِلم *to know*, come the second form عَلَّم *to teach*, and the fifth تَعَلَّم *to be taught*.

The sixth form is derived immediately from the third, and signifies the co-operation and mutual action of two or more persons, as تَضَارب *the one beat the other*; تَلَعَب غِلمَان *the boys played together*.

The seventh and eighth forms have usually a passive meaning, derived mostly from the first, but sometimes from the second, as from قَطع *to cut*, comes the seventh إِنقَطع *to be cut*, from نصر *to help*, the eighth أَنتَصر *to be helped*.

The ninth and eleventh forms designate colors; the eleventh, with more intensity, إِصفَر *to be yellow*; إِصفَار *to be very yellow*. These conjugations are also verbs, expressing deformity, as أَضجَم and إِضجَام *to have the face or mouth distorted*; إِعوَج *to be crooked*.

The tenth form expresses the desire of, or petition for, the action indicated by the first, as غَفر *to pardon*, إِستَغفِر *to beg pardon*, سَقى *to water*, إِستَسقى *to beg for water, to put up prayers for rain*.

The twelfth and thirteenth forms are of very rare occurrence, and generally add intensity or energy to the primitive signification; thus from خَشن *to be harsh*, is derived إِخشَوشَن *to be very harsh or rude*, from عَلطا *to adhere*, comes إِعلَوط *to adhere firmly*.

Upon the various significations of the different forms or conjugations of the verb, much more might be said, and some grammarians enter into long details ; but, although well worth the notice of the curious investigator, these inquiries are wholly undeserving the attention of the student. The brief remarks here made will not be found without use, but it is only by reading and consulting the dictionary, that a knowledge can be gained of the significations of the various forms. However minute might be the observations made upon the different meanings of the verb, we should still find many exceptions ; these can only be learned by use, and the same must be said as to the forms in which any given verb is to be found. Some roots are only met with in one conjugation, most are in several, none in all.

Quadriliteral verbs, it will be seen, have but four forms; the first answers to the first of triliterals, the second to the fifth, the third to the seventh, and the fourth to the ninth.

Every variation of which the verb is susceptible, whether in forming the derivatives from the primitive, or in the voices, tenses, persons, numbers and genders, or in verbal nouns, is by the Arabians comprised under the term تصريف *exchange*, peculiarly applied to grammatical inflection, and almost equivalent to conjugation.

The regular verb is termed سالم *sound or perfect*, and follows in all its inflections the common rule, or paradigm فعل. The irregular verb, غير سالم *unsound or imperfect*, has among its radicals one or more of the feeble letters ا, و, ى, or has its second and third radicals alike.

In the Arabic language there are a few verbs which may be regarded as primitives of five or six letters, or as derivatives belonging to forms not included among those we have enumerated. Such are اِبْلَنْدَج ,ثَعْجَر ,اِعْتَنْدَر, but these examples are rare, and it is to be observed that ن, always, or almost always, enters into the formation of these derivatives of forms not used, and that by subtracting it, it is easy to reduce them to a quadri-literal root.

There are two voices, the active, denominated صِيفَةُ ٱلْفَاعِل *the form of the agent*, or simply فَاعِل *agent*, and the passive مَفْعُول ,صِيفَةُ ٱلْمَفْعُول, *the form of the thing done*, or merely مَفْعُول, *the object on which the action falls, the patient.*

Neuter verbs, of whatever form they may be, by their very nature, are destitute of a passive voice, whether these verbs simply express a mode of being, as مَرِض *to be ill*, or an energy not passing out of the energizer, and which we more particu-larly call intransitive verbs, as مَشَى *to walk*, نَام *to sleep*; the Arabian grammarians consider them as active, and their sub-ject is always called فَاعِل, or *agent*.

In Arabic verbs there are but three principal modifications, of which two are of *time*, زَمَان, and the third of *command*, أَمْر.

CONJUGATION OF THE FIRST FORM فَعَلَ OF REGULAR TRILITERAL VERBS.

Active Voice.

Preterite.

	Plu.			Dual.			Sing.		Pers.
Fem.	Com.	Mas.	Fem.	Com.	Mas.	Fem.	Com.	Mas.	
كَتَبْنَ		كَتَبُوا	كَتَبَتَا		كَتَبَا	كَتَبَتْ		كَتَبَ	3
كَتَبْتُنَّ		كَتَبْتُمْ		كَتَبْتُمَا		كَتَبْتِ		كَتَبْتَ	2
	كَتَبْنَا			كَتَبْتُ			كَتَبْتُ		1

Indef.

	Plu.			Dual.			Sing.		
يَكْتُبْنَ		يَكْتُبُونَ	تَكْتُبَانِ		يَكْتُبَانِ	تَكْتُبُ		يَكْتُبُ	3
تَكْتُبْنَ		تَكْتُبُونَ		تَكْتُبَانِ		تَكْتُبِينَ		تَكْتُبُ	2
	نَكْتُبْ			أَكْتُبُ			أَكْتُبُ		1

Imper.

	Plu.			Dual.			Sing.		
اكْتُبْنَ		اكْتُبُوا		اكْتُبَا		اكْتُبِي		اكْتُبْ	

Participle.

	Plu.			Dual.			Sing.		
كَاتِبَاتٌ		كَاتِبُونَ	كَاتِبَتَانِ		كَاتِبَانِ	كَاتِبَةٌ		كَاتِبٌ	

Infinitive.

كَتْبًا

OF TENSES.

Of these there are in the Arabic verb only two; the first ماضٍ or the *past*, we denominate the preterite; the second مُضَارِع or *resembling**, being susceptible of both present and future, may be called the indefinite tense.

The compound tenses are formed by the addition of the verb substantive كَانَ. The preterite of this verb being joined to that of any other, gives to the latter the signification of the pluperfect, كَانَ كَتَبَ *he had written*. Joined to the indefinite tense of another verb, it gives it the force of the imperfect, كَانَ يَكْتُبُ *he was writing*.

The indefinite tense of كَانَ which is يَكُونُ, joined to another verb in the preterite, forms the future subjunctive, يَكُونُ كَتَبَ *he will have written*.

These compound tenses are not given in the paradigm of the verb, the Arabian grammarians not considering this union of two verbs, for the determination of the circumstances of time, as forming compound tenses of one verb.

Numbers.

In the Arabic language there are three numbers, عَدَد, pl. أعداد. The *singular* المفرد or الفرد. The *dual* المُثَنَّى or

---

* So called, because in many of its accidents it resembles the noun.

اَلتَّثْنِيَةِ, and the *plural* اَلْجَمْعِ or اَلْمُكَثِّرُ. These distinctions take place in the verb as well as in nouns, adjectives and pronouns.

Genders and Persons.

In Arabic there are three genders, جِنْسٌ, pl. أَجْنَاسٌ, the *masculine* اَلْمُذَكَّرُ, the *feminine* اَلْمُوَنَّثُ, and the *common* اَلْمُسْتَوَى. These are also used in the verb.

The first person is called اَلْمُتَكَلِّمُ *he who speaks*, the second اَلْمُخَاطَبُ *he who is spoken to*, and the third اَلْغَائِبُ *he who is absent*. The first person plural is named نَفْسُ اَلْمُتَكَلِّمِ مَعَ اَلْغَيْرِ *he who speaks conjointly with others*.

ON THE TENSES OF THE REGULAR TRILITERAL VERBS.

The Preterite.

THE persons of the preterite are formed by adding one or more letters after the radicals. According to the system of the Arabian grammarians, there is no person of the verb without a pronoun expressed or understood, that pronoun being the agent or subject; several of the letters added to the root in order to form the persons, are, therefore, considered by them as pronouns.

The middle radical of the preterite of some verbs takes *Kasrah* in place of *Fathah*, as transitively عَلِمَ *he knew*; but

5

this is more peculiarly the characteristic of intransitive or neuter verbs, as فَرِحَ *he was glad,* حَزِنَ *he was sorrowful;* sometimes the middle radical of the preterite takes *Dammah;* but this only in a neuter sense, as قَبُحَ *he was ugly,* حَسُنَ *he was hand-some.* The vowels of the two first radicals do not vary in the other persons, but the last is changed to *Dammah* in the third person masc. plu., and is jazmated in most of the other persons.

The preterite usually corresponds with the English prete-rite perfect, as اُذْكُرُوا نِعْمَتِىَ ٱلَّتِى اَنْعَمْتُ عَلَيْكُمْ و اَنِّى فَضَّلْتُكُمْ عَلَى ٱلْعَالَمِينَ *Remember the benefits that* I have conferred *upon you, and (remember) that* I have rendered you superior *to other men.*

When the preterite is preceded by the particle قَدْ, it always signifies a past time, which is also the case when it follows the adverb لَمَّا, *when.*

The preterite is often employed to express the present, as

وَقَعَ ٱلشَّوَائِبَ شَيَّبَ و ٱلدَّهْرُ بِالنَّاسِ قُلَّبٌ .

إِنْ دَانَ يَوْمًا لِشَخْصٍ فَفِى غَدٍ يَتَغَلَّبُ .

The violence of affliction makes grey the hairs, *and fortune with mankind* changes.

Although she stoops *to day to a man, yet on the morrow she will overwhelm him.*

The particle لَوْ *if,* conveying a supposition, and connecting two correlative propositions, gives to the preterite the signification of the pluperfect. Suppositive propositions are distinguished from conditional, as implying that the case supposed is never realised, while in the conditional there is a simple enunciation of one proposition depending on another.

In the suppositive proposition, the first preterite is to be rendered by the pluperfect of the indicative, and the second, to which is prefixed the particle لَ, by the preterite of the potential mood, as لَوْ عَلِمْتَ هٰذَا لَنَصَحْتُكَ *if I had known this, I would have admonished thee.* If the second member be negative, the indefinite tense is used with the particle لَمْ, which, as will he hereafter explained, gives to the indefinite the power of the preterite, as لَوْ كُنْتَ هَاهُنَا لَمْ يَمُتْ أَخِى *if you had been here, my brother would not have died.*

If after لَوْ the verb of the first proposition is in the indefinite tense, and the second in the preterite, they take a future sense, and the first may be translated by an imperfect subjunctive, and the second by a conditional future, as لَوْ يَمَسُّ الْبَخِيلَ رَاحَةَ يَحْيَى لَسَخَتْ نَفْسُهُ بِبَذْلِ النَّوَالِ *if the miser* touched *the palm of Yahya, his soul* would become generous *in bestowing gifts.*

The negative لَا gives to the preterite the meaning of the future; this is particularly observable in the taking of an oath.

اَلَيْتَ لَا خَامَرَتْنِى الْخَمْرُ مَا عَلِقَتْ

رُوحِى بِجِسْمِى وَ أَلْفَاظِى بِأَفْصَاحِى

I have sworn (I swear) *that wine* shall not disturb me, *while my soul is in my body, and my words in my power of speaking.*

In the Korán and in the Poets, examples are found of the preterite preserving its own meaning after لَا . لَا وَ صَدَّقَ فَلَا صَلَّى وَ لٰكِن كَذَّبَ و تَوَلَّى *he has not believed and he has not prayed; but he has denied the truth and has been perverse.*

The preterite is used in Arabic to express the optative. Thus in speaking of God, after his name, is added تَعَالَى *may he be exalted!* After the name of Muhammad, صَلَّى ٱللَّهُ عَلَيْهِ و سَلَّم *may God be propitious to him, and give him peace!* Such are these forms also, رَضِيَ ٱللَّهُ عَنْهُ *may God be pleased with him!* دَامَ مُلْكُهُ *may his reign be long!* دمتم سالِمِين *may you remain in good health!* لَعْنَةُ ٱللَّهُ *may God curse him!*

After إِذَا *when,* an adverbial particle of time especially applied to the future, as لَمَّا *when* is to the past, the preterite takes a future sense, as إِذَا كَتَبْتَ ذٰلِكَ أَحْمَدُكَ *when thou shalt have written that, I will praise thee.*

When this adverb is put at the head of two correlative propositions, of which the verbs are in the preterite, they both assume this future meaning, إِذَا جَاءَ وَعْدُ ٱلْآخِرَةِ جِئْنَا بِكُمْ لَفِيفًا *when the promise of the future life shall have come, we will bring you together.*

But this influence of إِذَا ceases when the preterite of كَان precedes it, and the two verbs may then be rendered the first by the pluperfect, the second by the imperfect, وَ كَانَ مِن عَادَةِ

تِيمُورَ وَ فِكْرِهِ أَنَّهُ كَانَ فِى أَوَّلِ أَمْرِهِ إِذَا نَزَلَ بِأَحَدٍ مُسْتَضِيفًا

إِنْتَسَبَهُ وَ حَفِظَ أَسْمَهُ وَ نِسْبَهُ *and it was a custom of Tímúr, and of his forethought, that in the beginning of his command, when he had alighted at the dwelling of any one and requested hospitality, he enquired into his family and remembered his name and his pedigree.*

To have this effect, it is not even necessary that the preterite of the verb كَانَ should be expressed ; it is sufficient that before إِذَا there be a verb in the preterite, upon which the conjunctive proposition depends, لَا تَكُونُوا كَالَّذِينَ كَفَرُوا وَ قَالُوا

لِإِخْوَانِهِمْ إِذَا ضَرَبُوا فِى ٱلْأَرْضِ أَوْ كَانُوا غُزًّى لَوْ كَانُوا عِنْدَنَا مَا

مَاتُوا وَ مَا قُتِلُوا *be not like those who have been incredulous, and who have said of their brothers, when travelling in the country, or on a military expedition, if they had remained with us, they would not have died, and would not have been killed.*

It is the verb قَالُوا which here deprives إِذَا of its usual effect. To occasion the cessation of this influence of إِذَا, it suffices that what precedes it should contain necessarily the idea of the past.

Whenever the two particles حَتَّى, *in order that, until, &c.,* and إِذَا *when,* are united at the head of two conjunctive propositions ; the temporal power of the verbs of those two propositions depends upon the antecedents, and accordingly as they express a past, or future sense, the verbs of the conjunctive propositions, although put in the preterite, must be translated by the past or future. و يوم نَحشُرُ مِن كُلِّ أُمَّةٍ فَوجًا مِمَّن

يُكَذِّبُ بِآيَاتِنَا فَهُم يُوزَعُون حَتَّى إِذَا جَاؤُا قَالَ أَكَذَّبتُم بِآيَاتِى

on the day when we shall assemble from every nation, a crowd of those who have treated our revelations as falsehoods, they shall be driven, until when they shall have come, he will say, *have you then treated my revelation as falsehood?*

The preterites جَاؤُا and قَالَ have a future sense, on account of the indefinite نَحشُر, by which حَتَّى إِذَا is preceded.

What has been said of the tenses of verbs coming after إِذَا, إِذَا مَا, is equally applicable to إِذَا.

After the conditional particle إِن *if*, the preterite acquires the force of the subjunctive future : كُتِبَ عَلَيكُم إِذَا حَضَرَ أَحَدَكُم
ٱلمَوتُ إِن تَرَكَ خَيرًا ٱلوَصِيَّةُ. *It is written to you, when death shall come to one of you*, if he (should or shall) leave property (*let there be) a will.*

If the verb كَانَ come between إِن and a verb in the preterite, the latter expresses a past sense, as إِن كُنتُ أَجرَمتُ أَو
جَنَيتُ. *If I have committed a crime or been guilty of a fault.*

When after إِن, a present is to be expressed, the preterite of كَانَ, and the indefinite tense of the verb required is employed.

Thus, اُشْكُرُوا لِلَّهِ إِنْ كُنْتُمْ إِيَّاهُ تَعْبُدُونَ. *Give thanks to God,* if it be him you serve.

When the conjunction إِنْ comes before two correlative propositions, of which the first is conditional and the second dependent on the first, the verbs in the preterite may be rendered, the first by the subjunctive or hypothetical present, and the second by the future, إِنْ فَعَلْتَ ذَلِكَ ضَيَّعْتَ مَالِي, *if I do that, I shall lose my property.*

The preterite of the verb كَانَ is often employed without conveying any idea of time, and merely connecting a subject and an attribute, as أُولَئِكَ مَا كَانَ لَهُمْ أَنْ يَدْخُلُوهَا إِلَّا خَائِفِينَ *Those (people), it is not for them to enter, unless with fear.*

Examples without number may be met with, where the preterite of كَانَ, is thus used without any indication of time past, and merely as the opposite of the negative verb لَيْسَ, which has no tense but the preterite, with the power of the indefinite present.

The Indefinite.

The indefinite, (or future of Erpenius) is formed by prefixing to the different persons, one of the four letters comprised in the technical word أَتَيْنِ, and by adding one or two of those contained in the other technical word يُونَا. The prefixed serviles have constantly *Fathah,* excepting in the second, third and fourth of the triliterals, and the first of the quadriliterals, where they take *Dammah;* they jazmate the first radical. If the second radical of the preterite has *Dammah*, it remains also *Dammah* in the indefinite, but if *Kasrah*, it is changed in the indefinite to *Fathah*, excepting نَعِمَ *it was pleasant*; حَسِبَ *he thought*; يَئِسَ *he despaired*; يَبِسَ *it dried up*; فَضِلَ *he excelled*; قَنِطَ *he despaired*; عَرَضَ *he met*, which may be pronounced both with *Fathah* and *Kasrah*, and even sometimes with *Dammah*; as يَفْضُلُ, يَفْضِلُ, يَفْضَلُ, يَنْعَمُ, يَنْعِمُ, يَنْعَمُ; but if the second radical takes *Fathah* in the preterite, in the indefinite it is changed to *Dammah*; as كَتَبَ *he wrote*, يَكْتُبُ; or to *Kasrah*, as ضَرَبَ *he struck*, يَضْرِبُ; unless the second or third radical is a guttural letter, in which case it sometimes remains *Fathah*, as شَغَلَ *he laboured*, يَشْغَلُ; مَنَحَ *he presented*; يَمْنَحُ; and in the same manner رَكَنَ without a guttural, *he reclined* يَرْكَنُ, and أَبَى *he refused* يَأْبَى. The last radical has *Dammah*, but when followed by the serviles يُونَا it is sometimes dropped, sometimes changed, as is seen in the paradigm.

The indefinite, however, when preceded by certain particles, admits of several variations in the termination which are classed under the grammatical heads of Apocope, Antithesis, and Paragoge.

Apocope not only converts the *Dammah* of the last radical into *Jazmah*, but cuts off the final ن every where, excepting in the feminine plural. The particles which occasion the Apocope are لَمْ *not*; لَمَّا *not yet*; لَا *no, not*; and لِ when prefixed to the future in an imperative sense. لَمْ يَنْصُرْ *he did not assist*, may answer as a general example.

Plural.	Dual.	Singular.
لَمْ يَنْصُرْنَ لَمْ يَنْصُرُوا لَمْ يَنْصُرْ	لَمْ يَنْصُرَا لَمْ تَنْصُرَا لَمْ يَنْصُرْ	لَمْ تَنْصُرْ لَمْ يَنْصُرْ
لَمْ تَنْصُرْنَ لَمْ تَنْصُرُوا لَمْ تَنْصُرْ	لَمْ تَنْصُرَا	لَمْ تَنْصُرِى لَمْ تَنْصُرْ
لَمْ نَنْصُرْ		لَمْ أَنْصُرْ

To the above particles may be added the following : إِنْ *if;*
مَنْ and أَىُّ *whoever;* مَا *whatever,* and its compounds كُلَّمَا *all
that,* and كُلَّمَا *every time that;* أَنَّى and أَيْنَ , حَيْثُمَا *every where;*
مَتَى and إِنَّمَا, مَهْمَا *as often as;* كَيْفَ and كَيْفَمَا *however;*
أَيَّانَ *when, whenever,* and in poetry إِذَا *when;* provided, however, another verb in the retributive sense (as whatever you
will do, I will do) is subjoined in the same sentence. If both
verbs are in the indefinite, they conform to this rule; if only
the first, that does the same; but if the last alone is indefinite,
it follows either this, or the general rule; as مَا تَصْنَعْ أَصْنَعْ
whatever you will do, I will do; مَا تَصْنَعْ صَنَعْتُ *whatever you
will do, I did;* مَا صَنَعْتَ أَصْنَعْ or مَا صَنَعْتَ أَصْنَعْ, *whatever
you did, I will do.*

This rule takes place likewise, when an imperative precedes,
to which the indefinite is responsive; as أَنْصُرْنِى أَنْصُرْكَ *assist
me, I will assist you.*

Antithesis, by the influence of another set of particles, cuts
off the final ن in the same manner, and changes the *Dammah*
of the third radical to *Fathah;* these are لَنْ *by no means,
not at all;* لِ, أَنْ, كَى, لِأَنْ, كَى, لِكَى, كَيْلَا, لِكَيْلَا *that, in order*

to, *because*; اِلَّا , لَيِّلًا *lest not, so as not*; أَو *or*; حَتَّى *until*. Also

فَ , prefixed to an indefinite, referring to a preceding word, as

اُنْصُرْنِى فَأَنْصُرَكَ *assist me and I will assist you*; likewise وَ *when*

it implies *and at the same time*; as لَا تَأْكُلِ ٱلسَّمَكَ وَ تَشْرَبِ ٱللَّبَنَ

do not eat fish and at the same time drink milk; and also

اِذَا *or*, اِذَنْ *well! do so! come on! &c.* لَنْ يَنْصُرَ *he will by

no means assist*, is here put for a general example.

Plural.			Dual.			Singular.	
لَنْ يَنْصُرْنَ	لَنْ يَنْصُرُوا	لَنْ تَنْصُرَا	لَنْ يَنْصُرَا	لَنْ يَنْصُرَ		لَنْ تَنْصُرَ	لَنْ يَنْصُرَ
لَنْ تَنْصُرْنَ	لَنْ تَنْصُرُوا		لَنْ تَنْصُرَا			لَنْ تَنْصُرِى	لَنْ تَنْصُرَ
	لَنْ نَنْصُرَ						لَنْ اَنْصُرَ

Paragoge adds to the future نَّ or نْ ; but this last only
in the singular, and in the plural masculine and common, when
it denotes commanding, wishing, intreating, or asking about
futurity, in the manner following : هَلْ يَنْصُرَنْ *will he assist?*

Plural.			Singular.	
هَلْ يَنْصُرْنَانِ	هَلْ يَنْصُرُنَّ		هَلْ تَنْصُرَنْ	هَلْ يَنْصُرَنْ
هَلْ تَنْصُرْنَانِ	هَلْ تَنْصُرُنَّ		هَلْ تَنْصُرِنْ	هَلْ تَنْصُرَنْ
	هَلْ نَنْصُرَنْ			هَلْ اَنْصُرَنْ

Dual.

هَلْ تَنْصُرَانِ	هَلْ يَنْصُرَانِ
	هَلْ تَنْصُرَانِ

لَيْتَ يَنْصُرْنْ *would to God he would assist!*

Plural.			Singular.		
Com.	Mas.		Fem.	Com.	Mas.
	لَيْتَ يَنْصُرْنْ		لَيْتَ تَنْصُرْ	لَيْتَ	لَيْتَ يَنْصُرْنْ
	لَيْتَ تَنْصُرْنْ		لَيْتَ تَنْصُرِنْ	لَيْتَ	لَيْتَ تَنْصُرِنْ
لَيْتَ نَنْصُرْنْ				لَيْتَ أَنْصُرْنْ	

After this mode may be inflected لِيَنْصُرَّنْ and لِيَنْصُرْنْ *let him
assist* ; لَا تَنْصُرَّنْ and لَا تَنْصُرْنْ *do not assist* ; or when preceded
by an oath, as وَاللّٰهِ يَنْصُرَنْ *by God he will assist* ; or
لَنَقْتُلَنْ *then by God we will kill.*

The indefinite tense may be translated by the future of
the indicative. 1. When preceded by the particle سَوْفَ , or
one of its abridged forms سَوْ سَفْ سْ . 2. When preceded by
the negative لَا , provided, however, that neither of the other
negative particles لَمْ, مَا, or لَمَّا have occurred in the phrase
before. 3. When, as is often the case, there is a plain indication of a future sense.

When these rules do not operate, or when the indefinite is
preceded by مَا , it becomes a present tense, مَنْ يَفْعَلْ ذَلِكَ
عُدْوَانًا وَ ظُلْمًا فَسَوْفَ نُصْلِيهِ نَارًا *he who shall do that maliciously
and unjustly,* we will punish him *by fire.*

إِنَّ ٱلَّذِين يَكْتُمُون مَا أَنْزَل ٱللَّه مِن ٱلْكِتَاب و يَشْتَرُون بِه ثَمَنًا قَلِيلًا أُولَٰئِك مَا يَأْكُلُون فِي بُطُونِهِم إِلَّا ٱلنَّار وَلَا يَكْلِمُهم ٱللَّه يَوْم ٱلْقِيَامَة وَلَا يُزَكِّيهِم, *verily* they who hide *the book which God has sent down (from heaven), and* buy *with it a thing of small price, those* eat *nothing but fire, and God on the day of judgment will not speak to them nor approve them.*

In this passage are seen examples of the indefinite with a future signification after لَا, and with that of the present after مَا.

The particle لَن restricts it to the future, لَن يَضْرِب *he will not strike.*

The particles أَنْ and كَى *that, in order that,* with their compounds; also حَتَّى *until,* and لِ give to the indefinite a future meaning.

أَمْ حَسِبْتُم أَنْ تَدْخُلُوا ٱلْجَنَّة *do you think* you will enter *Paradise?*

إِجْعَل لِي وَزِيرًا مِن أَهْلِي هَرُون أَخِي — كَى نُسَبِّحَك كَثِيرًا *Give me an assistant out of my own family, my brother Hárún, in order that* we may praise thee *much.*

It will be often found, that a verb in the indefinite tense, depends upon a verb immediately preceding, without the interposition of any particle; in this case, the verb in the indefinite must be translated by the subjunctive, preceded by, *in order that;*

by the infinitive, or by the participle present. ظَعَنَ يَقْتَادُ ٱلْقَلْبَ

بِأَزِمَّتِهِ *he departed*, leading *my heart by the bridle.*

فَلَبِثْنَا نَرْقُبُهُ نَرْقَبَةَ أَهِلَّةِ ٱلْاَعْيَادِ *we continued* to watch *his*
return, like the watching for the festival new moons.

وَ أَمَّكُمْ دُونَ ٱلْاَنَامِ طُرًّا

يَبْغِى قِرًى مِنْكُمْ وَ مُسْتَقَرًّا

He seeks you above all other men, in order that he may
solicit *hospitality, and an abode.*

When preceded by لَمْ *not*, لَمَّا *not yet*, the indefinite assumes
a preterite sense ; لَمْ يَضْرِبْ *he has not struck*, لَمَّا تَخْرُجْ *he has*
not yet gone out.

This rule is liable to some exceptions ; and it is remarkable, that in the example given by M. de Sacy, the verb
following لَمْ, must really be translated by the present. أَلَمْ
تَعْلَمْ أَنَّ ٱللَّهَ لَهُ مُلْكُ ٱلسَّمَوَاتِ وَ ٱلْاَرْضِ do you not know
that to God belongs the empire of heaven and earth?

That the indefinite, preceded by لَمْ, may sometimes be translated by the present, was observed by Mr Richardson, who gives
the following instance :

وَ لَوْ لَمْ يَكُنْ فِى هَذِهِ ٱلْاَلْفَاظِ إِلَّا مَا يُشَكِّكُكَ فِى إِعْتِقَادِكَ

ٱلْمَوْرُوثِ لَكَفَى بِذَلِكَ نَفْعًا فَإِنَّ مَنْ لَمْ يَشُكَّ لَمْ يَنْظُرْ وَ مَنْ

لَمْ يَنْظُرْ لَمْ يَبْصِرْ وَ مَنْ لَمْ يَبْصِرْ بَقِىَ فِى ٱلْعَمَى وَ ٱلْحَيْرَةِ *but if there is nothing in these words, but what makes you doubtful of your hereditary belief, even that is sufficient for your good; for he who doubts not, considers not; and he who considers not, understands not; and he who understands not, remains in blindness and perplexity.*

When لِ is prefixed, the indefinite tense expresses command, when لَا comes before, it has a deprecative or prohibitive signification; فَمَنْ شَهِدَ مِنْكُمُ ٱلشَّهْرَ فَلْيَصُمْهُ *and he among you who shall see the month,* let him fast (*during*) *it.* لَا تَقْرَبَا هٰذِهِ ٱلشَّجَرَةَ *approach not you (two) this tree.*

The preterite of the substantive verb كَانَ, as has been before said, when put before the indefinite tense, gives it the sense of the imperfect indicative. Should the proposition be negative and the adverb لَمْ be employed, the indefinite يَكُنْ put before, gives to the following indefinite the same meaning. When however one or more verbs in the preterite have gone before, they communicate that sense to the following indefinite, without the intervention of كَانَ.

رَكِبَ جَعْفَرٌ إِلَى ٱلصَّيْدِ وَ جَعَلَ يَشْرَبُ تَارَةً وَ يَهْلُو أُخْرَى وَ تَحِفُّ ٱلرَّشِيدِ وَ هَدَايَاهُ تَأْتِيهِ وَ عِنْدَهُ بُخْتِيشُوعُ ٱلطَّبِيبُ وَ أَبُو زَكَّارٍ ٱلْعَمَى يَغَنِّيهِ *Jáfar rode to the chase; and sometimes drank and amused himself at others; and presents and gifts came to him from Rashíd; and Bakhtishuá the physician was with him, and Abú Zakkár the blind sang to him.*

It often, however, will be found, that the indefinite carries this meaning without being preceded by the preterite كَانَ, or any other verb in that tense ; the attending circumstances fixing the sense in which it must be taken.

قُلْ فَلِمَ تَقْتُلُونَ أَنْبِيَآءَ ٱللَّهِ مِنْ قَبْلُ

Say (to them) *why* did you kill *the prophets of God, before* (now).

Beside the pluperfect and imperfect, which the Arabians express by adding the preterite of the verb كَانَ to the preterite and indefinite of another verb, they form a past or retrospective future by prefixing the indefinite of كَانَ to a preterite, sometimes inserting the particle قد between the two verbs.

يَقُولُونَ مَتَى هَذَا ٱلْوَعْدُ إِنْ كُنْتُمْ صَادِقِينَ قُلْ عَسَى أَنْ يَكُونَ رَدِفَ لَكُمْ بَعْضُ مَا تَسْتَعْجِلُونَ *they say, when will this menace* (take effect) *if you be trustworthy? Say peradventure somewhat of that which you wish to hasten, will have* (already) *mounted behind you.*

أَغِيرُوا عَلَى نَعَمِهِمْ فَلْنَأْخُذْهُ فَنَكُونَ قَدْ أَخَذْنَا عِوَضًا مِمَّا صَنَعَ بِنَا

Rush upon their camels, take them, and then we shall have taken *reparation for what has been done to us.*

The use which is thus made of the verb كَانَ to modify the preterite and indefinite tenses, must not be considered as constituting it an auxiliary verb, in the sense in which that term is used by European grammarians. The use of the preterite or indefinite of the verb كَانَ has for its object only the expression of that double relation of time belonging to the preterite anterior or pluperfect, the limited preterite or imperfect, and the retrospective future; effecting this by the union of two verbs, either in the same tense, as كَانَ كَتَبَ *he had written*; or in different tenses, as كَانَ يَكْتُبُ *he did write, or was writing*; and يَكُونُ كَتَبَ *he will have written*.

The imperative, as well as the future, sometimes takes the paragogical نِ, as اَنْصُرَنَّ or اَنْصُرَنْ *assist thou*. This mood is formed by prefixing ا, which, when beginning a sentence, always has *Kasrah*; as اِعْلَمْ *know thou*; اِضْرِبْ *strike thou*; unless the vowel of the penult. radical, which is always the same with that of the future, be *Dammah*; when ا also takes *Dammah*; as اُكْتُبْ *write thou*, the first and last radicals take *Jazmah*. In the formation of the genders and numbers, the final serviles يُونَا are employed, as in the future. The imperative is only used in the second person; the others being supplied by the future; لِ with *Kasrah* being then prefixed, as لِيَنْصُرْ *let him assist*; لِنَنْصُرْ *let us assist*; which is also sometimes the case with the second, as لِتَنْصُرْ *assist thou*; but لِ drops *Kasrah*, and takes *Jazmah*, when فَ or وَ are prefixed, as فَلْيَنْصُرْ *then let him assist*.

The office of the imperative of triliteral verbs is sometimes performed by an indeclineable word, of the form فَعَالِ or فِعَالِ. Thus, from نَزَلَ *to alight*, is formed نَزَالَ or نِزَالِ *alight thou*.

The participle of the primitive triliteral verb in the active voice is of the form فَاعِل ; and in the passive of the form مَفْعُول . There are however many other forms; and particularly فَعِيل and فَعُول , which are both active and passive.

It has been objected that these participles are merely verbal adjectives, conveying no idea of time; but I have preferred the authority of Erpenius. It would seem they are rather of all times, and as in the following instance, often appear to be true participles, و ٱللَّه بَصِير بِمَا يَعْمَلُون , *God is seeing (sees) what they do.*

The Infinitive differs greatly from those of other languages, being merely a verbal noun substantive in the accusative case; corresponding, in some measure, to the Latin gerund in *do*. It is often used adverbially, and by a peculiar idiom is joined sometimes to its own verb, to give a greater energy to the meaning.

Although it is not considered that the nature of the participle, partaking both of verb and adjective, should exclude it from a place in the paradigm; or that the infinitive should be rejected, because, in truth, it is a verbal noun; which all infinitives really are; a more minute account of each will be given hereafter under the heads of "Name of Agent and Patient," and "Noun of Action."

The account here given of the use of the tenses, may seem to be somewhat difficult and complicated, yet it will be found that the times of Arabic verbs are subject of very little doubt, unless it be in the Korán, the elliptical, figurative, and somewhat incoherent style of which, leads to different interpretations.

6

The following principles may be regarded as general. 1. That the two tenses of Arabic verbs, have each its determined value, the one of the past, the other of the present and future. 2. It is often unimportant whether this second tense be translated by the present or future, and when that distinction is really necessary, the sense is never dubious. 3. In an infinite number of cases, the time of a proposition is fixed, not by the forms of the verbs, but by the conjunctions, or adverbial conjunctions of time, by the negative adverbs, or other particles to the influence of which the propositions are subjected; or finally, by the relation which the propositions bear to each other.

PASSIVE VOICE.

Preterite.

Plural.			Dual.			Singular.			Pers.
Fem.	Com.	Mas.	Fem.	Com.	Mas.	Fem.	Com.	Mas.	
كُتِبْنَ		كُتِبُوا	كُتِبَتَا		كُتِبَا	كُتِبَتْ		كُتِبَ	3
كُتِبْتُنَّ		كُتِبْتُمْ		كُتِبْتُمَا		كُتِبْتِ		كُتِبْتَ	2
	كُتِبْنَا						كُتِبْتُ		1

Indefinite.

Plural.			Dual.			Singular.			Pers.
Fem.	Com.	Mas.	Fem.	Com.	Mas.	Fem.	Com.	Mas.	
يُكْتَبْنَ		يُكْتَبُونَ	تُكْتَبَانِ		يُكْتَبَانِ	تُكْتَبُ		يُكْتَبُ	3
تُكْتَبْنَ		تُكْتَبُونَ		تُكْتَبَانِ		تُكْتَبِينَ		تُكْتَبُ	2
	نُكْتَبُ						أُكْتَبُ		1

Participle.

Plural.			Dual.			Singular.		
Fem.	Com.	Mas.	Fem.	Com.	Mas.	Fem.	Com.	Mas.
مَكْتُوبَاتٌ		مَكْتُوبُونَ	مَكْتُوبَتَانِ		مَكْتُوبَانِ	مَكْتُوبَةٌ		مَكْتُوبٌ

The passive preterite only differs from the active by the first radical always having *Dammah* for its vowel, and the second *Kasrah*.

In the indefinite tense, the incremental letters أَتِين, always have *Dammah* for their vowel, and that of the second radical is always *Fathah*.

The want of the imperative is supplied by the indefinite tense with لِ prefixed, as لِيَنْصَرْ *let him be assisted.*

6—2

PARADIGM OF THE QUADRILITERAL VERBS.

Active Voice.

Infin.	Part.	Imper.	Indef.	Preter.	
قمطارا	مقمطر	قمطر	يقمطر	قمطر	1
تقمطرا	متقمطر	تقمطر	يتقمطر	تقمطر	2
اقمنطارا	مقمنطر	اقمنطر	يقمنطر	اقمنطر	3
اقمطارا	مقمطر	اقمطرر	يقمطر	اقمطرّ	4

Passive Voice.

Part.	Indef.	Preter.	
مقمطر	يقمطر	قمطر	1
متقمطر	يتقمطر	تقمطر	2
مقمنطر	يقمنطر	اقمنطر	3
مقمطر	يقمطر	اقمطرّ	4

DERIVATIVES OF THE FIRST CLASS OF REGULAR TRILITERAL VERBS.

Active Voice.

Infin.	Part.	Imper.	Indef.	Preter.	
تَكْتِيبًا	مُكَتِّب	كَتِّب	يُكَتِّب	كَتَّب	2
مُكَاتَبَةً	مُكَاتِب	كَاتِب	يُكَاتِب	كَاتَبَ	3
إِكْتَابًا	مُكْتِب	أَكْتِب	يُكْتِب	أَكْتَبَ	4

Passive Voice.

Part.	Indef.	Preter.	
مُكَتَّب	يُكَتَّب	كُتِّب	2
مُكَاتَب	يُكَاتَب	كُوتِب	3
مُكْتَب	يُكْتَب	أُكْتِب	4

Of Quadriliterals, and Derivatives of the First Class.

Quadriliterals and derivatives of the first class, are conjugated in nearly the same manner, and only differ from the preceding in the following particulars.

1. The radical penultima in the preterite active always has *Fathah*, and in the indefinite *Kasrah*, except in the second quadriliteral, where it retains *Fathah*. أَتَّين in the indefinite active as well as passive bears *Dammah*, as دَحْرج , يدَحْرج , but the second, third, and fourth quadriliterals active keep *Fathah*.

2. The imperative is formed from the future by dropping أتين and the vowel of the last radical, as دَحْرج , كَسَر . If the preterite commences with *Alif* servile, that letter takes the place of the incremental letters of the indefinite.

3. In the fourth form أَفْعل , *Alif* is dropped whenever a servile precedes the radical letters, thus يَنْصِر and not يَأْنْصِر . Initial *Alif*, forming the derivative verbs, is dropped with its vowel whenever the serviles أتين come before; whence in the imperative, where those serviles are lost, *Alif* and its vowel return, as أَنْصِر , where it is not to be regarded as being *Alif* of union forming the imperative.

DERIVATIVES OF THE SECOND CLASS OF REGULAR TRILITERAL VERBS.

Active Voice.

Infin.	Part.	Imper.	Indef.	Preter.	
تَكَتُّبًا	مُتَكَتِّب	تَكَتَّبْ	يَتَكَتَّبُ	تَكَتَّبَ	5
تَكَاتُبًا	مُتَكَاتِب	تَكَاتَبْ	يَتَكَاتَبُ	تَكَاتَبَ	6
إِنْكِتَابًا	مُنْكَتِب	إِنْكَتِبْ	يَنْكَتِبُ	إِنْكَتَبَ	7
اِكْتِتَابًا	مُكْتَتِب	اِكْتَتِبْ	يَكْتَتِبُ	اِكْتَتَبَ	8
اِكْتِبَابًا	مُكْتَبّ	اِكْتَبِبْ	يَكْتَبُّ	اِكْتَبَّ	9

Passive Voice.

Part.	Indef.	Preter.	
مُتَكَتَّب	يَتَكَتَّبُ	تُكُتِّبَ	5
مُتَكَاتَب	يَتَكَاتَبُ	تُكُوتِبَ	6
مُنْكَتَب	يُنْكَتَبُ	أُنْكُتِبَ	7
مُكْتَتَب	يُكْتَتَبُ	أُكْتُتِبَ	8

DERIVATIVES OF THE THIRD CLASS OF REGULAR TRILITERAL VERBS.

Active Voice.

Infin.	Part.	Imper.	Indef.	Preter.	
اِسْتَكْتَابًا	مُسْتَكْتِبْ	اِسْتَكْتِبْ	يَسْتَكْتِبْ	اِسْتَكْتَبَ	10
اِكْتِيَابًا	مُكْتَابْ	اِكْتَابِبْ	يَكْتَابّ	اِكْتَابَّ	11
اِكْتِيتَابًا	مُكْتَوْتِبْ	اِكْتَوْتِبْ	يَكْتَوْتِبْ	اِكْتَوْتَبَ	12
اِكْتَوَّابًا	مُكْتَوِّبْ	اِكْتَوِّبْ	يَكْتَوِّبْ	اِكْتَوَّبَ	13

Passive Voice.

Part.	Indef.	Preter.	
مُسْتَكْتَبْ	يُسْتَكْتَبْ	اُسْتُكْتِبَ	10
مُكْتَوْتَبْ	يُكْتَوْتَبْ	اُكْتُوتِبَ	12
مُكْتَوَّبْ	يُكْتَوَّبْ	اُكْتُوِّبَ	13

Of the other Derivatives.

In the remaining derivative conjugations, the penultima of the preterite active always has *Fathah*.

The indefinite is formed from the preterite, by prefixing أَتِينَ with *Fathah;* the initial *Alif,* if there be one, being dropped, according to the rule just given, and the last *Fathah* regularly changed into *Dammah,* the penultima receiving *Kasrah,* except in the fifth and sixth forms, which retain it, as اِجْتَمَعَ ، يَجْتَمِعُ، يَتَبَاعَدَ ، تَبَاعَدَ ، يَتَكَسَّرَ ، تَكَسَّرَ ، but those two forms beginning with ت, sometimes drop that letter, when ت of أَتِينَ is prefixed, as تَبَاعَدَ for تَتَبَاعَدَ ، تَكَسَّرَ for تَتَكَسَّرَ ، which the vowels will easily prevent being taken for the future of the second and third conjugations, their future actives being يَفْعَلُ and يَفَاعَلُ، and the passive يُفْعَلُ and يُفَاعَلُ.

The imperative is formed, as in the quadriliterals, يَتَكَسَّرَ تَكَسَّرْ، the *Alif* which had been dropt returning with *Kasrah,* in those forms to which it appertains, as اِسْتَعْمِلْ يَسْتَعْمِلُ.

The ninth and eleventh have no passives, the others form the passive preterite from the active, the first two vowels being changed into *Dammah,* and the penultima into *Kasrah,* as تُفُعِّلَ تَفَعَّلَ; the indefinite is also formed from the indefinite active, the *Fathah* of the letters أَتِينَ being converted into *Dammah,* and the penultimate *Kasrah* into *Fathah,* as يُسْتَفْعَلُ يَسْتَفْعِلُ.

THE SURD VERB.

Active Voice.

Preterite.

Fem.	Com.	Mas.	Fem.	Com.	Mas.	Fem.	Com.	Mas.	Pers.
	Plural.			Dual.			Singular.		
فَرَرْنَ	فَرُّوا		فَرَّتَا		فَرَّا	فَرَّتْ		فَرَّ	3
فَرَرْتُنَّ	فَرَرْتُمْ			فَرَرْتُمَا		فَرَرْتِ		فَرَرْتَ	2
	فَرَرْنَا						فَرَرْتُ		1

Indefinite.

Fem.	Com.	Mas.	Fem.	Com.	Mas.	Fem.	Com.	Mas.	Pers.
يَفِرِرْنَ	يَفِرُّونَ		تَفِرَّانِ		يَفِرَّانِ	تَفِرُّ		يَفِرُّ	3
تَفِرِرْنَ	تَفِرُّونَ			تَفِرَّانِ		تَفِرِّينَ		تَفِرُّ	2
	نَفِرُّ						أَفِرُّ		1

Imperative.

Fem.	Com.	Mas.	Fem.	Com.	Mas.	Fem.	Com.	Mas.
إِفْرِرْنَ	إِفِرُّوا			إِفِرَّا		إِفِرِّي		إِفْرِرْ

Participle.

Fem.	Com.	Mas.	Fem.	Com.	Mas.	Fem.	Com.	Mas.
فَارَّاتٌ	فَارُّونَ		فَارَّتَانِ		فَارَّانِ	فَارَّةٌ		فَارٌّ

Infinitive.

فَرًّا

OF THE IRREGULAR VERBS.

1. *Of the Surd Verb.*

The triliteral verbs, of which the third radical is the same as the second, are called surd verbs, الأصمّ, as مَدَّ for مَدَدَ *he* extended. All the irregularity of surd verbs is reduced to the following rule. In all the inflections where, according to the conjugation of the regular verb, the last radical bears a vowel, the penultimate radical is inserted in the last by *Tashdíd*, the vowel of the penultimate radical is then suppressed, unless the letter preceding it has *Jazmah*, for then the vowel of the penultimate radical is given to the latter, which would otherwise have *Jazmah*. In all the inflections where, on the contrary, the last radical has *Jazmah*, these verbs are conjugated regularly. Thus in the third person of the preterite singular and masculine, حَبِبَ becomes حَبَّ. The second person of the singular of the same tense is regularly حَبِبْتَ.

In the third person of the singular masculine of the indefinite tense, يَحْبِبُ is contracted into يَحَبُّ, the *Dammah* of the second radical passing to the first, in place of its *Jazmah*. If the indefinite follows a particle producing *Jazmah*, or an apocope, it becomes regularly يَحْبِبْ, because the last radical having *Jazmah*, no contraction takes place. Under the influence of these particles, *Fathah* or *Kasrah* may be given to the last radical in lieu of *Jazmah*; in this case the contraction returning يَفِرّ, يَفُرّ for يَفْرِرُ. In verbs of which the second radical in the indefinite tense bears *Dammah*, the same vowel may also be given to the last. Thus, instead of يَمْدُد we may write with the contraction يَمُدّ, يَمَدّ, or even يَمِدّ.

The imperative preserves its regular form. According to the rule of the surd verb we should write اِفْرِرِى, اِفْرِرَا and اِفْرِرُوا, but the reason why the rule is not here followed, is, that the *Alif* of union is always followed by a letter bearing *Jazmah*.

But beside the regular form, the imperative has another, in which the insertion of the second radical in the third does take place, except in the plural feminine. *Alif* of the imperative is omitted here, according to the rule, by which it is never prefixed to a letter bearing a vowel.

	Masc.		Fem.		Masc.		Fem.
S. فِرّ or فُرّ			فِرِّى	D. فِرَّا	P. فِرُّوا		اِفْرِرْنَ

Surd verbs follow in the passive voice the same rules as in the active, thus فُرّ is for فُرِرَ, *Kasrah* being dropt, because the preceding letter already bears a vowel; in the indefinite tense it is يُفَرّ for يُفْرَرُ, *Fathah* being given to the preceding letter which before had *Jazmah*; but in the third person plural feminine without contraction يُفْرَرْنَ. The derivative verbs follow the same rule of contraction in those forms which admit it. The contraction in these derivative verbs takes place or not, following the same rules as the primitive.

Derivative Verbs bearing contraction.

	Preter.			Indef.	Imp.
3	فَارَّ	for	فَارَرَ	يَفَارَّ	فَارِرْ
4	أَفَرَّ		أَفْرَرَ	يُفِرَّ	أَفْرِرْ
6	تَفَارَّ		تَفَارَرَ	يَتَفَارَّ	تَفَارَرْ
7	إِنْفَرَّ		إِنْفَرَرَ	يَنْفَرَّ	إِنْفَرِرْ
8	إِفْتَرَّ		إِفْتَرَرَ	يَفْتَرَّ	إِفْتَرِرْ
10	إِسْتَفَرَّ		إِسْتَفْرَرَ	يَسْتَفِرَّ	إِسْتَفْرِرْ
12	إِفْرَوَّرَّ		إِفْرَوْرَرَ	يَفْرَوِرّ	إِفْرَوِرِرْ

In these derivative forms, as in the primitive, the contraction may be preserved in the indefinite tense, and in the imperative, whenever the third radical ought (in the indefinite tense by the influence of a particle preceding,) to bear *Jazmah*, by giving to that third radical a vowel أَدِلَّهْ for أَدْلِلْه, and أَقِلَّهْ for أَقْلِلْه.

The derivative forms to which *Tashdíd* naturally belongs are not susceptible of contraction.

Forms.	Pret.	Indef.	Imp.
2	فَرَّرَ	يُفَرِّرُ	فَرِّرْ
5	تَفَرَّرَ	يَتَفَرَّرُ	تَفَرَّرْ
9	إِفْرَرَّ	يَفْرَرُّ	إِفْرَرِرْ
11	إِفْرَارَّ	يَفْرَارُّ	إِفْرَارِرْ
13	إِفْرَوَّرَ	يَفْرَوِّرُ	إِفْرَوِّرْ

Verbs ending in ت or ن double these letters by *Tashdíd* in those persons, whose final characteristic serviles are ت or ن, as زَيَّنَّا *we adorned*, for زَيَّنْنَا; and سَكَتَّ *thou wert silent*, for سَكَتْتَ; but neither these, nor the verbs beginning with ت or ن, when they coalesce with the initial characteristics of the fifth, seventh, and other conjugations, are considered as irregulars, إِنْقَبَّ *it was dug through*, for إِنْنَقَبَ and إِتَّجَرَ *it was negotiated*, for إِتْتَجَرَ being in every respect perfect verbs.

2. *Of Verbs having Hamzah for one of their Radicals.*

Verbs which have *Hamzah* or *Alif* moveable for one of their radicals, are called مَهْمُوز or hamzated.

The conjugation of hamzated verbs is almost the same as that of regular verbs; it is only necessary to observe the rules of permutation, in virtue of which وُ or يُ are substituted for the radical *Hamzah*.

As *Hamzah* may be either the first, second or third radical, there are three sorts of hamzated verbs.

Verb Primitive.

Active Voice.

Pret. اَثَرَ —Indef. يَاْثُرُ —Imper. اِيثُرْ —Part. اَثِرٌ for اَلثِرُ —

Infin. اَثْرًا.

If the imperative has *Dammah* for its vowel, the radical *Alif* is changed into و, as اوْمُلْ from the root اَمَلَ. The three verbs اَخَذَ, اَمَرَ and اَكَلَ, make in the imperative خُذْ, مُرْ and كُلْ; sometimes however اوْكُلْ and اوْمُرْ are written regularly. When the imperative of the verb اَمَرَ is preceded by the conjunctions و or فَ, it is also written فَامُرْ, وَامُرْ.

Passive Voice.

Pret. اُثِرَ   Indef. يُوْثَرُ for يُاْثَرُ   Part. مَاْثُورٌ

Derivatives.

	Pret.	Indef.	Imp.	P.
2nd form Act.	اَثَّرَ	يُؤَثِّرُ	اَثِّرْ	مُؤَثِّرٌ
Pass.	اُثِّرَ	يُؤَثَّرُ		مُؤَثَّرٌ
3rd Act.	آثَرَ or اَاثَرَ	يُواثِرُ	آثِرْ	مُواثِرٌ
Pass.	اوثِرَ	يُواثَرُ		مُواثَرٌ

4th form Act.   مُؤَثِّرٌ   يُؤَثِّرُ   أَثَّرَ

Pass.   مُؤَثَّرٌ   يُؤَثَّرُ   أُثِّرَ

Inf. 2nd تَأْثِيرًا   3rd مُوَاثَرَةً   4th إِيثَارًا

It is only necessary to apply the same rules to all the
other forms of derivative verbs, in order to find their root,
when *Hamzah* is changed into و or ى. Thus اُسْتُوصِل is the
passive voice of إِسْتَأْصِل. In the sixth form it must be observed
that the *Hamzah*, preceded by *Fathah*, followed by *Alif* quiescent,
may be changed into و; thus from the primitive verb, أَكَّل may
be written in the sixth form تَآكَل or تواكل.

In order to conjugate the verbs where *Hamzah* is the
second or last radical, it is only necessary to equally apply
the rules of permutation common to the three letters ا, و, ى,
or those which are peculiar to *Alif-Hamzah*.

For example, if *Hamzah* be the second radical, it is preserved or changed into و or ى, according to the vowel belonging
to it, or immediately preceding it; thus, in the preterite is written
سَأَل, بوس, in the indefinite يَسْأَل, صَاب for صَئِب, بَاس for بَئِس,
and in the
forms derived from the primitive لَأَم.
and in the passive voice it is سُئِل, يَبُوس, يَصَاب

	Pret.	Indef.	Imp.	P.
3rd form	لاَعَم	يلاَعِم	لاَعِم	مُلاَعَم
4th	اَلاَم	يلِيم	أَلِيم	مُلِيم
8th	إِلتَام	يلتِيم	اِلتِيم	مُلتَيم
10th	إِستَلَم	يستلِيم	إِستلِيم	مُستلِيم

Inf. 3rd مُلاَعَمَة   4th اِلاَ مَا   8th اِلتِيَامًا   10th اِستِلاَمًا

If the *Hamzah* is the last radical, care must equally be taken to preserve or change it into وُ or ىُ, according to the rules of permutation;

3rd Pers. Mas.	Fem.	3rd Pers. Mas.
بَرَأ	بَرَأَت	بَرَاءَت
هَنَأ	هَنَأَت	هَنَاءَت
دَنُو	دَنُوت	دَنُوت
خَرِى	خَرِءَت	خَرِءَت

Indef.   يَبرو يَهنِى يَدنو يَخرَا or يَخرو.

Impera.   أبرو إهنِى ادنو إخرَا

The case is the same in the passive voice, and derivative forms.

	Pret.	Indef.
2nd form	جَشَّى	يَجَشِّى
5th	تَجَشَّا	يَتَجَشَّا
10th	إِستَخذَا	يستَخذِى

7

The quadriliteral verbs, such as دَأدَأَ جَاجَأَ, present no new
difficulty; the rules are always the same: thus from طَمْأَن comes
in the fourth form, the preterite اِطْمَأَنَّ, in the indefinite يَطْمَئِنُّ,
in the impera. اِطْمَأْنِنْ, and by contraction اِطْمَئِنَّ.

Verbs having *Hamzah* for their second radical are sometimes conjugated like concave verbs, of which we shall soon
speak: and in which *Alif* is quiescent, coming from و or ى
radical, this is particularly observable in the verb سَأَل to *ask*,
which is often written سَال, Indef. يَسَال or يَسَل, Imp. سَل
for أُسْأَل: where both the *Alifs* drop, radical *Hamzah* by the
third general rule, and the servile *Alif* by the following letter
having a vowel. Verbs, of which the last radical is *Hamzah*,
are often confounded also with verbs properly called defective,
that is, having their last radical و or ى.

Of Imperfect Verbs in General.

These have among their radicals one or more of the letters و
and ى, and are divided into different classes; the first comprehends those which have و or ى for their first radical, the second
class those in which either of the same letters is the second radical,
and the third those having و or ى as last radical, whether the
root be triliteral or quadriliteral. The fourth class, and the
following two, are verbs in which two of the letters و and ى
are contained. The fourth class contains verbs in which these
letters are the second and third radicals. In the fifth class
they are the first and third radical. The sixth class is of verbs

where the three radicals are all و or ى: but not more than
one or two examples of these can be found.

Of Imperfect Verbs, of which the first Radical is و *or* ى.

These verbs are called by the Arabians مِثَال or *similar
verbs*, because their conjugation in the preterite is conformable
to the regular verb: amongst these verbs, those having و for
their first radical are subject to more irregularity, than those
whose first radical is ى.

The principal irregularity of the verbs having و for their
first radical, consists in their sometimes losing that letter in
the indefinite and imperative; this most frequently occurs in
those verbs, of which the second radical in the indefinite bears
Kasrah; it is to be observed, however, that several verbs of
this class, of which the second radical bears *Kasrah* in the
preterite, and should consequently take *Fathah* in the indefinite, nevertheless preserve *Kasrah*, and therefore lose و.

وَعَدَ يَعِدُ for يُوعِدُ

وَرِثَ يَرِثُ يُورِثُ

وَمِقَ يَمِقُ يُومِقُ

It is the same with the imperative.

أَوْعِدْ for عِدْ   أُومِقْ for مِقْ

7—2

When the second radical in the indefinite does not bear *Kasrah*, that tense is regularly formed, as يُوجَلَ from وَجِلَ, and يُودُّ from وَدَّ. When the indefinite is regular, the imperative is so likewise, as إِيدَدْ, إِيجَلْ, أُوجَهْ. In the two last examples, the ى is substituted for و radical, according to the rules of permutation; thus إِيدَدْ imperative of وَدَّ, is for أُودُدْ.

Several verbs lose و in the indefinite though their second radical in that tense bears *Fathah*; these verbs are, وطِئ *to tread under foot*, which is for وطَأَ; وسِع *to be large*; وقع *to fall*; ودع *to leave*; وهب *to give*; وضع *to place*; which make in the indefinite يَضَع, يَهَب, يَدَع, يَقَع, يَسَع, يَطَأ.

The verb وذر is only used in the indefinite and imperative, يذر and ذَر.

The irregularity of all these verbs exists only in the active voice of the first form. In the passive voice of that form, and in all the derivative forms, they present no irregularity except indeed in the eighth form, as will be observed immediately.

Verbs having ى for first radical, are not, properly speaking, irregular; thus يَبِس, يِيبَس: يَسَر, يَيْسِر, وَيَسَر, يَبِسَر. It must only be observed that the radical ى is changed into و when it is quiescent after *Dammah*; thus يَسَر makes in the indefinite of the third form يُوسِر, instead of يَيْسِر; the rule of permutation is merely to be observed.

It has been already said that verbs having for their first radical و or ى usually change it in the eighth conjugation into ت, which unites by *Tashdíd* with the ت characteristic of that conjugation; اِتَّعَدَ and اِتَّسَرَ are written therefore for اِوْتَعَدَ and اِيْتَسَرَ. Sometimes however the regular form is preserved, the و, when quiescent after *Kasrah*, being changed into ى, and the ى, when quiescent after *Dammah*, being similarly changed into و; and both changing into *Alif*, when quiescent after *Fathah*.

There are some similar verbs which at the same time have *Hamzah* وَاَرَ, وَنَأَ, وَطِئَ · Indef. يَبَرُ, يَنَأُ, يَطَأُ, but this presents no new difficulty.

Of Imperfect Verbs, of which the Second Radical is و or ى, called Concave Verbs.

Verbs having their second radical و or ى, are called by the Arabians أَجْوَفُ, that is to say, concave, and ذُو الثَّلَاثَةِ or verbs of three letters, because one of their characteristics is, to have only three letters in the first person singular of the preterite, where the regular and defective verbs have four, as may be seen by comparing قُلْتُ concave verb, with كَتَبْتُ *I have written*; مَضَيْتُ *I have passed by*; غَزَوْتُ *I have made war*. These verbs, and those of the next class, are they which depart most widely from the regular forms; their number is very great, and it is therefore essential to be well acquainted with their conjugation.

THE CONCAVE وَ.

Active Voice.

Preterite.

Plural Fem.	Plural Com.	Plural Mas.	Dual Fem.	Dual Com.	Dual Mas.	Singular Fem.	Singular Com.	Singular Mas.	Pers.
قُلْنَ	قَالُوا		قَالَتَا		قَالَا	قَالَتْ		قَالَ	3
قُلْتُنَّ	قُلْتُمْ			قُلْتُمَا		قُلْتِ		قُلْتَ	2
	قُلْنَا						قُلْتُ		1

Indefinite.

Plural Fem.	Plural Com.	Plural Mas.	Dual Fem.	Dual Com.	Dual Mas.	Singular Fem.	Singular Com.	Singular Mas.	Pers.
يَقُلْنَ	يَقُولُونَ		تَقُولَانِ		يَقُولَانِ	تَقُولُ		يَقُولُ	3
تَقُلْنَ	تَقُولُونَ			تَقُولَانِ		تَقُولِينَ		تَقُولُ	2
	نَقُولُ						أَقُولُ		1

Imperative.

Plural Fem.	Plural Com.	Plural Mas.	Dual	Singular Fem.	Singular Mas.
قُلْنَ	قُولُوا		قُولَا	قُولِي	قُلْ

Participle.

Plural Fem.	Plural Com.	Plural Mas.	Dual Fem.	Dual Mas.	Singular Fem.	Singular Mas.
قَائِلَاتٌ	قَائِلُونَ		قَائِلَتَانِ	قَائِلَانِ	قَائِلَةٌ	قَائِلٌ

Infinitive.

قَوْلًا

Passive Voice of the Concave و.

Preterite.

Plural			Dual			Singular			Pers.
Fem.	Com.	Mas.	Fem.	Com.	Mas.	Fem.	Com.	Mas.	
قُلْنَ		قِيلُوا		قِيلَتَا	قِيلَا	قِيلَتْ		قِيلَ	3
قُلْتُنَّ		قِلْتُمْ		قِلْتُمَا		قِلْتِ		قِلْتَ	2
	قُلْنَا						قِلْتُ		1

Indefinite.

Plural			Dual			Singular			Pers.
Fem.	Com.	Mas.	Fem.	Com.	Mas.	Fem.	Com.	Mas.	
يُقَلْنَ		يُقَالُونَ		تُقَالَانِ	يُقَالَانِ	تُقَالُ		يُقَالُ	3
تُقَلْنَ		تُقَالُونَ		تُقَالَانِ		تُقَالِينَ		تُقَالُ	2
	نُقَالُ						أُقَالُ		1

Participle.

مَقُولَاتٌ	مَقُولُونَ	مَقُولَتَانِ	مَقُولَانِ	مَقُولَةٌ	مَقُولٌ

THE CONCAVE ی.

Active Voice.

Preterite.

Fem.	Plural. Com.	Mas.	Fem.	Dual. Com.	Mas.	Fem.	Singular. Com.	Mas.	Pers.
سِرْنَ		سَارُوا	سَارَتَا		سَارَا	سَارَتْ		سَارَ	3
سِرْتَنَّ		سِرْتُمْ		سِرْتُمَا		سِرْتِ		سِرْتَ	2
	سِرْنَا						سِرْتُ		1

Indefinite.

Fem.	Com.	Mas.	Fem.	Com.	Mas.	Fem.	Com.	Mas.	Pers.
يَسِرْنَ		يَسِيرُونَ	تَسِيرَانِ		يَسِيرَانِ	تَسِيرُ		يَسِيرُ	3
تَسِرْنَ		تَسِيرُونَ		تَسِيرَانِ		تَسِيرِينَ		تَسِيرُ	2
	نَسِيرُ						أَسِيرُ		1

Imperative.

Fem.	Com.	Mas.	Fem.	Com.	Mas.	Fem.	Com.	Mas.
سِرْنَ		سِيرُوا		سِيرَا		سِيرِى		سِرْ

Participle.

Fem.	Com.	Mas.	Fem.	Com.	Mas.	Fem.	Com.	Mas.
سَائِرَاتٌ		سَائِرُونَ	سَائِرَتَانِ		سَائِرَانِ	سَائِرَةٌ		سَائِرٌ

Infinitive.

سَيْرًا

Verbs having و or ى for their second radical are irregular only in the first, fourth, seventh, eighth, and tenth forms.

In these verbs, the second radical letter always loses its vowel, and sometimes disappears altogether. When it is quiescent it undergoes various changes. All the rules indicating the anomalies of these verbs will be found among the rules of permutation common to و and ى .

It is in conformity with those rules, that in the third person singular masculine of the preterite, قَالَ is written instead of قَوَلَ, and خَافَ for خَوِفَ , that in the second and first person of the same tense, قَلْتَ, قُلْتُ and خِفْتَ are written for قَوَلْتَ, خَوِفْتُ, and that in the indefinite يَقُولُ, خِفْتُ and قَوَأَتْ, قَوَلْتُ are written for يَخَافُ, يَقُولُ, or under the influence of a particle producing apocope, يَخَفْ يَقُلْ ; it is so with all the other irregularities. Thus, in the feminine plural, و and ى drop, on account of the subsequent *Jazmah*. These radicals are also dropped in the singular masculine, and plural feminine of the imperative, but they return when the paragogical ن is added, as قُولَنْ *say thou*; سِيرَنْ *go thou*; خَافَنْ *fear thou*.

Verbs having و for their second radical, take *Dammah* in the indefinite, when the preterite is either of the form فَعَلَ or فَعُلَ ; as يَقُولُ the indefinite of قَالَ, which is for قَوَلَ ; and يَطُولُ indefinite of طَالَ, which is for طَوُلَ : but if the second radical have *Kasrah* for its vowel in the preterite, the inde-

finite takes *Fathah*, as يُخَاف for يَخْوَف, indefinite of خَاف
which is for خَوِف .

Verbs having ى for their second radical, generally take
Kasrah in the indefinite, because they are of the form فَعَل,
indefinite يَفْعِل, as يَسِير indefinite of سَار, which is for سِير .   There
are some however of the form فَعَل, indefinite يَفْعَل, these take
Fathah in the indefinite, as يَهَاب for يَهْيَب, indefinite of هَاب,
which is for هَيِب .

The imperative has no *Alif* of union, because the first radical
bears a vowel, as in قُل and سِر, and *Alif* of union can only
come before a letter bearing *Jazmah*.

The radical *Alif* in the participle, following the character-
istical quiescent *Alif*, ought to have a vowel, as two quiescent
letters cannot meet, but *Hamzah* or moveable *Alif* is substituted for it; which by the first canon, *Alif* is changed to ىِ.
قَائِل being for قَاأِل, and that for قَاوِل, سَائِر for سَاأِر, and that
again for سَايِر .

There is no difference in the preterite and indefinite of the
passive voice, between verbs whose second radical is و, or those
having ى .

In the participle of the passive voice however, the *Dammah*
of the second radical being removed to the first, the letter و
is thrown out, to prevent the concurrence of two quiescent
letters after one vowel, مَقُول being for مَقْوُول; but in concave,
ى *Dammah* is also changed to *Kasrah*, as مَسِير for مَسْيُور .

In approved authors however, particularly among the Poets, many of these participles are regularly formed, as مصوون guarded; but especially those of concave ى, as مخيوط sewed together; مكيول measured.

It is well to observe that in concave verbs whose last radical is ت, this ت is incorporated by *Tashdíd*, with the ت forming the second person of the preterite, and first person singular of the same tense; thus from مات comes in the first person singular مت, and in the second persons متما, مت, مت.

In concave verbs whose last radical is ن, the same occurs whenever this ن, being jazmated, is followed by ن forming the person. Thus from صان is made in the third person plural feminine of the preterite, and in the second person plural feminine of the imperative صن; in the first person plural of the preterite صنا; and in the third person plural feminine of the indefinite يصن.

These observations equally apply to the derivative verbs, and are of importance in finding the root when reading Arabic written without vowels, or orthographical signs.

Verbs derived from Concave Roots.

As has been before observed, in forms derived from concave verbs, the fourth, seventh, eighth, and tenth only are irregular, in these derivative forms, no difference exists between those whose second radical is و and those where it is ى. It will be sufficient to give a paradigm of these forms, presenting the first word of each tense.

Active Voice.

Infinitive.	Participle.	Imperative.	Indefinite.	Preterite.	
اِقَالَتًا	مُقِيلٌ	أَقِلْ	يُنِّيلٌ	أَقَالَ	4
اِسَارَتًا	مُسِيرٌ	أَسِرْ	يَسِيرُ	أَسَارَ	
اِنْقِيَالًا	مُنْقَالٌ	إِنْقَلْ	يَنْقَالُ	إِنْقَالَ	7
إِنْسِيَارًا	مُنْسَارٌ	إِنْسَرْ	يَنْسَارُ	إِنْسَارَ	
اِقْتِيَالًا	مُقْتَالٌ	اِقْتَلْ	يَقْتَالُ	اِقْتَالَ	8
اِسْتِيَارًا	مُسْتَارٌ	اِسْتَرْ	يَسْتَارُ	إِسْتَارَ	
اِسْتِقَالَةٌ	مُسْتَقِيلٌ	اِسْتَقِلْ	يَسْتَقِيلُ	اِسْتَقَالَ	10
اِسْتِسَارَةٌ	مُسْتَسِيرٌ	اِسْتَسِرْ	يَسْتَسِيرُ	إِسْتَسَارَ	

Passive Voice.

Participle.	Indefinite.	Preterite.	Participle.	Indefinite.	Preterite.	
مُسَارٌ	يُسَارُ	أُسِيرَ	مُقَالٌ	يُقَالُ	أُفِيلَ	4
مُنْسَارٌ	يُنْسَارُ	أُنْسِيرَ	مُنْقَالٌ	يُنْقَالُ	أُنْقِيلَ	7
مُسْتَارٌ	يُسْتَارُ	أُسْتِيرَ	مُقْتَالٌ	يُقْتَالُ	اُقْتِيلَ	8
مُسْتَسَارٌ	يُسْتَسَارُ	اُسْتُسِيرَ	مُسْتَقَالٌ	يُسْتَقَالُ	أُسْتُقِيلَ	10

In forming the different persons of each tense of these derivative forms, it is only necessary to apply the same rules as
in the primitive verb. Thus, in the third person singular feminine, of the preterite of the fourth form, أقومت for أقامت, and
in the second person singular masculine of the same tense, أقمت
for أقومت.

The other derivatives are regular; it is to be observed however, that in the passive voices of the third form فاعل, and the
sixth form تفاعل of concave verbs, whose second radical is و,
that the *Alif* characteristic of these forms, and which is changed
into و on account of the *Dammah* preceding, does not unite by
Tashdíd with the radical و that follows it, thus قووم and not
قوم. If the second radical is ى, the و and the ى must be
kept distinct; thus بايع makes in the passive voice بويع.

There are a few concave verbs conjugated regularly, as عور
to be one-eyed, and صيد *to hunt*. Some other concave verbs,
though irregular in the first form, may be conjugated either
regularly or irregularly in the fourth, such are راح *to do any
thing at night;* غام *to be cloudy;* which in the fourth form
are أروح or أراح, أغيم or أغام. It is the same with the tenth
form of verbs, whose second radical is و, as إستجاب and إستجوب
he answered; and إستصاب or إستصوب *he approved.* The irregular conjugation is however most in use.

Of Imperfect Verbs, which are at the same time Concave and Hamzated.

Of these there are two sorts, the first class comprehends those which have أ for first, and و for second radical, such are أَثَرَ and آبَ for أَوَّلَ and أَوَبَ; they are conjugated like قَالَ and آبَ, آبَتْ, آبْتُ, آبْتَ; thus in the preterite like قَالَ, قَالَتْ, قُلْتُ, قُلْتِ.

In the indefinite يَوُوبُ like يَقُولُ, observing the change of *Alif-hamzah* into و in the imperative أُبْ and أُوبِي, like قُلْ and قُولِي. Inf. أُوبًا. Part. آبُبٌ.

The second class comprehends those which have و or ى for second radical, and أ for the third, as سَآءَ for سَوَءَ, جَآءَ for جِيًا, and شَآءَ for شَيَأَ. The first is conjugated like قَالَ and هَنَا, the second like سَارَ and هَنَا, and the third like هَابَ and هَنَا. Thus, Pret. سَآءَ, سَآءَتْ, سُوتُ, سُوتَ, &c. Indef. يَسُوءُ. Impera. سُوْ. Pret. جَآءَ, جَآءَتْ, جِئْتُ, جِئْتَ, &c. Indef. يَجِىءُ. Impera. جِىْ. Pret. شَآءَ, شَآءَتْ, شِئْتُ, شِئْتَ, &c. Part. سَوَآءٌ. Inf. سَوَآءٌ. Part. سَائِءٌ. Impera. شَأْ. Indef. يَشَآءُ. Inf. شِيَّةً. Part. شَائِءٌ. Inf. جِيَّةً and مَجِيَّاءً. Part. جَائِءٌ.

In the passive voice the same rules are to be observed; thus
جِيءَ for جِىءَ. and سُوءَ for سِىءَ.

When several *Hamzah's* come in succession, it is usual to suppress one in order to soften the pronunciation; this is called تَسهِيل or *softening*, the contrary being called تَحقِيق or *verifying*.

Of Imperfect Verbs, whose last Radical is و or ى, and which are called Defective Verbs.

Verbs whose last radical is و or ى, are called by the Arabian grammarians نَاقِص defective, and also ذَوُ الأَربَعة, or verbs of four letters, because they have four letters in the first person singular of the preterite, as غَزوتُ.

The last radical undergoes changes resembling those to which the second radical is subject in concave verbs, sometimes it is changed into another letter, sometimes it disappears, sometimes its vowel passes to the preceding letter, and at other times it is totally suppressed. The chief anomalies of these verbs are founded on the rules of permutation.

THE DEFECTIVE ,و.

Active Voice.

Preterite.

Plural.			Dual.			Singular.			Pers.
Fem.	Com.	Mas.	Fem.	Com.	Mas.	Fem.	Com.	Mas.	
غَزَوْنَ		غَزَوْا	غَزَتَا		غَزَوَا	غَزَتْ		غَزَا	3
غَزَوْتُنَّ		غَزَوْتُمْ		غَزَوْتُمَا		غَزَوْتِ		غَزَوْتَ	2
	غَزَوْنَا						غَزَوْتُ		1

Indefinite.

يَغْزُونَ		يَغْزُونَ	تَغْزُوَانِ		يَغْزُوَانِ	تَغْزُو		يَغْزُو	3
تَغْزُونَ		تَغْزُونَ		تَغْزُوَانِ		تَغْزِينَ		تَغْزُو	2
	نَغْزُو						أَغْزُو		1

Imperative.

أُغْزُونَ		أُغْزُوا		أُغْزُوَا		أُغْزِى		أُغْزُ

Participle.

غَازِيَاتٌ		غَازُونَ	غَازِيَتَانِ		غَازِيَانِ	غَازِيَةٌ		غَازٍ

Infinitive.

غَزْوًا

THE DEFECTIVE ى.

Active Voice.

Preterite.

Plural.			Dual.			Singular.			Per.
Fem.	Com.	Mas.	Fem.	Com.	Mas.	Fem.	Com.	Mas.	
رَمَيْنَ		رَمَوْا	رَمَتَا		رَمَيَا	رَمَتْ		رَمَى	3
رَمَيْتُنَّ		رَمَيْتُمْ		رَمَيْتُمَا		رَمَيْتِ		رَمَيْتَ	2
	رَمَيْنَا						رَمَيْتُ		1

Indefinite.

يَرْمِينَ		يَرْمُونَ	تَرْمِيَانِ		يَرْمِيَانِ	تَرْمِى		يَرْمِى	3
تَرْمِينَ		تَرْمُونَ		تَرْمِيَانِ		تَرْمِينَ		تَرْمِى	2
	نَرْمِى						أَرْمِى		1

Imperative.

أَرْمِينَ		أَرْمُوا	أَرْمِيَا		إِرْمِى			إِرْمِ

Participle.

رَامِيَاتٌ		رَامُونَ	رَامِيَتَانِ		رَامِيَانِ	رَامِيَةٌ		رَامٍ

Infinitive.

رَمْيًا.

8

In the third person masculine singular of the preterite, غَزَا is for غَزْوَ , and رَمَى for رَمَىَ . In the third person singular feminine, and in the dual of the same gender, the last radical and its vowel are dropped altogether, and غَزَتْ is for غَزَوَتْ , and غَزَتَا for غَزَوَتَا .

In the third person plural masculine, the last radical with its vowel disappear, and غَزَوُوا and رَمَوُا are contractions for غَزَووا and رَمَيُوا , according to the rule of permutation. If after this third person, or those of the indefinite which terminate in the same way, *Waslah* or *Alif* of union occur, *Dammah* is given to the و , in order that the union may take place, دَعَوُا آللَّه .

The *Fathah* which the second radical bore in the preterite, in the indefinite changes into *Dammah* if the last radical be و , or into *Kasrah* if it be ى . Sometimes, however, in verbs whose last radical is ى , the *Fathah* remains in the indefinite on account of meeting a guttural letter, يَرْعَى from رَعَى . This last radical, in the indefinite, loses its vowel and becomes quiescent, according to the rules of permutation. After the و thus quiescent, *Alif* mute is not put however in the singular, يَغْزُو not يَغْزُوا (see و , 15, rule of permutation) this is not always strictly observed, the *Alif* being sometimes added. When preceded by particles changing, by antithesis, the *Dammah* of the third radical into *Fathah*, the last radical retakes its vowel, as يَرْمِى , يَغْزُو , because that vowel being *Fathah* there is no reason for its suppression.

When subject to apocope, the third radical wholly disappears, as يَغْزُ and يَرْمِ .

When subjected to paragoge, the third radical is preserved, as يَغْزُونْ, يَغْزُونَّ, يَرْمِيَنْ, يَرْمِيَنَّ .

In the second person singular feminine of the indefinite, as well as in the second and third person plural masculine of the same tense, a contraction occurs, تَغْزُونَ, يَغْزُونَ, تَرْمِينَ, تَغْزِينَ for تَغْزُوِينَ, تَرْمِيِينَ, يَغْزُوونَ, تَغْزُوونَ, يَرْمِيُونَ and تَرْمُونَ, يَرْمُونَ, تَرْمِيُونَ . It may be observed that in عَزَا, and verbs similarly conjugated, the second and third persons masculine plural are like the feminine, and that in رَمَى, and verbs of the same form, the second person singular feminine is the same as the second person plural of the same gender.

When the second person singular feminine of the indefinite, and second and third person plural masculine of the same tense are subject to paragoge however, the و and the ى, which remain after the contraction, are wholly dropped, on account of the ن quiescent, which then follows them agreeably to the rule (gen. 3) this is written with *Tashdíd* تَغْزُنَّ, تَرْمِنَّ, يَغْزُنَّ, تَغْزُنَّ, تَرْمُنَّ, يَغْزُنَّ, &c. Among the verbs, whose last radical is و, it is only those having *Fathah* for vowel of the second radical in the preterite which wholly follow the paradigm غَزَا; those whose second radical bear *Dammah*, form the preterite regularly, except in the third person plural masculine; thus

سَرُوَ, in the third person singular feminine, is سَرُوَت, and in that of the dual feminine سَرُوَتَا; but in the third person plural masculine, it is by contraction سَرُوا for سَرُووا agreeably to the rules. In other respects these verbs are conjugated like غَزَا.

As to those having *Kasrah* for vowel of the second radical in the preterite, they are conjugated in a peculiar manner, which it is necessary to explain by giving an example, observing that in this case و radical is changed into ى; thus رَضِى is written for رَضِو.

DEFECTIVE , PRECEDED BY KASRAH, رَضِوَ FOR رَضِى.

Active Voice.

Preterite.

Plural.			Dual.			Singular.			pers.
Fem.	Com.	Mas.	Fem.	Com.	Mas.	Fem.	Com.	Mas.	
رَضِين		رَضَوا	رَضِيَتَا		رَضِيَا	رَضِيَتْ		رَضِى	3
رَضِيتنّ		رَضِيتم		رَضِيتمَا		رَضِيت		رَضِيت	2
	رَضِينَا						رَضِيت		1

Indefinite.

Plural.			Dual.			Singular.			pers.
Fem.	Com.	Mas.	Fem.	Com.	Mas.	Fem.	Com.	Mas.	
يَرضِين		يَرضَون	تَرضَيَان		يَرضَيَان	تَرضَى		يَرضَى	3
تَرضِين		تَرضَون		تَرضَيَان		تَرضِين		تَرضَى	2
	نَرضَى						أَرضَى		1

Imperative.

Plural.			Dual.			Singular.		
Fem.	Com.	Mas.	Fem.	Com.	Mas.	Fem.	Com.	Mas.
إِرضِين		إِرضَوا		إِرضَيَا		إِرضِى		إِرض

Participle.

Plural.			Dual.			Singular.		
Fem.	Com.	Mas.	Fem.	Com.	Mas.	Fem.	Com.	Mas.
رَاضِيَات		رَاضَون	رَاضِيَتَان		رَاضِيَان	رَاضِيَة		رَاضٍ

Infinitive.

رَضًى

The preterite is conjugated regularly, excepting the third person plural masculine, where the third radical is dropt, and its vowel given to the second radical which loses its *Kasrah*, رَضِيُوا for رَضُوا.

In the indefinite, يَرْضَى is for يَرْضُوُ; the suppression of the last vowel, and change of و into ى, are in conformity to the rule (و 7,) but it must be observed that this change of و into ى which, conformably to the rule quoted, takes place in the third person because the و is final, continues in those persons of the indefinite where the و ceases to be final. Thus in the plural feminine, تَرْضُونَ and يَرْضُونَ for تَرْضِينَ and يَرْضِينَ. For the same reason in the second person singular feminine ought to be written تَرْضِيِينَ, and in the plural masculine يَرْضِيُونَ and تَرْضِيُونَ; as in the dual يَرْضِيَانِ; but instead of these regular forms a contraction takes place in these different persons, and تَرْضُونَ and يَرْضُونَ , تَرْضِينَ are written agreeably to the rule of permutation. When the indefinite bears antithesis, يَرْضَى cannot be written in conformity to the conjugation of regular verbs, in consequence of the rule of permutation (ى 3,) it is therefore written يَرْضَى in the common form.

When paragoge occurs, ى resumes its vowel, because it is no longer at the end of a word, تَرْضَيَنَّ and يَرْضَيِنَّ. When apocope takes place the third radical is dropt, as in يَغْزُ and وَيِرْمِ and we write يَرْضَ.

When receiving antithesis, or apocope, the second person

singular feminine of the indefinite is written ترضى and not

ترضِى ; but the ى then bears *Jazmah*, and if it be followed

by *Waslah*, or *Alif* of union, it receives *Kasrah*. This occurs

also in the second person feminine singular of the imperative

اِرضى. In this case, therefore, they are written ترضِي and

اِرضِي. In the second and third persons plural masculine of the

indefinite, when receiving either antithesis or apocope, a similar

contraction occurs, and يرضوا and ترضوا are written for يرضيوا ,

ترضيوا . *Jazmah* is then put over the و, and if it be followed

by an *Alif* of union, it receives *Dammah* ; ترضوا , يرضوا . The

same takes place in the second person plural masculine of the

imperative.

The *Kasrah* and the *Dammah* used in the cases just men-

tioned, are equally used in the persons enumerated when paragoge

occurs, thus يرضون and ترضون , ترضين . Impera. اِرضين and

اِرضون .

In the singular masculine of the participle, و final after

Kasrah is changed to ى (by 14 canon غازى (و being put for

غازٍو ; and as ى final after *Kasrah* cannot take *Dammah*, it

rejects it, and throwing the nunnation on the preceding letter,

drops, as غازٍ for عازى ; but if the nunnation is removed by the

article, ى then returns, as الغازى for الغازى . The same pre-

vails in the defective ى ,و as رامٍ for رامى ; and as ى final after

Kasrah refuses another *Kasrah*, غَازٍ and رَامٍ are used also in the genitive for غَازِي and رَامِي . The accusative is however regular, as غَازِيًا and رَامِيًا . In غَازِيَةً and رَامِيَةً, the rejected ى returns, as not being final, and غَازُون makes a contraction, as in the future.

In the passive voice, the defective verbs of the four forms غَزَا , سَرْوَ , رَمَى , رَضِيَ are all conjugated in the same way, رَضِيَ , رَمِيَ , سَرِيَ , غَزِيَ . All the inflections of the preterite, and the indefinite of these passive voices, resemble those of the active voice رَضِيَ . It is only necessary to give *Dammah* to the first radical in the preterite, and also to the formative letters of the different persons of the indefinite. Thus in the preterite is written غَزِيَ , غَزِيتَ , غَزِيتِ , غَزِيتُ , &c. In the indefinite يُغْزَى , dual يُغْزَيَانِ , plural يُغْزَوْن , &c.

In the derivative forms there is no difference between the verbs whose last radical is و and those having ى , both take ى for their final letter through all these forms.

In the active voice ى is quiescent after *Fathah*, as غَزَّى and رَمَّى . In the passive voice it bears *Fathah* after *Kasrah*, رُمِّيَ , غُزِّيَ .

All the derivative forms follow, in the active voice, the conjugation of رَمَى , and in the passive voice that of رَضِيَ .

DEFECTIVE DERIVATIVES.

Passive Voice		Active Voice		
Indefinite.	Preterite.	Indefinite.	Preterite.	
يُرْضَى	رُضِّيَ	يُرَضِّى	رَضَّى	2
يُرَاضَى	رُوضِيَ	يُرَاضِى	رَاضَى	3
يُرْضَى	أُرْضِيَ	يُرْضِى	أَرْضَى	4
يُتَرَضَّى	تُرُضِّيَ	يَتَرَضَّى	تَرَضَّى	5
يُتَرَاضَى	تُرُوضِيَ	يَتَرَاضَى	تَرَاضَى	6
يُرْتَضَى	أُرْتُضِيَ	يَرْتَضِى	إِرْتَضَى	8
يُسْتَرْضَى	أُسْتُرْضِيَ	يَسْتَرْضِى	اُسْتَرْضَى	10

Of Verbs, being at the same time Defective and Hamzated.

These verbs are divided into two classes; the first containing those which have اُ for the first radical, and for last و or ى. Such are أَتَى *to come,* أَبَى *to refuse,* أَدَّى *to pay.* They are conjugated like أَثَرَ and غَزَا, or سَرُوَ, رَمَى or رَضِيَ.

Pret. أَتَى, أَتَتْ, اتَيْتَ, &c. Indef. يَأْتِى. Impera. اُئْتِ. Irregularly تِ or تَهْ. Part. آتٍ. Inf. إِتْيَاً. The verb أَتَى in the third form, sometimes changes the radical *Alif* into ه, it is then written هَاتَى, instead of آتَى. Indefinite يُهَاتِى. Impera. هَاتِ. The second class contains those whose second radical is اُ, and the third و or ى, as نَأَى *to be distant.* These verbs are conjugated like سَأَل and غَزَا, رَمَى or رَضِيَ. Pret. نَأَى, نَأَتْ, نَأَيْتَ, &c. Indef. يَنْأَى or يَنْأَى. Impera. إِنْأَ. Part. نَاءٍ. In verbs of this class, the second radical preserves in the indefinite tense the *Fathah* which it bore in the preterite; this is caused by the *Alif-hamzah* being a guttural letter.

The verb رَأَى *to see,* being in very common use, almost always loses its *Alif-hamzah* in the indefinite and imperative.

Indefinite.

Plural.		Dual.		Singular.
یَرَیْنَ	یَرَوْنَ	تَرَیانِ	یَرَیانِ	تَرَی	یَرَی
تَرَیْنَ	تَرَوْنَ	تَرَیانِ	تَرَیانِ	تَرَیْنَ	تَرَی
	نَرَی				أَرَی

With Antithesis,	یَرَوْا , &c.		یَرَیا , &c.	یَرَی , &c.
Apocope,	یَرَوْا , &c.		یَرَیا , &c.	یَرَ , &c.
Paragoge,	یَرَوْنَ , &c.		یَرَیَنِّ , &c.	یَرَیانِّ , &c.
Impera.	رَوْا رَیْنَ		رَیا	رَ or رَهْ
Paragoge,	رَوْنَّ رَیْنانِ		رَیانِّ	رَیَنَّ رَیْنَ

The passive voice of رَأَی رَای is رُئِیَ, which is conjugated like رُمِیَ. In the indefinite, *Alif-Hamzah* may be dropped, as in the active voice, یُرَی for یُرْأَی.

In the fourth form, the verb رَأَی always loses its second radical; thus, Pret. أَرَی , أَرَتْ , أَرَیْتَ , أَرَیْتُ , &c. Indef. یُرِی. Imp. أَرِ. The imperative of the verbs رَأَی , أَتَی , and others being, on account of their double irregularity, reduced to a single letter, as رَ , تِ , a quiescent ه is added whenever they are followed by a pause رَهْ , تِهْ.

Of Verbs Doubly Imperfect.

Verbs having two of the letters و and ى among their radicals are divided into two classes. In the first these two letters make the first and third radicals. Those which have *Fathah* for the vowel of the second radical, are conjugated like وَعَدَ and رَمى; those having *Kasrah*, like وَجِلَ and رَضِىَ.

1. وَقَى , وَقَتْ , وَقَيْتُ , &c. Indef. يَقِى . Imp. قِ or قِه . Part. وَاقٍ .

2. وَجِىَ , وَجِيَتْ , وَجِيتُ , &c. Indef. يَوْجَى . Imp. إِيجَ . Part. وَاجِ . إِوَجْ for

The Imperative قِ in the other persons resumes ى , contracted however in the plural masc. as قِ , قِى , قِيَا , قُوا , قِينَ .

The second class contains the verbs in which the letters و and ى occupy the second and third places; thus, شَوَى *to roast*; قَوِىَ *to be strong*; حَيِىَ *to live*. These verbs are concave and defective, but the second radical is subject to no irregularity; thus شَوَى is conjugated like رَمى , and قَوِىَ like حَيِىَ , follows غَزَا . Some follow رَضِىَ .

Pret. شَوَى , شَوْتُ , شَوَيْتُ , &c. Indef. يَشْوِى . Imp. إِشْوِ , &c.

إِقْوَ   يَقْوَى   &c. قَوِى , قَوِيتُ , قَوِيَتْ

حَيِرَ for حَيِىَ .

Pret. حَيِىَ ,حَيِيتَ ,حَيِيتُ . Indef. يَحْيَا, &c. Dual يَحْيِيَانِ .

Plural يَحْيِونَ .

Impera. إِحْيَى إِحِى . Dual إِحْيَيَا . Plural إِحْيُوا ,إِحْيِينَ .

Part. حَاىٍ ,قَاوٍ ,شَاوٍ .

Inf. حَيوةٌ ,قوةٌ ,شَيًّا .

The final و of the indefinite يَحْيُو ought to be changed into ى according to the rule of permutation (و, 7,) but here *Alif* is substituted for ى following another rule (ى, 4,) on account of the ى which precedes it, and to distinguish it from the proper name يَحْيَى .

The infinitive شَيًّا is put for شَوْيًا and (و, ى, 3,) and قوةٌ for قووةٌ . Instead of the participle حَاىٍ, the adjective حَىٌّ is most generally used.

The verb حَيِىَ is often contracted in the manner of surd verbs, in the third persons of the preterite; excepting that of the plural feminine, حَيًّا ,حَيِيتُ ,حَيَّ and حَيَّتَا ,حَيُّوا .

Verbs of this kind preserve in their derivatives the analogy of those whose last radical is و or ى, but it must be observed, that the verb حَيِىَ, in its tenth form, often has a particular irregularity, losing its second radical, the vowel of which passes to the first. Thus,

Pret. يَسْتَحِمِى or يَسْتَحِيِى .Indef — .إِسْتَحَى or إِسْتَحِيِى

Imp. إِسْتَحِمِ or إِسْتَحِمِى .

Of Verbs Doubly Imperfect and Hamzated.

Of these, there are two classes, the one has for its first radical أُ, and for second and third و or ى; such is أَوَى, أَوَيت, أَوتَ, أَوَى, which is conjugated like أَثَّرَ and شَوَى . Pret. &c. Indef. يَأْوِى, &c. Imp. وإِأْوُ, &c. Par. أَوٍ . Inf. أَيَّاً .

In the second class of these verbs the second radical is أ, and the letters و and ى are the first and third; as وَأَى *to promise*; which is conjugated like وَقَى and سَأَل, being at the same time similar, defective, and hamzated.

Pret. وَأَى, وَأْتُ, وَأَيتُ, &c. Indef. يَأْى, تَأَى, تَأْى, &c. Indef. with antithesis, يَأَى, أُحَى, &c. With apocope, إِى, يَأْ, تَأْ, تَأَى, أَحْ, &c. Imp. إِ or إِأ—إِى, &c. Part. وَأٍ, &c. Inf. وَأَيَّا .

Of the Negative Verb.

The Arabians have a negative verb, possessing only the preterite tense but unlimited in time, and the conjugation of which much resembles that of the concave verb. It is the verb لَيسَ *is not, was not, will not be,* &c.

Plural.			Dual.			Singular.		
Mas.	Com.	Fem.	Mas.	Com.	Fem.	Mas.	Com.	Fem.
لَسْنَا		لَيْسُوا	لَيْسَتَا	لَيْسَا	لَيْسَتْ	لَيْسَ		
	لَسْتُنَّ	لَسْتُمْ	لَسْتُمَا		لَسْتِ	لَسْتَ		
	لَسْنَا					لَسْتُ		

In some cases لَاتَ is used instead of لَيْسَ. This admits of no inflection, and the Arabian grammarians are not agreed upon its nature.

Verbs of Praise and Blame.

Those verbs which the Arabians denominate أَفْعَالُ الْمَدْحِ وَالذَّمِّ or verbs of praise and blame, do not admit of conjugation. They are نِعْمَ, which is also pronounced نَعِمَ, نِعِمَ and نَعْمَ, to be good, and بِئِسَ to be bad. They may be regarded as a species of interjectional verbs; they receive a feminine termination also, as بِئِسَتْ, نِعْمَتْ. They are sometimes, but very rarely, written نِعْمَا in the dual; and نِعْمُوا in the plural. The word حَبَّذَا may be looked upon as a verb of this kind; it is compounded of حَبَّ and ذَا, and signifies, to be excellent, or worthy of love. To these three verbs may be also added سَآءَ to be bad; and حَسُنَ for حَسُنَ, to be beautiful; but these under other acceptations are regularly conjugated.

Of Verbs of Admiration.

Verbs called افعال التَّعجب, verbs of admiration, are rather
a kind of admirative formula than a particular species of verb.
There are two. In the first مَا أَفعَل, the form of the third
person singular masculine of the preterite of the fourth conjugation أفعَل is used, preceded by the monosyllable مَا, and
followed by an accusative. In the second, the second person
singular masculine of the imperative of the fourth conjugation
مَا أَفعَل is employed, followed by the preposition بِ, as أَفضَل بِزيدٍ
or زيداً *Zaid is very excellent.*

OF NOUNS.

Nouns إِسْم are divided into proper names, عَلَم , as مُحَمَّد

Muhammad; مَكَّة *Mecca*; جَيْحُون the *Jaihun* (river); or appel-

latives, إِسْمُ الجِنْسِ (name of kind or genus), as نَبِّى *a prophet*;

مَدِينَة *a city*; نَهْر *a river*; and into adjectives, صِفَة , (quality

or qualificative); as صَغِير *little*; أَبِيض *white*.

They are either primitive, deriving their origin from no
other words; or derivative, from either a verbal or substantive
origin.

The servile letters employed in the derivation of nouns are
comprised in the word يَتَسَمَّنَا .

ى is added at the end, as فَرْسِى *a Persian*; it is placed
after the vowel of the second syllable, so forming diminutives,
as كُلَيْب *a little dog*; and sometimes, though rarely, before
the radicals, as يَنْبُوع *a fountain*.

ت is employed at the beginning, as تَطْوِيل *prolongation*;

تَكَبُّر *pride*; in the middle, as in nouns, from the eighth conjugation إِعْتِرَاف *confession*; or at the end, where it is represented by ة , as رَحْمَة *mercy*.

9

س never serves alone, but with two others, as in nouns from the tenth conjugation, as اِسْتِغْفَار *deprecation*; مُسْتَخْرِج *a leader*.

م is servile at the beginning, as مَمْلَكَة *a kingdom*; and, though very rarely, at the end, as اِبْنَم *a son*.

ن serves in the beginning with ا, as in nouns from the seventh conjugation, as اِنْقِطَاع *abstinence*; or at the end, then forming nouns of action from the primitive triliteral verb, as غُفْرَان *pardon*, from غَفَرَ; or adjectives, as سَكْرَان from سَكِرَ.

أ is used at the beginning, as أَسْوَد *black*; أَحْسَن *handsomer*; أَسْوَار *a horseman*; or after the radicals, as كِبْرِيَاء *haughtiness*; in this case it is represented by *Hamzah* only, and has quiescent ا before it.

Under the head of verbal derivatives, are comprehended almost all adjectives, and participles used adjectively, together with those substantives which signify the Agent or Patient, the Time or Place of Action, the Instrument, and the Action itself.

Name of the Agent and Patient.

Adjectives derived from verbs, or as they are considered by Erpenius, active participles, received in a substantive sense, denote the agent, as نَاصِر *assisting, an assistant*; مَالِك *ruling, a king or ruler*.

These verbal adjectives, when derived from the triliteral primitive verb, are for the active voice of the form فَاعِل, and for the passive voice of the form مَفْعُول. Thus حَاكِم from حَكَمَ *to judge*; رَاغِب from رَغَبَ *to desire*; مَوْجُود from وَجَدَ *to be found, to exist*; مَرْغُوب from رَغَبَ *to be desired*.

From the verbal adjective of the form فَاعِل is derived another of the form فَعَّال, which adds to the primitive idea, that of intensity, or constant habitude; thus حَسَّان signifies *very handsome*; أَكَّال *a great eater*; كَذَّاب *one habituated to lying*; عَلَّام *very learned*.

This form of verbal adjectives supplies the names of trades, &c., as خَبَّاز *a baker*; نَجَّار *a carpenter*; سَقَّاء *a water-carrier*.

Name of Place and Time.

The place and time of action are denoted by the same noun, as مَكْتَب *place and time of writing*; مَجْلِس *place and time of sitting*; it is formed from the indefinite tense of triliteral verbs, by substituting م for the incremental letters أَتَين. When the second radical of the indefinite tense has for its vowel *Fathah* or *Kasrah*, this vowel is preserved in the noun of time and place; but if that letter have *Dammah* for its vowel, it usually becomes *Fathah*; thus from يَكْتُب is formed مَكْتَب *a school, a place where writing is taught*. There are, however, twelve nouns of this kind, which change *Dammah* into *Kasrah*, as

مَشْرِق *the place of rising, the east.*

مَغْرِب *the place of setting, the west.*

مَرْفِق *a place on which the elbow rests.*

مَنْبِت *the place where a plant grows.*

مَسْقَط *the place where a thing falls.*

مَجْزِر *the place where a camel is slaughtered or flayed.*

مَنْخِر *the place of breathing, the nostrils.*

مَنْسِك *the place where the victim is sacrificed.*

مَطْلِع *the place of rising of the stars.*

مَفْرِق *the place on the head where the hair divides.*

مَسْكِن *the place of residence, a house.*

مَسْجِد *the place of worship, a mosque.*

Of these nouns, the last five, and according to some grammarians, the first six, may take indifferently *Fathah*, or *Kasrah* for vowel of the second radical; the seventh may also have *Kasrah* for the vowel of م, as مَنْخِر. In nouns derived from a similar verb, whose first radical is و, the second radical always has *Kasrah* for its vowel, and the و is preserved, even when dropped in the indefinite, thus مَوْعِد *time and place of promise,* from وَعَد *to promise,* of which the indefinite is يَعِد, from وَضَع

to place, the indefinite of which is يَضَعُ, is formed مَوْضِعٌ place or time of position, or place in general, from وَجَهَ to go towards a place, the indefinite of which is يُوجَهُ, is formed مُوَجَّهٌ the place towards which we direct our way.

In concave roots, if the first radical have for its vowel, in the indefinite tense, Fathah or Dammah, the noun of time and place is made by substituting an Alif quiescent for the second radical, and carrying to the first radical the Fathah which belonged to the second; thus from قَامَ to stand erect, indefinite يَقُومُ is formed, مَقَامٌ, for مَقْوَمٌ place where we stand upright, or place where we stand in general. If the first radical have Kasrah for its vowel in the indefinite, the second radical undergoes no change; thus from صَارَ, indefinite يَصِيرُ to arrive somewhere, is formed مَصِيرٌ the place of arrival, from خَاطَ, indefinite يَخِيطُ to crawl, is formed مَخِيطٌ the place in which a serpent crawls. In defective roots whose third letter is و or ى, the noun of time and place is regularly formed by observing the rules of permutation; thus from نَجَا to save himself, is formed مَنْجَى the place of refuge, for مَنْجُو; from رَعَى to graize, comes مَرْعَى the place of pasture; مَأْوَى the place where we live, is, however, sometimes written مَأْوٍ. It often happens that these nouns of place take the final ة, as مَقْبَرَةٌ place of burial, a cemetery; مَشْرِقَةٌ the place of sun-rising; مَغَارَةٌ a deep place, a cavern; مَنَارَةٌ a place proper for a light-house, a tower; مَرْعَاةٌ

place of pasture. When the noun of place takes this final ة, the second radical sometimes bears *Dammah;* thus مَقْبُرَة *a cemetery;* there are some nouns of time and place of the form مِفْعَال; these nouns belong to roots whose first radical is و, thus مِيلَاد *the time of birth;* مِيقَات *the time fixed for a thing.*

The noun of time or place coming from quadriliteral roots, or derivative verbs, is formed from the indefinite tense of the passive voice, by substituting م for the incremental letters of that tense, so that they differ nothing from the name of the patient (the participle passive of Erpenius); thus from يَلْتَقِى passive indefinite of اِلْتَقَى *to meet,* is formed مُلْتَقًى *the place of meeting, the confluence of two rivers;* from إِنْصَرَف *to return,* مُنْصَرَف *place or time of return,* from صَلَّى *to pray,* مُصَلًّى *a place of prayer.*

Nouns indicating the place in which any thing abounds, are nearly allied to nouns of time and place; they are of the form مَفْعَلَة or مَفْعِل, such are مَأْسَدَة and مَسْبَعَة *a place in which there are many lions,* derived from أَسَد and سَبُع, which signify *a lion.* مَقْثَأَة *a field of cucumbers,* derived from قِثَّاء *a cucumber;* مَبْطَخَة *a melonry,* derived from بِطِّيخ *a melon.*

Name of Instrument or Vessel.

These nouns are usually of one of these three forms, مِفْعَلَة, مِفْعَال, مِفْعَل. They are distinguished from nouns of time and place by their first letter م bearing *Kasrah*, as مِحْلَب

a *milk-pail*, from حَلَب *milk*; مِفْتَاح a *key*, from فَتَح *to open*;

مِيزَان a *balance*, from وَزَن *to weigh*; مِكْسَحَة a *broom*, from كَسَح

to sweep; مِحْلَاج an *instrument employed in cleaning cotton*.

There are a few nouns of this class of the two forms مِفْعَل

and مِفْعَلَة; as مِنْخَل a *sieve*, from نَخَل *to sift*; مِدَقّ an *instrument with which flax or cotton is beaten*, from دَقّ *to beat*;

مِدْهَن a *vessel for holding perfumes*; مِكْحَلَة a *vessel containing*

collyrium, from كَحَل. The form of this word distinguishes it

from مِكْحَل, which signifies *the instrument with which that collyrium is applied*; these two last forms, however, are rather
names of vessels than instruments of action. Besides the species
of derivative nouns here mentioned, whose forms constantly indicate the ideas, added to those of the primitive, there are other
forms not classified by the grammarians, but which may be reduced
to a system, almost as regular as that of the forms we have
just described.

Such is the form فِعْلَة which usually indicates, as well as
the form فِعْل a passive sense; and particularly the quantity
contained in a place or vessel, resembling somewhat our words
a handful, a mouthful, a pinch, &c. لُقْمَة *a mouthful*; قَبْضَة
a handful; بُلْغَة *what suffices to prevent starvation*; شُرْبَة *a sip*.
In the following forms it merely shews a passive attribute,

جَمَعَة a crowd or assembly collected together; جَمَلَة the total, that which is added up; نَحَفَة a present, that which is given; the form فَعَلَة which is much like the preceding, designates a fragment, or piece broken off, as قَطَعَة a portion; جِذَمَة a splinter; خِرْقَة a rag.

The form فِعَال indicates diseases, as كَبَاد the liver complaint; and the form فَعَالَة a piece remaining, or thrown away, as طَفَافَة the surplus of any thing sold by measure; عَجَالَة a bite.

Noun of Action.

This is an abstract noun, signifying the action or manner of being, expressed by the verb, without the least regard to subject, object, or time; it is named مَصْدَر the source; not as being the root of the verb, from which on the contrary it is often evidently derived, but as being the origin of the signification of the verb, and containing the primitive idea, to which the different forms of the verb only add accessory ideas. It is thus that the primitive idea contained in the word love, produces first the word, loving, which connects the idea of love with that of some being, and then all the forms of the verb to love.

Most of the Arabian grammarians consider the third person singular masculine of the preterite, as the root from which not only the whole verb, but also nouns of action, verbal adjectives, nouns of time and place, &c. are derived. The learned of the School of Kufah were of this opinion, while the School of Basrah held that the noun of action is the root,

from which comes the verb itself, and all nouns and verbal
adjectives.

Every noun indicating abstractedly the attribute contained
in the signification of the verb, is not to be regarded however
as a noun of action; thus علِم *learning*; ظِمْءٌ *thirst*; are not
the nouns of action of the verbs علِم *to learn;* ظِمِى *to be thirsty;*
their nouns of action are عِلم and ظِمَأ. The Arabian grammarians call these simply *nouns* إسم, in contradistinction to the
noun of action مصدر; the difference between these is often
almost imperceptible, and they are frequently used for each
other.

The noun of action is chiefly distinguished by being put
in the accusative case, or as it were adverbially, and joined to
the verb itself; adding to it a species of energy, thus,
كَلَّمَ ٱللَّهُ مُوسَى تَكْلِيمًا "*God spoke to Moses, speaking.*"

In treating of the verb, it has been observed, that the
noun of action, when put in the accusative case, supplies the
place of the infinitive, which in all languages is really the
verb's noun. These forms for the first conjugation, that being
most in use, are very numerous, and are in all 35. The
second, third, and fourth conjugations have a few variations;
the remaining nine have each but one form, which will be
found in the tables of the verbs, where they appear in the
accusative case as infinitives.

Nouns of Action of the Primitive Triliteral Verb.

1. فَعْل	10. فَعْلة	19. فُعْلَى	28. فِعِل
2. فُعْل	11. فُعْلة	20. فِعْلَى	29. فَعُول
3. فِعْل	12. فِعْلة	21. فَعْلَى	30. فَعُولة
4. فَعَل	13. فَعَلة	22. فَعَلان	31. فُعُولة
5. فَعُل	14. فَعِلة	23. فَعَلان	32. مَفْعِل
6. فِعَل	15. فَعَالة	24. فِعْلان	33. مَفْعِلة
7. فَعَال	16. فِعَالة	25. فُعْلان	34. مَفْعَل
8. فِعَال	17. فُعَالة	26. فَعُول	35. مَفْعَلة
9. فُعَال	18. فَعْلَى	27. فَعِيل	

Nouns of Action of Derivatives.

2nd Conj. فَعَّال, فِعَّال, تَفْعِلة, تَفْعَال, فِعَّال, تَفْعِيل.

3rd فِيعَال, فِعَال, مُفَاعلة.

4th فَعَالة, فِعَال, إِنْعَال.

This multitude of forms of nouns of action belonging to
the primitive triliteral verb, need not however alarm the student,

for very few verbs have more than one or two, and those are
indicated in the dictionaries. In the nouns of action derived
from فَعَّل, the form تَفْعِيل is most used; in those derived from
فاعل, the most common form is مُفَاعَلَة. In the nouns of action
derived from أفعل, the form أفعال is almost always observed.

Nouns of Action formed from Surd Verbs.

In forming nouns of action from surd verbs, the same rules
take place as in fixing the contraction of the second and third
radical; thus from مَدَّ, the noun of action is مَدّ for مدد; from
غرر, the noun of action is تغِرَّة for تغرِرة.

Several nouns of action, where the two first radicals bear
Fathah, suffer no contraction, as علل, دبب, سدد, &c.

In the noun of action of the third form of these verbs,
the contraction may or may not take place, مَمادّة or مَمَادَدَة.

Nouns of Action of Hamzated Verbs.

The rules of permutation of *Alif* must be observed here,
as in the verbs themselves; thus the third form of the verb
أثر has for noun of action مواثَرَة or مواثرة, the *Alif-Hamzah*
being changed into و or و; the eighth form has إِئتِثار, and
so on.

Verbs having أ for second or third radical follow the same
rules, as سوَال noun of action of سأل; ملومة from لأم; and

مُلَاءَمَة from لَاءَم, the third form of the same verb; اِلتِّئَام

from إِلتَأَم, eighth form of the same root.

Nouns of Action of Similar Verbs.

Similar verbs, whose first radical is و, lose this letter in the indefinite tense, and imperative in certain cases; this irregularity takes place also in their nouns of action, which then have *Kasrah* or *Fathah* for vowel of the second radical, as in the indefinite.

عِدَة	from	وَعَد	Indef. يَعِد,
دَعَة		وَدَع	يَدَع,
زِنَة		وَزَن	يَزِن,
دِيَة		وَدَى	يَدِى.

In this form the final ة is regarded as a compensation for the first radical suppressed, and the noun of action is considered to be of the form فِعَل; many similar verbs, though irregular in the indefinite, have their nouns of action regularly of the form فَعَل; as وَجَر, noun of action of وَجَر; Indef. يَجَر; several have at the same time the regular and irregular form.

All the forms except فَعَل of nouns of action derived from similar verbs are regular;

وُلُوج	from	وَلَج	Indef. يَلِج
وِجْدَان		وَجَد	يَجِد

Indef. وَزَفَ from وَزِيفٌ يَزِفُ

يَصِى وَصَى وِصَاءٌ

Nouns of Action derived from Concave Verbs.

The rules of permutation observed in the conjugation of these verbs must be followed here.

There is however a particular form occurring, of nouns of action of concave verbs; it is this, فَعْلُولَة; here the place of the second radical is always filled by ى; thus from دَامَ ,بَانَ, and غَابَ, for دَوَمَ ,بَيَنَ and غَيَبَ, are formed دَيْمُومَةٌ, and غَيْبُوبَةٌ ,بَيْنُونَةٌ and غَيْبُوبَةٌ.

Nouns of action, of the fourth and tenth forms, have a peculiar irregularity; instead of writing regularly إِقْوَام and إِسْتِقْوَام, as إِفْعَال ,إِسْتِفْعَال; we write إِقَامَة for the noun of action of the fourth form; and إِسْتِقَامَة for that of the tenth.

Nouns of Action of Defective Verbs.

Nouns of action coming from defective verbs, having و or ى for their last radical, have no irregularity when they are of one of the forms where the second radical bears *Jazmah*; as غَزْو ,رَمْى ,لَقْى ,رِضْوَان, &c.

Those of the forms فَعِل ,فَعَل ,فَعُل, change the third radical, if it be و, into ى; and this third radical is always quiescent; as رَضِى and لَقِى; it is the same where the third radical is followed by ة, as شكوة for شكاة ; علاة or صلوة for حيوة . And in the form مفعل, as حيوة for حياة ; صلوة for حياة . And in the form مفعل, as مثوى for منوى, from ثوى .

In those of the forms فعول and فعولة an irregularity occurs; if their last radical be و, the و quiescent of this form unites by *Tashdíd* with the و radical, as علو for علوو; if it be ى, the و changes into ى, the *Dammah* into *Kasrah*, and the two ى unite by *Tashdíd*, as رقى for رقوى ; thus from شصا for شصو is formed the noun of action شصو, and from شصى for شصا comes the noun of action شصى.

Nouns of action of the form فعيل unite the last radical by *Tashdíd* with the quiescent ى, changing it into ى if it be و; as هوى for هويى from هوى .

The forms فعال, فعال, فعال, change the last radical into *Hamzah*, as سراء, سراو, بكاى, and سراء for بكاء .

In nouns of action of derivative verbs from defective roots, there is no difference between those whose third radical is و or those in which it is ى.

In the second form, the noun of action is of the form تفعلة, as تسمية, from سمى . In the third form the noun of action is either مفاعلة or فعال, as منادية, مناداة for منادية, and نداء for نداى .

In the fourth, seventh, and all the following forms, the last radical is changed into *Hamzah*, according to the rule of permutation; (4. و and ى), thus إِعْطَآءٌ is derived from أَعْطَى, إِرْتِجَآءٌ from إِرْتَجَى.

Nouns of Action of Verbs doubly imperfect.

It is here only necessary to observe, that triliteral verbs, having the second and third radical infirm letters, in nouns of action when the first bears *Jazmah*, unite them both by *Tashdíd*, as قُوَّةٌ for قُوْوَةٌ, noun of action of قَوِىَ; and if one of these letters be و and the other ى, the و is changed into ى; as شِىٌّ for شِوْىٌ from شَوَى, and أَىٌّ for أَوْىٌ from أَوَى. This is in conformity with one of the rules of permutation (3. و and ى).

In the same way مَجِىٌّ is written for مَجِيىٌ of the form مَفْعِلٌ; or مَجِيَةٌ of the form مَفْعِلَةٌ, coming from the verb جَآءَ, Indef. يَجِىُ. This verb has a noun of action belonging to no acknowledged form, إِتْجَآءٌ.

Noun of Unity.

The Arabians have a particular form for an action occurring but once; this verbal noun is called إِسْمُ الْمَرَّةِ, or noun of unity, and is regarded as a noun of action. It is derived from the noun of action of the simple triliteral verb, by substituting *Fathah* for the nunnated vowel of the third radical, and adding ة, as نصرة from نصر , قومة from قام, which signify the action of assisting and of standing up, once only.

The noun of unity, of imperfect verbs, follows the same rule; thus from وعد similar verb, is formed وعدة ; from قام a concave verb, comes قومة ; from عدا and رمى defective verbs, عدوة and رمية. This noun is formed in the same way, from the quadriliteral and derivative verbs; thus from دحراج *the action of rolling*; إخراج *the action of sending out*; are formed دحراجة and إخراجة, which signify the action of rolling, and of sending out, once only. If the noun of action should itself end in ة, this kind of noun cannot be formed; the word واحدة is then added after the noun of action, as إقامة واحدة *the action of establishing once*. Here may be classed another species of nouns, of unity, or rather of individuality; formed from primitive nouns indicating a whole species, or a collection of homogeneous parts. By adding ة at the end, nouns are formed which signify a portion, or an individual; thus from تبن *straw*, is formed تبنة *a single straw*, from ذهب *gold*, comes ذهبة *a grain of gold*, from حمام *the genus pigeon*; حمامة *a single pigeon* only.

Another kind of verbal noun, regarded also by the Arabians as a noun of action, and the form of which differs little from that of the noun of unity, is by them named إسم النوع *noun of species*, or specificative noun; because it serves to restrain

a general expression to a particular idea, as when we say, this
man excels in writing, the general idea *to excel*, is determined
and restrained by the word of action, *writing*. This noun, derived
from the primitive triliteral verb, regular or irregular, is always
of the form فِعْلَة, and differs only from the noun of unity by
the first vowel being *Kasrah*; thus كِتْبَة signifies the action of
writing once, and كُتْبَة the action of writing considered abstractedly, and rather as a faculty than as an immediate action; thus
هُوَ حَسَن كِتْبَة *he excels in writing*. When this noun is formed
from quadriliteral or derivative verbs, it is of the same form
as the noun of unity, and the context can alone distinguish them.
The poets sometimes confound the two forms.

Possessive Nouns.

The possessive is the noun adjective, signifying possession,
or relation of origin, quality, &c. It is named by the Arabian
grammarians ٱلِٱسم ٱلْمَنْصُوب *noun relative*, or نِسْبَة *relation*.
It is derived from the substantive by adding ـِى, as سَمَاوِى

heavenly from سَمَآء *heaven*; شَمْسِى *solar* from شَمْس *the sun*;
مِصْرِى *Egyptian* from مِصْر *Egypt*; عُثْمَانِى *a man of the*
family of Othman; سَعْدِى *a freed man of Saâd*. When the
noun from which this relative adjective is formed ends in
ة or ىة, this termination is dropt; thus from مَكَّة *Mecca* comes

10

مَكِّيّ *a native of Mecca*; from طَبِيعَة *nature*, is formed طَبِيعِيّ
natural.

When the third radical is suppressed in the primitive, but
replaced by ة, it is restored in the possessive noun, or relative
adjective; as from لُغَة *language* or *dialect*, comes لُغَوِيّ.

Diminutive Nouns.

The diminutive noun is named by the Arabians إِسْم مُصَغَّر
diminished noun, or تَصْغِير *diminution.* In triliterals it is of the
form فُعَيْل: if the primitive is quadriliteral, the diminutive is
of the form فُعَيْلِل, as رُجَيْل *a little man,* from رَجُل *a man;*
عُقَيْرِب *a little scorpion,* from عَقْرَب *a scorpion.*

Of Adjectives.

The Arabians do not consider the adjective as forming a
different part of speech from the noun, and under the names
of *agent and patient,* that class which Erpenius denominates
participles has been already noticed; another has just appeared
under the name of *possessive nouns,* or *relative adjectives* derived
from nouns.

There are other verbal adjectives derived from the primitive
triliteral verb of the forms فَعُل, فَعِل, فَعْل, فَعِيل, فُعَل, فُعُل,
فَعَلَان and فَعْلَان, فَعَال, فَعَّال, أَفْعَل, فَعَال, فَعُول. This sort of verbal
adjectives belongs in general to neuter verbs, as شَهِيد *witness-*

ing, *a witness*, *or martyr*, from شَهِدَ *to witness*; رَحِيمٌ *merciful*, from رَحِمَ *to have mercy*; حَسَنٌ *handsome*, from حَسُنَ *to be handsome*; صَعْبٌ *difficult*, from صَعُبَ *to be difficult*; رَوُوفٌ *compassionate*, from رَأَفَ *to be compassionate*; غَفُورٌ *forgiving*, from غَفَرَ *to pardon*; سَكْرَانُ *intoxicated*; غَضْبَانُ *angry*; عُرْيَانٌ *naked*; أَمْرَدُ *smooth* or *beardless*; أَحْمَرُ *red*; عَجَّابٌ *wonderful*. Most of these forms are only used to express an habitual and constant quality; others convey the idea of intensity and energy.

Of Genders.

Genders are of two kinds, masculine and feminine. Feminine nouns are known by their signification or termination.

Those of which the gender is determined by the signification, are:

1. The names of women, as مَرْيَم *Mary*; هِنْد *Hinda*; and those whose signification carries with it the idea of a woman, as عَرُوس *a bride*; أُمّ *a mother*.

2. The names of provinces or towns, as مِصَّر *Egypt*; مَكَّة *Mecca*; ٱلشَّام *Syria*.

3. The names of parts of the body which are twofold; as يَد *the hand*; رِجْل *the foot*; كَتِف *the shoulder*. Nouns or adjectives feminine, the gender of which is fixed by their termination, are

1. Those terminated by ة, as خِلَاة *friendship*; جَنَّة *a garden*; صَغِيرَة *little* (fem.).

2. Those ending in ا not radical, as كِبْرِيَاء *pride*; صَحْرَاء *a field*.

3. Those having for final letter ى *servile*, or *Alif* short, quiescent after *Fathah*; as ذِكْرَى *remembrance*; أُولَى *the first* (fem.); دُنْيَا for دُنْيَى *the world*.

To these are to be added أَرْض *the earth*; خَمْر *wine*; بِئْر *a well*; نَار *fire*; رِيح *the wind*; نَفْس *the soul*; شَمْس *the sun*; and others, which must be learned by use; on the contrary, a few words having the feminine termination ة, are of the masculine gender, as خَلِيفَة *a Khalif*; it is the same with those verbal adjectives, which ending in ة, become a species of intensitives, as عَلَّامَة *very learned*; ضُحَكَة *habituated to laugh*; رَاوِيَة *relating from memory*. Substantives and adjectives not comprised under these heads are masculine; as قَمَر *the moon*; بَيْت *a house*.

The names of the letters of the alphabet are of both genders; but more usually made feminine.

The manner of forming the Feminine Gender.

Adjectives, and some substantives applicable to both sexes, pass from the masculine to the feminine. This they generally do by dropping the nunnated vowel and adopting ة at the end of the masculine, as عَظِيم *great*; عَظِيمَة *great*, (fem.); جَدّ *a grandfather*; جَدَّة *a grandmother*; فَتَى *a young man*; فَتَاة *a young woman* (for فَتِيَة).

Verbal adjectives of the form اَفْعَل, when not of the comparative or superlative degree, take in the feminine form فَعْلَاء; as اَصْفَر *yellow*; fem. صَفْرَاء.

Verbal adjectives of the same form, but of the comparative or superlative degree, take in the feminine the form فُعْلَى; as اَكْبَر *greater*; كُبْرَى *greater*, (fem.); اَوَّل *first*, which is for اَوْءَل, or وَوَّل, and آخَر *another*, which is for الْاَخِر; make in the feminine agreeably to this rule اُولَى and اُخْرَى.

The word اَحَد *one*, makes in the feminine اِحْدَى. Verbal adjectives of the form فَعْلَان become in the feminine فَعْلَى, as سَكْرَان, feminine سَكْرَى; غَضْبَان, feminine غَضْبَى. These very adjectives sometimes take their feminine in the common form, as سَكْرَانَة, غَضْبَانَة.

Those of the form فُعْلَان having *Dammah* for vowel of the first radical, make their feminine by adding ة, as عُرْيَان *naked*, fem. عُرْيَانَة.

Verbal adjectives of the forms فَعُول and فَعِيل, which are often of both genders, sometimes however take final ة to make the feminine. The form فَعُول when of the passive signification, always admits the variation of gender; as رَسُول *a messenger*, or *one sent*, fem. رَسُولَة. When neuter or active, as كَذُوب *a liar*; شَكُور *a grateful person*; غَشُوم *one of violent temper*; they are of both genders if the substantive to which they relate is expressed; if it be not, they then admit the difference of genders. The form فَعِيل when of active or neuter signification, as نَصِير assisting; عَفِيف abstinent, is subject to the variation of gender; when of passive signification, as حَبِيب beloved; قَتِيل a person slain, the gender is distinguished only when the noun to which they relate is not expressed.

Verbal adjectives of the forms فَعْلَة, فَعُولَة, فَعَّالَة, فَعَالَة, مِفْعَلَة, مِفْعَال, مِفْعِيل, are of both genders; مِسْكِين makes however fem. مِسْكِينَة.

The Arabians have no neuter gender, whence adjectives used as neuter substantives, are expressed by the feminine gender, as وَاحِدَة تَعْوَزُكَ one thing is wanting to you.

Of Numbers.

There are three numbers in the nouns, as in the verbs, the singular, the dual, and the plural.

The dual is formed from the singular, by adding ان, and substituting ت for the ة final; thus كِتَاب a book; كِتَابَان two books; مَدِينَة a city; مَدِينَتَان two cities.

When the last letter is و or ى, and in the singular, a short Alif represented either by ا or ى has been substituted for them; in order to make the dual the original form is restored; as ذِكْرَى for فَتَى a young man, for فَتًى, dual فَتَيَان

ذِكْرَى *remembrance;* dual ذِكْرَيانِ . عَصًا for عَصْوٌ *a staff;* dual عَصَوانِ .

In words of three letters, the radical, whether و or ي , re- turns in the dual; but if the word have more than three letters, the و is changed into ى; thus مَرْضًى passive verbal adjective of the root رَضِوَ , makes in the dual مَرْضِيانِ , and not مَرْضَوانِ .

When the singular ends in *Hamzah,* preceded by servile *Alif,* forming the feminine, the *Hamzah* becomes و in the dual; as صَفْراءُ feminine of أَصْفَرُ *yellow;* dual صَفْراوانِ .

If the *Hamzah,* preceded by *Alif,* is in the place of و or ى radical, in forming the dual it may be preserved or changed into و ; thus رِداءٌ for رِدَاى *a mantle;* dual رِدَاءَانِ , or رِدَاوانِ ; if the *Hamzah* be radical, it must be preserved, قَرَّاءٌ *a reader,* from قَرَأَ *to read;* dual قَرَّاءَانِ .

There are two sorts of plurals, the one uniform and regular, called by the Arabians جَمْعٌ سالِمٌ or *perfect plural,* because it preserves all the letters and vowels of the singular. The other, which adopts a great number of different forms, is called جَمْعٌ مُكَسَّرٌ *broken plural.*

The regular plural is formed for the masculine by adding ـونَ , and for the feminine by changing ةٌ into ـاتٌ . When the feminine does not in the singular end in ةٌ , the final vowel of the singular is dropt for the termination, thus سارِقٌ *a robber,* plu. سارِقونَ *robbers,* سارِقَةٌ *a female thief,* plu. سارِقاتٌ .

If the singular masculine end in ى quiescent after *Kasrah*, or *Fathah*; in the plural a contraction occurs, according to the rules of permutation, thus قَاضُوْنَ for قَاضِىُوْنَ *a judge*, plu. قَاضٍ for قَاضِىٌ; مُوْسِيُوْنَ for مُوْسُوْنَ. مُصْطَفَى *Moses*, plu. مُوْسَى *Mustafa*, plu. مُصْطَفَوْنَ for مُصْطَفِيُوْنَ.

Feminine nouns of the forms فَعَلٌ or فَعَلَةٌ, coming from a regular root, experience a change in the plural, the *Jazmah* of the second radical in the singular, being in the plural changed into *Fathah*. دَعَدُ *name of a woman*, plu. دَعَدَاتٌ; قَصْعَةٌ *a saucer*, plu. قَصَعَاتٌ.

If the singular be of the form فُعْلٌ or فُعْلَةٌ, the second radical takes, in the plural, *Dammah* or *Fathah*, or may preserve the *Jazmah*; ظُلْمَةٌ *darkness*, plu. ظُلُمَاتٌ, ظُلَمَاتٌ or ظُلْمَاتٌ.

If the singular be of the form فِعْلٌ or فِعْلَةٌ, the second radical in the plural takes *Kasrah* or *Fathah*, or preserves its *Jazmah*. سِدْرَةٌ *the lotus*; سِدَرَاتٌ, سِدِرَاتٌ or سِدْرَاتٌ.

The broken plural is that which is formed irregularly, and not by the addition of وْنَ and ـاتٌ. Of these there may be reckoned twenty-eight forms. It must be observed, however, that the application of these singular and plural forms to each other, has many exceptions, and is not to be taken strictly.

First form, فَعَل,

Is formed from the singulars فَعْلَة and فَعْلَى fem.; as تُحْفَة, تُحَف presents, كُبْرَى plu. كُبَر very great; and very rarely from the forms فِعْلَة, فَعْلَة; as قَرْيَة, plu. قُرَى villages; لِحْيَة, plu. لُحَى mustaches, for قُرَى and لُحَى.

Second form, فُعُل.

This form belongs, first to nouns of the form فَعَال and فِعَال, whose root is neither surd nor defective; and to those of the forms فَعِيل, فَعِيلَة, فَعُول, not coming from a defective root: as كِتَاب, plu. كُتُب books; سَرِير plu. سُرُر, thrones; عَمُود plu. عُمُد columns; سَفِينَة plu. سُفُن ships; صَحِيفَة plu. صُحُف leaves of a book. Second to a few nouns of the forms فَعَل, فِعْل, فُعْلَة; as أَسَد plu. أُسُد lions; نَمِر plu. نُمُر leopards; بُسْرَة plu. بُسُر glass beads. Third to verbal adjectives of the forms فَعِيل, فَعُول, not having a passive signification; as نَذِير plu. نُذُر preachers.

Third form, فُعْل.

This belongs to masculine adjectives of the form أَفْعَل and to their feminines فَعْلَاء; as أَحْمَر red, and حَمْرَاء red, (fem.) حُمْر red (mas. and fem.)

Fourth form, فُعَل.

This comes from the singular, فُعْلَة as سُكَّة plu. سِكَك coins,
بِيعَة plu. بِيَع churches.

Fifth form, فِعَال.

The fifth form appertains first to singulars of the forms
فَعْل, فِعْل, فُعْل, as قَدَح a dart without a point; plu. قِدَاح;
رُمْح a spear, plu. رِمَاح, رَجُل a man, plu. رِجَال.

2. To the forms فَعْل and فَعْلَة; as كَعْب the heel, plu.
كِعَاب, قَصْعَة a saucer, plu. قِصَاع; ثَوْب a vest, plu. ثِيَاب,
(و being changed into ى after Kasrah) فَيْف a desert, plu.
فِيَاف.

3. To the forms فِعْل, فَعْل, فَعْلَة, not having a surd or defective
root, (that is, the third radical like the second, or the third
radical و or ى), as جَبَل a mountain, plu. جِبَال, رَقَبَة the neck,
plu. رِقَاب.

4. To the adjectives فَعِيل and فَعِيلَة, as شَرِيف and شَرِيفَة
noble, plu. شِرَاف; but not when these are taken in a passive
sense, as in قَتِيل a person killed.

5. To adjectives of the forms فَعْلَان and فَعْلَانَة; as نَدْمَان
and نَدْمَانَة penitent, plu. نِدَام.

6. To adjectives of the forms فَعْلَان and فَعْلَانة, as خَمْصَان and خَمْصَانة *famishing*, plu. خِمَاص.

Sixth form, فُعُول.

This belongs to substantives of the forms فَعْل, فِعْل, فُعْل and فَعَل; and sometimes to adjectives of the form فَاعِل, as بَحْر *the sea*, plu. بُحُور, جُنْد *an army*, plu. جُنُود, أَسَد *a lion*, plu. أُسُود, شَاهِد *a witness*, شُهُود.

Seventh and eighth forms, فُعَّل and فُعَّال.

These belong to adjectives of the forms فَاعِل and فَاعِلة, with this only difference, that the form فُعَّال is exclusively appropriated to the masculine, thus كَاتِب *a writer*, plu. كُتَّاب; حَاكِم *a judge*, plu. حُكَّام and حُكَّم; غَازٍ *a combatant*, for غَازِو, plu. غُزَّاء; غَايِب *one who is absent*, plu. غُيَّب, for غُيَّاو; بَاهِلة *a female camel*, بُهَّل.

Ninth form, فَعَلَة.

This appertains to verbal adjectives of the form فَاعِل, when applied to rational beings, and not coming from a defective root, as كَامِل *perfect*, plu. كَمَلَة; قَائِم *standing erect*, plu. قَوَمَة; بَارّ *innocent*, plu. بَرَرَة.

Tenth form, فَعَلَة .

This belongs almost exclusively to verbal adjectives of the form فَاعِل coming from a defective root, and applied to rational beings; as رَامٍ *an archer*, plu. رُمَاةٌ for رَمَيَة , غَازٍ *a combatant*, plu. غُزَاةٌ for غَزَوَة , قَاضٍ *a Kadhi*, plu. قُضَاةٌ for قَضَوَة .

Eleventh form, فِعَلَة .

This belongs to substantives of the form فُعْل , and to a few of the forms فَعْل and فِعْل , as دُبّ *a bear*, plu. دِبَبَة ; كُوز *a pitcher*, plu. كِوَزَة ; زَوْج *a spouse*, plu. زِوَجَة , قِرْد *an ape*, plu. قِرَدَة .

Twelfth form, فُعْلَة .

This belongs to substantives of the forms فَعْل , فِعْل , فُعْل , فَعَال , فِعَال and فَعِيل , as ثَوْر *a bull*, plu. ثِيَرَة ; أَخ for أَخْو *a brother*, plu. إِخْوَة ; غُصْن *a branch*, plu. غِصَنَة ; غَزَال *an antelope*, plu. غِزَلَة ; غُلَام *a slave*, plu. غِلَمَة ; صَبِيّ for صَبِيو *an infant*, plu. صِبْيَة .

Thirteenth form, أَفْعَل .

This belongs to substantives of the form فَعْل , and sometimes فِعْل , فُعْل and فَعَل , not coming from a concave root, as وجْهة *the face*, plu. أوجهة; دلْو *a bucket*, plu. أدْلٍ for أدْلُو; رجْل *the foot*, plu. أرْجل. عصًا *a staff*, plu. أعْصٍ for أعْصُو; It also appertains to feminine substantives of four letters, not ending in ة, and of which the penultima is a quiescent letter, as ذراع *the arm*, plu. أذْرع; يمين *an oath*, plu. أيْمن. It also belongs, by custom, to several forms different from those indicated, and even to singulars coming from concave roots, as سبع *a lion*, plu. أسْبع; نهار *the day*, plu. أنْهر; عين *the eye*, plu. أعْين; دار *a house*, plu. أدْور.

Fourteenth form, أفعال.

This belongs to substantives of three letters, and of all forms, though but rarely to the forms فعْل and فعل; as مطر *rain*, plu. أمْطار: مرض *a disease*, plu. أمْراض; كتف *the shoulder*, plu. أكْتاف; إبل *a camel*, plu. آبال; عين *the eye*, plu. أعْيان; يوم *the day*, plu. أيّام; رطب *a date*, plu. أرْطاب.

Fifteenth form, أفعلة.

This belongs to nouns of four letters, the penultima of which is ا or و, and ى quiescent, as قلاد *a necklace*, plu. أقلدة; إله *God* (which is an abbreviation of إله) plu. آلهة; عمود *a column*, plu. أعمدة. This plural form belongs particularly to the singular forms فَعَالٌ and فِعَالٌ, coming from a surd or defective root; as بِتَاتٌ *an article of furniture*, plu. أَبِتَّةٌ; إِمَامٌ *an Imám*, plu. أَيِمَّةٌ for أَأْمِمَةٌ; قَبَاءٌ *a tunic or shirt*, plu. أَقْبِيَةٌ.

Sixteenth form, فَوَاعِلُ.

The sixteenth form belongs to substantives of the forms فَاعَلٌ and فَعَالٌ, and to substantives and adjectives feminine of the forms فَاعِلَةٌ and فَاعِلَاءٌ, and, though rarely, to verbal adjectives masculine of the form فَاعِلٌ, thus طَابِقٌ *a frying pan*, plu. طَوَابِقُ; صَاعِقَةٌ *death*, plu. صَوَاعِقُ; فَارِسٌ *a cavalier*, plu. فَوَارِسُ.

Seventeenth form, فَعَائِلُ.

This belongs to substantives singular feminine, of four letters, of which the third is و, ى, or ا servile or quiescent, after a vowel of the same kind; and to feminine substantives of the same forms, but adding ة at the end; as سَحَابَةٌ *a cloud*, عَجُوزٌ *an old woman*, plu. عَجَائِزُ; عَجِيبَةٌ *a wonder*, plu. عَجَائِبُ; سَحَائِبُ.

Eighteenth form, فِعْلَانٌ.

This belongs to substantives singular of the forms فَعَالٌ, فِعْلٌ, فُعْلٌ, and to some nouns of the forms فَعَلٌ and فَاعِلٌ, coming from concave roots, as غُلَامٌ *a young man, a slave*, plu. غِلْمَان ; غَزَال *an antelope*, plu. غِزْلَان ; حُوت *a fish*, plu.

حِيتَان ; تَاج *a crown*, plu. تِيجَان : أَجْ *a brother*, plu. إِخْوَان.
Some nouns, whose singulars belong to other forms, admit this
plural also.

Nineteenth form, فُعْلَان.

This belongs to substantives of the forms فَعْل , فُعَل , فَعِيل ,
not being of concave roots; as سَقْف *a roof*, plu. سَقْفَان : بَلَد
a region, a province, plu. بُلْدَان ; رَغِيف *a cake*, رُغْفَان.

Twentieth form, فَعَلَا ء.

This form is applied to adjectives masculine, of the form
فَعِيل , not having a passive sense; and to some of the form
فَاعِل not coming from a concave, or defective root, but applied
to a rational being, فَقِير *a poor man*, plu. فُقَرَا ء ; أَمِير *a prince*,
plu. أُمَرَا ء ; رَئِيس for رَائِس *a chief*, plu. رُؤَسَا ء ; شَاعِر *a poet*,
plu. شُعَرَا ء . The word خَلِيفَة *Khalif*, also makes the plural
خُلَفَا ء .

Twenty-first form, أَفْعِلَا ء.

This belongs also to singulars of the form فَعِيل , but is
almost peculiar to those whose root is concave or defective, as
حَبِيب *a friend, one beloved*, plu. أَحِبَّا ء ; غَنِيّ *a rich man*,
plu. أَغْنِيَا ء ; صَدِيق *veracious*, plu. أَصْدِقَا ء .

Twenty-second form, فَعْلَى .

This is made from adjectives of the form فَعِيلٌ , and sometimes also فَاعِلٌ and فَعِلٌ , signifying *pain*, or *destruction*; as هَالِكٌ *wounded*, plu. قَتْلَى ; قَتِيلٌ *slain*, plu. جَرْحَى ; جَرِيحٌ *perishing*, plu. هَلْكَى .

Twenty-third form, فَعَالَى .

This belongs to substantives singular, of the forms فَعْلَا ٪, فَعْلَى ,فُعْلَى ; and feminine adjectives of the forms فَعْلَا ٪ and فَعْلَى ; as فَتْوَى ; عَذَارَى عَذْرَا ٪ *a virgin*, plu. صَحَارَى ; صَحْرَا ٪, *the decree of a judge*, plu. فَتَاوَى — حَبْلَى *a pregnant woman*, حَبَالَى .

Twenty-fourth form, فَعَالَى .

This belongs, first to the same substantives and adjectives as the preceding; as عَذْرَا ٪ *a virgin*, plu. عَذَارَى .

2nd. To adjectives of the form فَعْلَان , as سَكْرَان *intoxicated*, plu. سَكَارَى .

3rd. To feminines of the form فَعِيلَة coming from a defective root, as هَدِيَّة *a gift*, plu. هَدَايَا .

Twenty-fifth form, فَعِيل .

This, which is very rare, belongs to singulars of the forms فَعَل , فِعَال and فَاعِل , as عَبْد a slave, plu. عَبِيد ; حِمَار an ass, plu. حَمِير ; كَلْب a dog, plu. كَلِيب ; غَازٍ a conqueror, plu. غُزَّى ; عَادٍ a courier, plu. عَدَّى .

Twenty-sixth form, فُعُولَة .

This, which is also of rare occurrence, belongs to singulars of the form فِعَل , as خَيْط a thread, plu. خَيُوطَة ; عَمّ a paternal uncle, plu. عُمُومَة ; عَيْر a wild ass, plu. عِيُورَة .

Twenty-seventh form, فِعَالَة .

This belongs to singulars of the forms فَعَل and فَاعِل , as صَاحِب a companion, plu. صَحَابَة ; حَجَر a stone, plu. حِجَارَة .

Twenty-eighth form, فُعَل .

A few singulars of the forms فَاعِل , فَعْلَة , فُعْلَة , have their plurals of the form فُعَل , as حَلْقَة a ring, plu. بَكَرة a pulley, plu. بُكَر ; حَلْقَة a ring, plu. حُلَق ; طَالِب a person who seeks, plu. طُلَب .

It may have been observed, that the same singular assumes various forms of plurals; some have at the same time a plural regular, and one or several irregular plurals; thus from نَفْس

11

the soul, are formed the plurals نفوس and أنفُس ; from غلام *a boy*, plu. غِلمَة and غِلمَان ; from عين *the eye*, أعيان , عيون ; from عبد *a slave*, عِبَاد , عبود , from سور *a wall*, أسوار . سيران ; from بحر *the sea*, بِحَار , بحر , البحر ; and also from عبدان ; شاهد *a witness*, شَوَاهد , شاهدون , شُهُود . It must not be supposed, however, that a singular admits indifferently all the plurals of which its form is susceptible; thus نفس does not admit نفَاس , أعبد , nor does عبد adopt the plurals نفسة , نفسان , رجُل عبدة , عبدة , &c. Sometimes one only is formed, as from *a man*, the only plural is رجال , and أمر *an affair, a command*, makes only أمور . This must be learnt by the use of the dictionary.

When a singular, having several meanings, admits several plurals, it will be often found that certain plurals are peculiarly, or exclusively attached to certain significations; for example, عين signifies *the eye, a fountain, the substance*, or *essence of a thing*, and *a person of rank*. In the plural it has عيون , أعين and أعيان .

The two first of these answer to the two first meanings, and the third only to the two last.

The regular plurals, and those of the twelfth, thirteenth, fourteenth, and fifteenth forms, are called جُموع قلّة *plurals of small number*, in contradistinction to the other forms, which

are called جُمُوعُ كَثْرَةٍ *plurals of great number*. This obser-
vation applies, however, only to nouns having several forms of
plural: when the plural of one of these four forms is its only
one, it is employed indiscriminately like those of the other forms.

All simple quadriliteral nouns, and most of those augmented, together with their feminines, take a broken, or irregular plural; assuming *Alif* quiescent after the second letter,
which, as well as the first, bears *Fathah*, as the third letter
has *Kasrah*. Thus they are of the form قَمَاطِر, as ضَفْدَع *a frog*,

plu. ضَفَادِع, مَدْخَل *a vestibule*, مَدَاخِل; final ة is dropt, as مَزْبَلَة
a dunghill, plu. مَزَابِل . If the last radical be preceded by either
of the letters ا, و, and ى quiescent, it remains, as قِنْدِيل *a lamp*,
plu. قَنَادِيل; if it be ا or و, the preceding *Kasrah* changes it
into ى; as سُلْطَان *a sultan*, plu. سَلَاطِين . Sometimes, however,
it is omitted, ة being put at the end as a compensation, thus
إِبْلِيس *the devil*, أَبَالِيس and أَبَالِسَة; إِسْكَاف *a shoemaker*,
أَسَاكِيف and أَسَاكِفَة . Final ة is sometimes found in the plural
of quadriliteral nouns not having quiescent letters before the
last radical in the singular; this is particularly applicable to
foreign words, and possessive nouns, or relative adjectives of

four letters, as أُسْقُف *a bishop*, plu. أَسَاقِف or أَسَاقِفَة; بَغْدَادِى
a native of Baghdád, plu. بَغَادِدَة; قَيْصَر *an emperor*, (Cæsar)
plu. قَيَاصِرَة; جَرْكَسِى *a Circassian*, plu. جَرَاكِسَة .

Adjectives of the form أفْعَل being comparatives, or super-latives, take in the plural the form of quadriliterals; but this is only when they are employed as substantives, as أسْوَد *black*, plu. أسَاوِد *serpents having a black skin*; أكْبَر *most great*, plu. أكَابِر *the great men of a kingdom*.

The forms of quadriliteral plurals serve also to make those plurals which are called جَمْعُ الْجَمْعِ, or *plurals of plurals*, and which are derived from other plurals; thus from ظُفُر *a finger nail*, is formed the plural أظْفَار, and from that, the plural of plural أظَافِير; from يَد for يَدَى *the hand*, comes أيْد for أيْدِى; and afterward أيَادِى; from سِوَار *a bracelet*, أسْوِرَة, and from that أسَاوِر. Words of five or more letters, not including ا, و, ى, or ة, quiescent, take the same form; these words then lose one of their letters of the singular number. This is sometimes the penultima, but usually the last, as سَفَرْجَل *a pomgranate*, plu. سَفَارِج; خُزَرِنق or عَنَاكِت, *a spider*, plu. عَنْكَبُوت *a spider*, plu. خَزَارِن, and خَزَارِق. If, however, the penultima is و or ى, forming a diphthong after *Fathah*, both remain; but و is changed into ى by the influence of the preceding *Kasrah*; as فِرْعَون *a crocodile*, plu. فَرَاعِين. Augmented words drop the ser-vile letters; مُدَحْرَج *the place in which a thing rolls*, plu. دَحَارِج. If, beside the servile م, there is also a ن, or the letters سْت, the م is preserved in the plural, while the other servile letters

disappear; as مُنْطَالَقْ plu. مَطَالَقْ *loosed*; مُسْتَنْخَرِجْ *a leader*, plu.
مَنْخَارِجْ. There are some nouns whose plurals are very irregular, or even borrowed from another root, thus طَرِيقْ *a road*,
plu. طَرُقَاتْ; أُمّ *a mother*, plu. أُمَّهَاتْ; فَمْ *a mouth*, plu. أَفْوَاهْ;
مَاءْ *water*, plu. أَمْوَاهْ or مِيَاهْ; in these two last words, it is
the singular which is irregular, for فَمْ is for فُوهْ, and مَاءْ for
مَاهْ. The singular أَمْرَاةْ *a woman*, has no plural, the place of
which is supplied by نِسَاءْ, نِسْوَةْ or نِسْوَانْ; the word إِنْسَانْ
a man, has in the plural أَنَاسْ, and by contraction نَاسْ.

Table shewing to what forms of the singular those of the plural usually belong.

	Form of Plural.	Singular.		Plural.
1	فُعَل	عُلْبَة	a milk pail,	عُلَب
2	فُعَل	كِتَاب	a book,	كُتُب
3	فُعْل	أَحْمَر	red,	حُمْر
4	فِعَل	كِسْرَة	a fragment,	كِسَر
5	فِعَال	رَجُل	a man,	رِجَال
6	فُعُول	بِزْر	seed,	بُزُور
7	فُعَل	} حَاكِم {	a judge,	حُكَّم
8	فُعَّال			حُكَّام
9	فَعَلَة	كَامِل	perfect,	كَمَلَة
10	فُعَلَة	قَاضٍ	a Kadhi,	قُضَاة
11	فِعَلَة	قِرْد	an ape,	قِرَدَة
12	فِعَلَة	غُصْن	a branch,	غِصَنَة
13	أَفْعُل	وَجْه	the face,	أَوْجُه
14	أَفْعَال	مَطَر	rain,	أَمْطَار
15	أَفْعِلَة	إِمَام	an Imam,	أَيِمَّة for أَئِمَّة

	Form of Plural.	Singular.		Plural.
		قِلَاد	a necklace,	اَقْلِدَة
16	فَوَاعِل	طَابِق	a frying pan,	طَوَابِق
17	فَعَائِل	شِمَال	the left hand,	شَمَائِل
18	فِعْلَان	غُلَام	a boy,	غِلْمَان
19	فُعْلَان	سَقْف	a roof,	سُقْفَان
		بَلَد	a country,	بُلْدَان
20	فُعَلَاء	شَرِيف	noble,	شُرَفَاء
		شَاعِر	a poet,	شُعَرَاء
21	أَفْعِلَاء	حَبِيب	a friend,	أَحِبَّاء for أَحْبِبَاء
22	فَعْلَى	جَرِيح	wounded,	جَرْحَى
23	فَعَالَى	صَحْرَاء	a desert,	صَحَارَى
24	فَعَالَى	سَكْرَان	intoxicated,	سَكَارَى

The twenty-fifth, twenty-sixth, twenty-seventh and twenty-eighth forms are of rare occurrence.

The details into which I have here entered, and the accompanying table, may be of some use, but no rules or tables can greatly assist the memory; those forms, however, which most often occur, will soon become familiar, and a dictionary will afford every necessary assistance with regard to the more uncommon.

Of Declension.

The Arabic nouns are classed under two heads with respect to declension: Triptots, which have three variations of case in the singular, or plural; and Diptots, which have only two, the dual being uniformly of this last class.

The first class of Diptots are the duals forming the nominative in ـانِ, and the oblique case in ـيَنِ.

The second regular masculine plurals, whose nominative is in ـونَ, genitive, &c. in ـيَنَ.

The third regular feminine plurals, having the nominative in ـاتُ, genitive in ـاتِ.

The fourth invariable nouns, whose last radical never admits the nunnation, having the nominative in ـُ, and other cases in ـَ.

These invariable nouns are:

1. Positive and comparative adjectives, of the same form as أَحْمَر *red*, حَمْرَا fem., except a few having their feminine in ة, as أَرْمَل *widowed*, mas. أَرْمَلَة fem.

2. Adjectives ending in ـَان servile, whose first radical has *Fathah*, and which do not form their feminines by adding ة, as غَضْبَان *enraged*; fem. غَضْبَى.

3. Substantives and adjectives singular, ending in *Alif* short, or ى quiescent after *Fathah*, as صُغْرَى *very little*; بُشْرَى *good tidings*; or in *Hamzah*, preceded by *Alif* bearing *Maddah*, as عَذْرَاءُ *a virgin*; بَيْضَاءُ *white*. If the ى or the *Hamzah* are radical, as in هُدًى *direction*, رِدَاءٌ *a cloak*, these words are Triptots.

4. All irregular plurals containing four syllables, of which the two first have *Fathah* for their vowels, and the third has *Kasrah*; as عَجَائِب *wonders*; مَدَارِس *colleges*; مَفَاتِيح *keys*; طَوَاحِين *mills*; أَقَارِب *relations*.

5. Some names of countries, cities, villages, castles, mountains, rivers, and other places.

6. Most proper names, and among others all those ending in ـَان, together with foreign names consisting of more than three letters; also all feminine names terminating in ة, and such as consist of four letters. The three letter female names, a few excepted, are occasionally either Triptots, or Diptots, which is sometimes the case, among the poets, with regard to other invariable nouns, whilst the variable or Triptots, are likewise sometimes converted into Diptots.

The declension is exceedingly simple, there being in writing, where vowel points are not used, no real difference of case, excepting in the addition of ا servile to the accusative. Where vowel points are used, the nominative singular and plural are distinguished by ٌ ; the genitive dative and ablative by ٍ ; and the accusative by ً ; the dual always ending in *Kasrah*. The ة, terminating a word, changes into ت, when being preserved, it ceases to be the last letter, as مَدِينَةٌ *a town*, dual مَدِينتَانِ. It disappears in the regular plural, as نَاصِرَةٌ *a woman* who assists, plu. نَاصِرَاتٌ.

1. Declension being Triptots singular and plural.

		Singular.	Dual.	Plural.
A house,	Nom.	بَيْتٌ	بَيْتَانِ	بُيُوتٌ
	Gen.	بَيْتٍ	بَيْتَيْنِ	بُيُوتٍ
	Accus.	بَيْتًا		بُيُوتًا

2. Being Triptots in the singular, and Diptots in the plural.

		Singular.	Dual.	Plural.
An assistant,	Nom.	نَاصِرٌ	نَاصِرَانِ	نَاصِرُونَ
	Gen.	نَاصِرٍ	نَاصِرَيْنِ	نَاصِرِينَ
	Accus.	نَاصِرًا		

		Singular.	Dual.	Plural.
An assistant,	(fem.) Nom.	نَاصِرَةٌ	نَاصِرَتَانِ	نَاصِرَاتٌ
	Gen.	نَاصِرَةٍ	نَاصِرَتَيْنِ	نَاصِرَاتٍ
	Accus.	نَاصِرَةً		

3. Being Triptots in the singular, and invariable Diptots in the plural.

		Singular.	Dual.	Plural.
A mosque,	Nom.	مَسْجِدٌ	مَسْجِدَانِ	مَسَاجِدُ
	Gen.	مَسْجِدٍ	مَسْجِدَيْنِ	مَسَاجِدَ
	Accus.	مَسْجِدًا		

4. Being invariable Diptots in the singular, and Triptots in the plural.

		Singular.	Dual.	Plural.
Red,	Nom.	أَحْمَرُ	أَحْمَرَانِ	حُمْرٌ
	Gen. and Accus.	أَحْمَرَ	أَحْمَرَيْنِ	حُمْرٍ
				حُمْرًا

5. Being invariable Diptots singular and plural.

		Singular.	Dual.	Plural.
Smaller,	Nom.	أَصْغَرُ	أَصْغَرَانِ	أَصَاغِرُ
	Gen. and Accus.	أَصْغَرَ	أَصْغَرَيْنِ	أَصَاغِرَ

When the last letter of a noun is و preceded by *Fathah*, or else ا, or ى, also preceded by *Fathah*, and called *short Alif*, أَلِفُ مَقْصُورَةٍ, the three cases are alike; if it be ى preceded by *Kasrah*, the nominative and the genitive alone are alike; in this case the ى not bearing either *Dammah* or *Kasrah*.

Thus in the three cases عَصًى *a staff*, is written for عَصَوٌ, عَصَوٍ,
عَصَوًا and رَحًى *a mill*, for رَحَيٌ, رَحَيٍ, رَحَيًا which are of the
first class, or Triptots. قَاضٍ *a Kadhi*, in the nominative and
genitive for قَاضِيٌ and قَاضِيٍ, of the same class, بُشْرَى *good
news*, for بُشْرَى in the nominative, and بُشْرَى in the genitive
and accusative of the second class, or Diptots. صَحَارَى *deserts*,
for صَحَارَى in the nominative, and صَحَارَى in the genitive and
accusative, irregular quadriliteral plural of the second class.

Six words have a variation of case peculiar to themselves
when in construction either with a noun, or an affixed possessive pronoun; viz. أَب *a father*; أَخ *a brother*; حَم *a father
in law*; هَن *a thing*; فَم for فُوه *the mouth*, when governing a
genitive, and ذُو *having, possessed of, endowed with*; which are
declined as follows:

Nom.	أَبُو زَيدٍ	the father of Zeid.
Gen.	أَبِى زَيدٍ	of the father of Zeid.
Accus.	أَبَا زَيدٍ	the father of Zeid.
Nom.	فَمٌ or فُو عُمَرٍ	the mouth of Omar.
Gen.	فَمٍ or فِى عُمَرٍ	of the mouth of Omar.
Accus.	فَمًا or فَا عُمَرٍ	the mouth of Omar.

Nom.	ذو رَحْمَةٍ	endowed with compassion.
Gen.	ذِى رَحْمَةٍ	of compassionate.
Accus.	ذَا رَحْمَةٍ	compassionate.

Nom.	أَخُوهُ	his brother.
Gen.	أَخِيهِ	of his brother.
Accus.	أَخَاهُ	his brother.

Nom.	حَمُوكَ	thy father in law.
Gen.	حَمِيكَ	of thy father in law.
Accus.	حَمَاكَ	thy father in law.

Nom.	هَنُوكَ	thy thing. (Res aliqua, pec. non magna.)
Gen.	هَنِيكَ	of thy thing.
Accus.	هَنَاكَ	thy thing.

When these words are prefixed to the pronoun of the first person, there is no change of case, as أَبِى *my father, of my father*, &c. When فَم is followed by an affixed pronoun, it varies only in the vowel points, as فَمُكَ *your mouth,* فَمِكَ *of your mouth,* فَمَكَ *your mouth.*

The accusative is substituted for the nominative, when certain particles go before, as إِنَّ *indeed, certainly;* أَنَّ *because,*

therefore; كَأَنَّ *as if*; لَكِنَّ *but*; لَيْتَ *would to God!* عَلَّ *and*
لَكِنَّ *perhaps*; as إِنَّ رَجُلاً يَقُومُ *indeed the man stands*;
اَلْمَلِكَ قَدِيرٌ *but the King is powerful.* No other word must
intervene, however, except a preposition with its case, as
إِنَّ فِى الدَّارِ رَجُلاً *certainly the man is in the house.*

لا *is not*, when immediately preceding any appellative, and
denying its very existence, gives it also the accusative termination, as لا رَيْبَ فِيهِ *there is no doubt in it.* In this case
the accusative loses the nunnation, but the noun must not be
definite, either as a noun proper, or as an appellative limited
by the article أَلْ, or by a word which it governs.

The vocative is expressed by the accusative with يا prefixed, as يا أُخْتا *Oh sister!*

فَاللهُ عَلَيْكُمْ يا ظَالِمِينَ فَهِيُّوا لِلْبَلايا جِلْبابا و لِلرَّزايا اترابا ۰
*For God is against you, O ye unjust! prepare ye, therefore,
weeds for wretchedness, and be ye the companions of sorrow!*

Except however a proper name, an appellative with an
article, or when the object addressed is in sight; where the
nominative without the nunnation, when that would otherwise
occur, is employed, as يا أَمِيرُ *O Prince!* يا عَثْمانُ *O Othman!*
The nominative thus employed, is naturally pronounced with rapi-
dity. Hence it is, that the nunnation is always dropped, and that
the affixed pronoun ـى is sometimes cut off, as يا قَوْمِ *O my
people!* رَبِّ *O my Lord!* Some words, chiefly proper names

in frequent use, throw off a whole syllable at the end, as يَا صَاحِ

for يَا صَاحِبِى *O my friend!* يَا مَنْصُ *O Mansur!* يَا مَرْوَ *O*

Marván! for مَنْصُور, &c.

On the other hand, when placed at the end of a sentence, and pronounced more strongly, the vowel is prolonged, and receives a kind of aspirate, as يَا غَلَامِيَّهْ for غُلَام *O my boy!* Sometimes this appears as final *áh*, as يَا غُلَامَاهُ or غُلَامَا for غُلَام.

When the name invoked, however, bears the article أَلْ, the pronoun هَذَا, or one of these words, أَيَّتُهَا, أَيُّهَا, أَيُّهَذَا, always comes between the name and the particle يَا, as يَا أَيُّهَا ٱلنَّاسُ *O men!*

In calling for help, لِ is often prefixed in the genitive, as يَا لَصَلَاحِ ٱلدِّينِ *help, O Saláh-addín!*

The dual and the perfect masculine plurals in ن, drop that letter, when followed by a noun in the genitive case, or by the affixed pronouns; as غَزَالَا يُوسُفَ *the two fawns of Joseph;* قَدَمَاهُ *his two feet;* بَنُوهُ *his sons.*

The nunnation is not only affected in the same manner as ن, when under these circumstances, but likewise before and after the article, as ٱلْمَلِكُ *the King,* دَارُ ٱلْمَلِكِ *the King's house.*

Of Comparison.

The comparative is formed from the positive, which is itself formed only from primitive triliteral verbs; by prefixing *Alif*, and is of the form أَفْعَل , as صغير *little* ; أصغر *less* ; حَبِيب *beloved* ; أَحَبّ for أَحَبّ *most beloved*. It in general takes مِن after it, as أعظم مِن المَلِك *greater than the King.*

The positive with مِن is used sometimes to express the comparative, as in the following couplet:

متى أصبح و أمسى .

و يومى خير مِن أمسى .

As long as morning and evening succeed, the present day is better than the past.

فِى however, and other particles, often follow the comparative instead of مِن , as أشهر فِى الحَرب *more glorious in war.*

In the feminine of the comparative, ى quiescent after *Fathah*, is added in place of ا prefixed, as كَبِير *great;* أكبر *greater,* (masc.) كُبرى *greater,* (fem.) Without مِن , but followed by a genitive, it forms the superlative, as أحسن النَّاس *the best of men.*

It has likewise a superlative sense, when placed absolutely, as الله أعلم *God is most wise.*

Verbal adjectives of the passive voice, and those which designate colours, or deformities, as أزرق *blue;* أسود *black;*

أعوج crooked; أعمى blind; أعور squinting; and which are themselves of the form أفعل do not generate comparatives.

These comparatives being formed only from certain adjectives; when it is necessary to give the accessory ideas of com-
parison and superiority, one of the following comparatives;
أشد stronger; أحسن handsomer; أقبح more ugly; أخير better;
أشر worse, &c. is used; with the infinitive or abstract noun of
the quality in question, as أشد حمرة stronger in redness; that
is, redder; أحسن تعليمًا و تأديبًا fitter to instruct and to teach.

THE ARTICLE.

THE Arabians have only one article, which they call ٱلْمَعْرِفَة *notification*, because it renders the noun to which it is prefixed definite, which would otherwise be general, or indetermined; as in the following distich:

ٱلدَّهْرُ دُولَابٌ يَدُورُ فِيهِ ٱلسُّرُورُ مَعَ ٱلشُّرُورِ.

بَيْنَا ٱلْفَتَى فَوْقَ ٱلسَّمَاءِ وَ إِذَا بِهِ تَحْتَ ٱلصُّخُورِ.

The world like a water-wheel rolls round, wherein pleasure with pain revolves.

Now the youth soars above the heavens, and now behold him low under the stones!

Here دُولَاب *a water-wheel*, being indefinite, is without an article.

When a definite substantive agrees with an adjective, the article is prefixed likewise to the adjective; as ٱلْكِتَابُ ٱلْعَظِيمُ *the excellent book.* When the noun is indefinite, the adjective becomes so too, as كِتَابٌ عَتِيقٌ *an old book.*

Proper names do not admit of the article, but it always accompanies the epithet, if any follows, as إِبْرَاهِيمُ ٱلْأَمِينُ *Abraham the faithful.* The article is likewise omitted when a possessive pronoun is affixed to the noun, as will be explained hereafter.

ل in the article is sometimes dropt; its place being supplied by *Tashdíd*, when the word to which it is prefixed begins also with ل; as ٱللَّيَل for ٱلْلَيَل. It frequently remains, however, and *Tashdíd* also; as

يَغُوصُ ٱلْبَحَرَ مَنْ طَلَبَ ٱللَّآلِى .

وَ مَنْ طَلَبَ ٱلْعُلَى سَهَرِ ٱللَّيَالِى .

He plunges into the sea who seeks for pearls;
And he who desires greatness, must have watchful nights.

The ل is always omitted in the masculine singular of the relative pronoun, ٱلَّذِى; the fem. sing. ٱلَّتِى; and the plural masculine ٱلَّذِينَ; being so written instead of ٱللَّذِى, &c. but never in the other cases, which seldom occur.

When the particle لِ is prefixed to a noun beginning with ل, and which being definite, ought to have the article, in order to avoid the meeting of three *láms*, the article is dispensed with, or represented by *Tashdíd*, as لِلَّيَلِ for لِلَّيَلِ, or لله for لِلّه, but when prefixed to nouns not beginning with ل, *Alif* alone is dropt; as

فَقُلْ لِلشَّامِتِينَ بِنَا رُوَيْدًا

أَمَامَكُمُ ٱلْمَصَايَبُ وَ ٱلْخُتُوبُ .

But say to the rejoicers in our distress, wait yet a little.
Before you are misfortunes, and great ones.

The article changes the substantives singular, and irregular plurals, which are diptots, into triptots, as

Nom.	Gen.	Accus.
السود *black,*	السود	السود
البيضآء *white,*	البيضآء	البيضآء

Of Numerals.

Numbers are either cardinal or ordinal. The cardinal numbers from 1 to 10 are of the two genders, thus

Fem.	Mas.		Fem.	Mas.	
إِثْنَتَانِ	إِثْنَانِ	2	واحدة	واحد	1
			or	or	
ثلاث	ثلاثة	3	إحدى	أحد	
			أربع	أربعة	4
ثَمَانِ	ثمانية	8	خمس	خمسة	5
تِسع	تسعة	9	ست	ستة	6
عشر	عشرة	10	سبع	سبعة	7

From three to ten, the termination ة, the usual sign of the feminine gender, here marks the masculine. All these numbers, except إِثْنَانِ and إِثْنَتَانِ, are Triptots; these two have only one inflexion, إِثْنَيْنِ and إِثْنَتَيْنِ for the genitive and accusative, like all the duals.

From three to ten, the cardinal numbers are employed either as adjectives or substantives; in the first case, they are

placed after the name of the thing numbered, with which they
agree in gender, and case; if employed as substantives, they
take for their complement the thing numbered, and then lose
their nunnation, as ثلاثة رجال *three men*. When ثَمَانٍ eight,
loses its nunnation, it recovers the ى, which had disappeared
according to the rule (6, ى), for ثَمَانٍ is for ثَمَانِيٌ; we then
write ثَمَانِى in the nominative and genitive, and ثَمَانِيَ in the
accusative.

From eleven to nineteen, the cardinal numbers are composed of units, and of the number ten, which in the masculine
is عشر, and in the feminine عشرَة or عشِرَة.

Feminine.		Masculine.
أُحدى عشرة	11	أحد عشر
إثنتا عشرة	12	إثنا عشر
ثلاث عشرة	13	ثلاثة عشر
أربع عشرة	14	أربعة عشر
خمس عشرة	15	خمسة عشر
ستّ عشرة	16	ستّة عشر
سبع عشرة	17	سبعة عشر
ثمانى عشرة	18	ثمانية عشر
تسع عشرة	19	تسعة عشر

All these numbers, from eleven to nineteen, are indeclinable, except اِثْنَا عَشَرَ and اِثْنَتَا عَشْرَةَ, which in the genitive and accusative make اِثْنَى عَشَرَ and اِثْنَتَى عَشْرَةَ.

سِتُّون	60	عِشْرُون	20
سَبْعُون	70	ثَلَاثُون	30
ثَمَانُون	80	أَرْبَعُون	40
تِسْعُون	90	خَمْسُون	50

The numbers from twenty to ninety, are the same for both genders; they are always employed as nouns, and are followed by the name of the thing numbered in the accusative; not however losing the ن final, as the regular plurals do when they govern a word. This rule, however, is not always strictly observed. These numbers are Diptots ending in the genitive and accusative in ـِين.

In the numbers composed of tens and of units, from twenty to ninety-nine, the conjunction و is inserted between the two numbers; the smallest number is put first, and both are declined, as أَحَدٌ و عِشْرُونَ; genitive أَحَدٌ و عِشْرِينَ; accusative أَحَدًا و عِشْرِينَ.

The numbers of the hundreds are for both genders:

سِتّ مِائَةٍ	600	مِائَةٌ	100
سَبع مِائَةٍ	700	مَائِتَانِ	200
ثَمانِ مِائَةٍ	800	ثَلاث مِائَةٍ	300
or			
ثَمانِى مِائَةٍ		أربع مِائَةٍ	400
تِسْع مِائَةٍ	900	خَمس مِائَةٍ	500

The numbers of thousands are

ثَلاثَة آلافٍ	3000	أَلفٌ	1000
أربعة آلافٍ	4000	أَلفَانِ	2000

and so on, up to ten thousand.

إِثْنَا عَشَر أَلفًا	12,000	أَحَد عَشَر أَلفًا	11,000

and so on, up to ninety-nine thousand.

ثَلثُمَائَة أَلفٍ	300,000	مِائَة أَلفٍ	100,000
&c.		مَائِتَا أَلفٍ	200,000

In numbers where units and tens are used, the units are always put first; but if hundreds and thousands are employed, the thousands may be placed first, then the hundreds, and then the units and tens; or first the units, then the tens, and then the hundreds and thousands.

The Ordinal Number.

Fem.	Mas.		Fem.	Mas.	
سَادِسَةٌ	سَادِسٌ	6th	أُولَى	أَوَّلُ	1st
سَابِعَةٌ	سَابِعٌ	7th	ثَانِيَةٌ	ثَانٍ	2nd
ثَامِنَةٌ	ثَامِنٌ	8th	ثَالِثَةٌ	ثَالِثٌ	3rd
تَاسِعَةٌ	تَاسِعٌ	9th	رَابِعَةٌ	رَابِعٌ	4th
عَاشِرَةٌ	عَاشِرٌ	10th	خَامِسَةٌ	خَامِسٌ	5th

The twentieth, and all above, are expressed by the cardinal numbers; the intermediate ones are formed nearly in the same manner as the cardinals; as

Fem.	Mas.	
حَادِيَةَ عَشْرَةَ	حَادِىَ عَشَرَ	11th
ثَانِيَةَ عَشْرَةَ	ثَانِىَ عَشَرَ	12th
ثَالِثَةَ عَشْرَةَ	ثَالِثَ عَشَرَ	13th
حَادِيَةً وَ عِشْرُونَ	حَادِى وَ عِشْرُونَ	21st
or	or	
وَاحِدَةً وَ عِشْرُونَ	وَاحِدٌ وَ عِشْرُونَ	

And thus with the others; but when they take the article, the first number is declined, and the second not; thus in the nominative اَلثَّالِثُ عَشَرَ, genitive اَلثَّالِثَ عَشَرَ; and thus with the others, as well in the masculine as feminine.

The cardinal numbers are often used in the place of the ordinals, and it is common to say indifferently أَرْبَعًا or اَلرَّابِعَة the fourth hour, day, week, &c.; وَقْت an hour, &c. being understood, according to the sense.

The Arabians denote fractional numbers from one third to one tenth, by particular numeratives; they are nouns of the first class, Triptots; as ثَلِيث , ثُلْث , ثُلُث one third; سُدْس and سُدُس one sixth; ثُمْن and ثُمُن an eighth. After one tenth, periphrasis is employed, as ثَلَاثَة أَجْزَاء مِنْ عِشْرِينَ جُزْءًا three parts of twenty parts, that is, three twentieths.

Distributive numbers, or those expressing the parts of a whole, divided into equal portions, are denoted in Arabic by repeating the cardinal number twice successively, as وَاحِدٌ وَاحِدٌ one by one; اِثْنَانِ اِثْنَانِ two by two; in the feminine وَاحِدَةٌ وَاحِدَةٌ , اِثْنَتَانِ اِثْنَتَانِ , or by using, from one to ten, particular numeratives of the forms فَعَال , or مَفْعَل , and which are employed either alone or double, as أَحَادَ أَحَادَ , or وُحَادَ وُحَادَ , مُوَحَّدَ مُوَحَّدَ one by one; or ثُنَاءَ ثُنَاءَ , or مَثْنَى مَثْنَى or مُوَحَّدَ مُوَحَّدَ two by two; رُبَاعَ رُبَاعَ or مَرْبَعَ مَرْبَعَ four by four; these numeratives are Diptots.

Numeratives denoting a periodical return, are of the form فَعَل . They are put in the accusative with or without an article, as اَلثَّلْث or ثَلْثًا every three days, months, &c.

From the cardinal numbers are formed relative adjectives
from one to ten; these present no difficulty. It must be
remarked, however, that from إِثْنَانِ *two*, a dual of which the
singular, if it could have one, would be إِثْنٌ for ثَنْوٌ; the relative adjective is formed by recurring to the form of the singular إِثْنِىّ and ثَنَوِىّ, like أَسَمِىّ.

From eleven to nineteen, the numeratives composed of two
indeclinable words, form their relative adjectives from the first
word only, wholly suppressing the second; whence it follows,
that these adjectives exactly resemble those derived from numeratives from one to nine; thus ثَنَوِىّ is the relative adjective
of إِثْنَانِ *two*, and of إِثْنَى عَشَرَ *twelve*, خَمْسِىّ is that of خَمْسَةٌ
five, and of خَمْسَةَ عَشَرَ *fifteen*.

From مِائَة *one hundred*, is formed the relative adjective
مِدْوِىّ or مِئِىّ; and from أَلْفٌ *a thousand*, أَلْفِىّ. Another sort
of relative adjectives, derived from numeratives from one to
ten, answers nearly to our addition of the monosyllable *fold*;
these are of the form فَعَالِى, thus رُبَاعِى *four fold*; خَمَاسِى
five fold, &c.

OF THE PRONOUN.

THE personal, demonstrative, and relative pronoun, have the same variation of gender and number, as nouns, but have no difference of case; the duals of the demonstratives and relatives excepted, which follow the modes of other duals.

The personal pronouns are as follows:

Plural.			Dual.		Singular.		
They	*You*	*We*	*These*	*You*	*He*	*Thou*	*I*
هُمْ	اَنْتُمْ		two	two	هُوَ	اَنْتَ		Mas.
		نَحْنُ	هُمَا	اَنْتُمَا			اَنَا	Com.
					She			
هُنَّ	اَنْتُنَّ				هِىَ	اَنْتِ		Fem.

The third persons of this pronoun are frequently used in place of the substantive verb كَانَ in every tense.

The demonstrative pronoun, implying an object near at hand, is expressed by ذَا *this* (hic.) and is declined as follows:

Plural.		Dual.		Singular.			
اُولَاءِ or اُولَا		نَذَيْنِ	نَذَانِ			ذَا	Mas.
Fem. The same.		تَيْنِ	تَانِ	نِى نِهِى نِه	تَا تِه تِهِى تِى		Fem.

(Oblique cases.)

The remote demonstrative, *that* (ille) is formed from the preceding by adding كَ.

Plural.	Dual.	Singular.
أُولَاكَ أُولَئِكَ	ذَانِكَ ذَيْنِكَ	ذَاكَ Mas.
Fem. The same.	تَانِكَ تَيْنِكَ	تَاكَ Fem.

(Dual column labelled *Oblique cases.*)

ل is often inserted before كَ, as ذَالِكَ, ذَلِكَ, ذَالِكُمْ, &c. هَا is frequently prefixed to ذَا and ذَاكَ, تِلْكَ, or تَاكَ the ا being generally dropt, and represented in pointed books by ◌, or a perpendicular *Fathah*, which is also the case where ذَا precedes any word beginning with ل or ا quiescent, in the following manner:

Plural.	Dual.	Singular.
هُولَاءِ	هٰذَانِ هٰذَيْنِ	هٰذَا Masc.
Fem. The same.	هٰتَانِ هٰتَيْنِ	هٰذِهِ Fem.

(Dual column labelled *Oblique cases.*)

The relative أَلَّذِى *who*, *which*, *that*, is compounded of ل and لَذِى; one ل being omitted in the singular, and in the masculine plural. It is declined as follows:

Plural.	Dual.	Singular.
ٱللَّائِي ٱللَّاؤُى ٱلَّذِينَ	ٱلَّذِينَ ٱللَّذَانِ	ٱلَّذِى Mas.
ٱللَّاءُ ٱللَّوَاتِى ٱللَّاتِى	ٱللَّتَيْنِ ٱللَّتَانِ	ٱللَّتِى Fem.

(columns labelled *Oblique cases.*)

This relative does not admit of any of the servile letters being prefixed, excepting ف , كَ , لِ , و ; the oblique cases are seldom used, and it is construed with the affixed pronouns annexed to the subsequent word, as أَلَّذِى بِهِ *in which*, for

اَلَّذِى رَأَيْتُهُ . مِنَ اَلَّذِى مِنْهُ اَلَّذِى *from which,* for بِالَّذِى

whom I saw, for اَلَّذِى رَأَيْتُ . مَنْ *he who, those who, whoever,*

and مَا *that which, those which, whatever,* are also relatives including the antecedent. The first is only applied to rational
beings, the second to irrational beings, animate or inanimate,
as in the proverb مَنِ اسْتَرْعَى اَلذِّئْبَ اَلْغَنَمَ فَقَدْ ظَلَمَ *he who*
commits the sheep to the care of the wolf does wrong.

The word أَىٌّ for the masculine, and أَيَّةٌ for the feminine,
who, which, what, of what kind, is generally used interrogatively, governing the substantive in the genitive, as أَىُّ كِتَابٍ

what book? It is often joined with مَنْ and مَا, as أَيْمَنْ *who-*
soever; أَيْمَا *whatever, whatsoever,* and sometimes plurally أَيُّهُمْ
mas., أَيُّهُنَّ fem. *which of them?* dual أَيُّهُمَا . ذُو is sometimes
employed in the same sense as اَلَّذِى; this word is indeclinable,
and used for both genders and all numbers; ذَاتُ is however
sometimes used for the feminine in the singular, and ذَوَاتُ
in the plural without any distinction of cases.

This is a peculiarity of the dialect of the tribe of Tai, as

فَإِنَّ اَلْمَاءَ مَاءُ أَبِى وَجَدِّى . وَبِئْرِى ذُو حَفَرْتُ وَذُو طَوَيْتُ .

Verily, the water is the water of my father, and of my
grandfather; and it is my well, which I dug, and which I
walled round.

The article أَلْ is also regarded as a relative by many of the Arabian grammarians, and is often indeed employed as one; this use of the article is particularly observable when it is placed before a verb, a preposition, or a nominal proposition, that is to say, commencing by a noun acting as the subject.

مَا أَنْتَ بِالْحَكَمِ آلْ تَرْضَى حُكُومَتَهُ *thou art not a judge* whose *decision ought to be accepted.*

مَنْ لَا يَزَالَ شَاكِرًا عَلَى الْمَعَهُ *the man who does not cease to testify his gratitude* to those who are with him. The relative pronoun أَلَّذِى is never interrogative.

أَىْ fem. أَيَّةٌ; being employed alone and interrogatively, receives all the numbers and cases; dual أَيَّانِ, fem. أَيَّتَانِ, plu. أَيُّونَ, fem. أَيَّاتٌ. The singular, as well as the plural, are declined as Triptots.

مَنْ employed interrogatively, also receives the genders, numbers, and cases; but nothing must then be added after this word.

Masculine.	Singular.	Dual.	Plural.
Nom.	مَنُو	مَنَان	مَنُون
Gen.	مَنِى		
Accus.	مَنَا	مَنِين	مَنِين

Fem.	مَنْتَ ,مَنْتِ ,مَنْهُ	Nom.	مَنْتَان	مَنَاتٌ
	for all cases.	Gen. & Acc. مَنْتِين		for all cases.

The use of these words thus declined, is, when any one has said, for example, رَأَيْتُ رَجُلًا " *I have seen a man*," he who is addressed replies أَيًّا or مَنَا *who or what is that man?* or when it is said مَرَرْتُ بِامْرَأَةٍ *I passed by a woman*, he is asked أَيَه or مَنْهُ *who is that woman?*

From the relative مَنْ is formed مَنِّى, answering precisely to the Latin cujus, cuja, cujum.

The following, which are called the affixed pronouns, are always annexed to a verb, a noun, or a preposition. When affixed to verbs or prepositions, they have a personal, and sometimes a relative sense; when joined to nouns, they are possessive, or relative; when added to verbs they are generally in the accusative, though often in the dative, particularly when another accusative comes immediately after, they are as follow:

Plural.		Dual.		Singular.		
هُمْ	كُمْ		كَ ﻫ		كَ	Mas.
		كَمَا نَا هُمَا		ى نِى		Com.
هُنَّ	كُنَّ		هَا ﻛ		كِ	Fem.

The words which take affixed pronouns undergo changes which may be reduced to the following rules.

1st. The nunnation of Triptot nouns disappears, and the vowel alone remains, as كِتَابٌ *a book*; كِتَابُهُ *his book*.

2nd. The affixed pronoun of the first person displaces the vowel itself, as كِتَابِى *my book*; there is then no difference in the three cases.

3rd. Nouns ending in ة‍, change it into ت‍, as نِعْمَة a benefit; نِعْمَتُهُ his benefit.

4th. The final نِ of the duals, and the final نَ of masculine plurals ending in ونَ disappear, as nom. كِتَابَانِ, gen. كِتَابَيْنِ two books, with the affixed pronouns كِتَابَاكُمْ and كِتَابَيْكُمْ your two books; nom. بَنُونَ, and gen. and accus. بَنِينَ sons; with the affixed pros. بَنُوكَ and بَنِيكَ thy sons.

5th. Nouns ending in Hamzah, change it into و if its vowel be Dammah, and into ى if it be Kasrah, as نِسَآءٌ women; نِسَاوُهُ his women; لِنِسَائِهِ to his women.

6th. In the third person mas. plu. of verbs, the quiescent Alif after و disappears, as نَصَرُوا they assisted; نَصَرُونِى they assisted me; رَمَوْا they threw; رَمَوْهُمْ they threw against them.

7th. After the verbal termination تُمْ, they add a Dammah over the مْ, and a و quiescent, as رَأَيْتُمْ you saw; رَأَيْتُمُوهُمْ you saw them.

8th. In those persons of the indefinite, which end in ونَ, as يَكْتُبُونَ, the final نَ is sometimes dropt before the affixed pronouns نِى and نَا, as تَأْمُرُونِى for تَأْمُرُونَنِى you order me.

9th. The ى quiescent after Fathah, may in nouns as well as verbs, be preserved or changed into Alif, as رَمَى he threw;

رمَاهُ or رميَهُ *he threw against him;* فَتًى *a boy;* فَتَاهُ *and*
فَتيَهُ *his boy.*

10th. In particles terminated by ى quiescent after *Fathah*,
the ى takes *Jazmah*, on account of the affixed pronouns, as
عَلَى *upon;* عَلَينَا *upon us;* إلَى *towards;* إليكَ *towards thee.*

The affixed pronoun of the first person ـى in place of *Kasrah*
preceding it, takes *Fathah* above it, when annexed to any word
ending in ا, و, ى, without vowels; if the letter preceding is
ى quiescent, or jazmated, it is joined by *Tashdíd* with that
of the affixed pronoun; if it is و quiescent after *Dammah*, the
و changes into ى, and also joins the affixed pronoun by *Tashdíd*,
the *Dammah* being changed into *Kasrah*, as خَطَايَا *sins;* خَطَايَاىَ
my sins; غَلَمَانَ *two slaves;* غَلَمَاىَ *my two slaves;* غَلَمَين *of*
two slaves; غَلَمَىَّ *of my two slaves;* عَلَىَّ *on me;* فِىَّ *in me;*
عَصًا *a staff;* عَصَاىَ *my staff;* قَاضٍ *Kadhi;* قَاضِىَّ *my Kadhi;*
مَسْلِمِين *of Muslims;* مَسْلِمِىَّ *of my Muslims;* مَسْلِمُونَ *in the nom.*
مَسْلِمِىَّ. makes in the same manner with the affixed pronoun
The ى affixed, pronoun of the first person, is sometimes suppressed; as رَبِّ for رَبِّى *my master;* إتَّقُونِ for إتَّقُونِى *fear me;*
this often happens when the noun is employed in a vocative
sense; and almost always, when the word to which the affixed
pronoun is joined ends in *Hamzah*, which by the influence of
the affixed pronoun becomes ى; as أَحْبَاىَ *my friends;* أبَاىَ
my fathers; for أحْبَائِى, and أبَائِى from أحْبَاءَ and ١٠.أبَاءَ

The affixed pronouns of the third person هُمَا ,هُم ,هُنَّ, ة,
change their *Dammah* into *Kasrah* when they are immediately preceded by *Kasrah*, or by ى quiescent after *Kasrah*, or
by ى jazmated, after *Fathah*, as حِمَارَةِ , حِمَارِهِمَا , فِيهِ , يُرمِيهِ,
عَلَيْهِ , عَلَيْهِمْ, &c.

نِي in place of ى, is used when joined to verbs, and also
to particles ending in ن ; such as وَمِن ,عَن ,إِنَّ ,أَنَّ, and also
to كَأَنَّ and لَكِنَّ. The affixed pronoun here always represents
an accusative case. The words إِنَّ and أَنَّ when taking the
affixed pronoun of the first person singular, are written إِنِّى
and أَنِّى, or إِنَّنِى and أَنَّنِى. It is the same with the first
person plural إِنَّا and أَنَّا, or إِنَّنَا and أَنَّنَا. It is the same
with كَأَنَّ . لَكِنَّ makes لَكِنِّى or لَكِنَّا.

Some other words, regarded as adverbs, also take the affixed
pronoun; such are عَلَّ and لَعَلَّ *may be*; لَيْتَ *would to God
that!*

Two affixes may be annexed to one word, when that of the
first person is always placed before the second, and the second
before the third; as أَعْطَانِيهِ *he gave it to me*; يَكْفِيكَهُمْ *it will
suffice you against them*. The same thing takes place with nouns
of action, as حَبِّيهِ *my love for him*.

These examples however are not common, and when a verb
governs two pronouns, the separate pronoun of which we are
about to speak is usually employed.

It often occurs, that the pronoun being required in the accusative, the affixes should be employed; but in such cases a separate pronoun is used, either on account of the meeting of several pronouns in the accusative, or on account of the ellipsis of the word which should serve as antecedent, and to which in consequence the affix ought to be annexed. In this case a separate pronoun is made of the word إِيَّا, which has no sense in itself, and of the affixed pronoun; as إِيَّاىَ *me*; إِيَّانَا *us*; إِيَّاكَ *thee*, (mas.); إِيَّاكِ *thee*, (fem.); إِيَّاكُمَا *you two*; إِيَّاكُمْ *you*, (mas.); إِيَّاكُنَّ *you*, (fem.); إِيَّاهُ *him*; إِيَّاهَا *her*; إِيَّاهُمَا *them* (*two*); إِيَّاهُمْ *them*, (mas.); إِيَّاهُنَّ *them*, (fem.).

This form of pronoun is also used when the pronoun personal is put before the verb which governs it, with the view of giving a greater emphasis; as إِيَّاكَ نَعْبُدُ وَ إِيَّاكَ نَسْتَعِينُ as *thee we adore, and thee we call to our help.*

Reflective pronouns, such as *myself, thyself*, &c. are expressed by the words نَفْس or ذَاتْ, as نَفْسِى *my soul*; نَفْسَكَ *thy soul*; انفسكم *your souls*; or ذَاتِى *my being*. These are sometimes joined, as بِذَاتِ نَفْسِه i. e. *by himself.*

OF PARTICLES.

PARTICLES are divided into inseparable, and separate; the first being always prefixed, and the second class, though not joined, always preceding the word which they govern. They occur in every line, and are of much consequence in acquiring a proper knowledge of the language, the inseparable adverbs, prepositions, and conjunctions especially; these, together with the servile letters, perplexing the learner in various ways, but more particularly by exhausting his patience in turning over, to no purpose, the leaves of a Dictionary for vocables, which he can never find till he has learned to analyse and separate those letters or particles from the words to which they are prefixed. It will be requisite, therefore, to pay very great attention to the observations upon them, in order that they may make a due impression on the memory; they consist of the following letters: أَ, this is an interrogative particle (an? num?) بِ *in*; تَ *by*; this is used in oaths. سَ, an adverb, indicating the future: فَ *and*; كَ *like*; لِ *for, in order to*; لَ *certainly*; and to these may be joined ع and م, which however are very seldom used; the first nine are contained in the technical words أَبْتَسَ ,فَكَلَوْ.

More than one of these particles may be prefixed to a word; thus the interrogative أ may be followed by فَ or وَ. These conjunctive particles فَ and وَ may likewise be followed by سَ,

indicating the future, or by the prepositions كَ, لِ, تَ, بِ,
ع, and مِ.

أ. This, as has been observed, is an interrogative particle,
as أَمَاتَ *has he died?* It is often joined to إِنَّ, and is then
written أَإِنَّ, as أَإِنَّكَ لَأَنْتَ يُوسُفُ *art thou indeed Joseph?*

When a second proposition follows, preceded by the separate
interrogative particle أَمْ, they both become disjunctives, signifying *whether—or,* thus إِنَّ ٱلَّذِينَ كَفَرُوا سَوَاءٌ عَلَيْهِمْ أَأَنْذَرْتَهُمْ
أَمْ لَمْ تُنْذِرْهُمْ *as to those who have disbelieved, it is the same with
them, whether you admonish them, or do not admonish them.*

2. It is a particle of invocation, as أَيُوسُفُ *O Joseph!* it
is then sometimes written thus آ.

ب.

This always bears *Kasrah,* and signifies

1. *In;* as بِٱلْمَسْجِدِ *in the mosque.*

2. *With;* especially when prefixed to a noun of instrument, as كَتَبْتُ بِقَلَمٍ *I wrote with a pen;* or when subjoined
to verbs of *coming* and *going,* which then assume the signification of *bringing* and *giving,* or *taking away,* as أَتَى بِٱلْكِتَابِ
he came with the book, i.e. *he brought the book;* ذَهَبَ بِٱلنُّورِ
he went away with the light, i.e. *he took away the light.*

3. *Because, for, on account of;* as النَّفْسُ بِالنَّفْسِ و الْعَينُ *life for life, and eye for an eye;* أللّٰهُ قَتلَكَ بِرجُوعِكَ عَن بِالْعَينِ *may God destroy thee on account of thy relapse from Islam!*

4. It is a particle of swearing, as بِاللّٰهِ *by God!*

5. It is often put before the predicate of a negative, and becomes a species of expletive, as مَا اللّٰهُ بِغَافِلٍ *God does not neglect;* literally, *God is not in neglecting;* لَسْتُ بِعَالِمٍ *I do not know.*

6. After إِذَا *behold,* بـ is prefixed to the name indicating the object of attention, as إِذَا بِرَجُلٍ *behold a man!*

7. It subserves to the construction of many verbs, as مَرَرْتُ بِرَجُلٍ نَائِمٍ *I passed near a man who was sleeping;* حَسَّ بِالشَّىءِ *he perceived the thing.*

ت .

This is a particle of swearing, as تَاللّٰهِ *by God!* it is employed in a few other forms of oath, as تَرَبِّى *by my Lord!* but is never applied but to God only.

س .

This is prefixed to the future tense, fixing it absolutely to a future signification.

ف .

This is a conjunction of very general use, signifying *and, then, therefore, so that,* &c.: and implies something that follows immediately; differing in that respect from ثُمّ *then, afterwards*, as well as from و *and;* both which denote a more remote consequence; as جَاءَنِي زَيد فَعمرو *came to me Zaid, and then Amru,* (he following Zaid immediately). It also differs from و, inasmuch as in the propositions connected by it, something is inferred from the preceding to the consequent; as غزَالٌ مَرَّةً عطَش فَأَتَى إِلَى عَين مَاءٌ *once a stag was thirsty, and came to a fountain of water.*

2. This conjunction is often used to indicate that the subject of the succeeding proposition differs from that of the preceding one. This should be particularly observed, as it may prevent the mistakes which might otherwise arise from the want of precision in expressing the subject which is sometimes found in Arabian authors. It is frequently prefixed to the imperative, and then in general marks the passage with peculiar emphasis. It frequently however appears as a mere copulative, like و.

ك.

This is an adverb of similitude, signifying *like,* or, *as,* and governs the genitive; as كَرَجُل *like a man.* It is prefixed also to the personal pronoun, as كَأَنَا *like me;* كَأَنتَ *like thee;* كَهُو *like him.* It is very rarely found with the affixed pronouns, as كِي *like me;* كَكَ *like thee;* كَّ *like him.* The word كَذَا composed of ك and of the demonstrative ذَا, is considered as a noun, and if governed by a preceding word, the antecedent loses the nunnation. فِى شَهْرِ كَذَا مِنْ سَنَةِ كَذَا *in such a month of such a year*. Of this particle, and the relative pronoun مَا, is formed the word كَمَا, signifying, *in the same manner as*.

ل.

This is a preposition employed in various senses, as

1. *To*, the sign of the dative case, as لِرَبٍّ *to the master;* اَلْحَمْدُ لِلّٰهِ *praise be to God*. With pronouns it bears *Fathah*, as لَكَ *to thee;* لَنَا *to us*, &c., except the affixed pronoun of the first person singular, as لِى *to me*.

2. *For, because, on account of;* تَأَجَّجَ كَرِبِى لِمُصَابِهِ بِنَاظِرَيْهِ *my grief was increased on account of what had happened to his two eyes*.

3. It expresses swearing with a mixture of surprise, as لِلّٰهِ *by God!*

4. When prefixed to a verb it sometimes means *in order to;* as اِلْتَمَسَ شَيْئًا لِيَأْكُلَهُ *he sought something that he might eat*.

5. It is elegantly prefixed, by way of pleonasm, to that part of the sentence which is called the predicate, or what is affirmed of any person or thing; particularly when إِنَّ is put before the subject, or the person or thing, of which somewhat is affirmed; as إِنَّ إِسْكَنْدَرَ لَقَدِيرٌ *for Alexander is powerful*.

6. With *Kasrah* before the future it forms the imperative passive, and occasions an apocope, as وَلْيَكْتُبْ بَيْنَكُمْ كَاتِبٌ

let a scribe write an agreement between you. It will be observed that when ﻑ or ﻭ are prefixed, it loses its *Kasrah.* With *Fathah* it is also used in calling for help, as يا لَزَيدٍ *help, O Zaid !*

It must be observed that when لَ comes before the article, the latter loses its *Alif;* وَ اَنّهُ لَلْحَقُّ مِنْ رَبِّكَ *verily that is the truth coming from thy Lord.* Here لَلْحَقُّ is for لَالْحَقُّ.

7. In conditional propositions it answers to the antecedent لَوْ *if;* or لَوْلَا *if not;* as لَوْ جِئتَنِى لَاكرمتكَ *if you come to me, I will certainly honour you.*

ﻭ.

This is, 1. The conjunction *and, also.*

2. It denotes swearing, as وَاللهِ *by God !*

3. It signifies *with,* indicating a simultaneous action, and then governs the accusative, as اَستوى الماءُ و الْحاشِية *the water is even with the bank;* جاءَ الاميرُ والجيشَ *the Amír came with the army.*

4. This conjunction is sometimes equivalent to اِذَا *when* or *whilst;* and then affects the indefinite tense with antithesis, as اَخافُ اَنْ تقتلنى وَ اَنَا اَشربُ *I fear that thou wilt kill me whilst I am drinking.*

عَ and مَ.

These are prefixed for عَنْ and مِنْ, the letter نْ being dropped; as عَمَّا for عَنْ مَا, and مِمَّا for مِنْ مَا.

Of Separate Particles.

These are divided into Prepositions, Adverbs, Conjunctions, and Interjections; it is rather the office of the dictionary than the grammar, to point these out; but as they very often occur, the learner will find great advantage in being well acquainted with them. I therefore here make a few remarks upon some of the principal.

The number of separate prepositions is not great, they are the following:

إِلَى. This indicates the term of an action, *to, until;* as جَاءَ إِلَى ٱلْمَدِينَةِ *he came to the city;* إِلَى حِينٍ *until the time.*

حَتَّى. This is used in four ways:

1. As a preposition, shewing the term or extremity, and is equivalent to *unto,* as حَتَّى مَطْلِعِ ٱلْفَجْرِ *unto the place of sun-rising.* When thus used it governs a noun in the genitive, or a conjunctive proposition beginning with أَنْ.

2. It is applied to time, then meaning *until,* as سَارُوا حَتَّى طَلَعَتِ ٱلشَّمْسُ *they travelled until the sun rose.*

3. It is equivalent to our word *even*, as أَكَلْتُ ٱلسَّمَكَةَ حَتَّى رَأْسِهَا *I have eaten the fish, even its head.* Had the particle إِلَى been used here instead of حَتَّى it would have meant, I have eaten the fish unto, or as far as its head.

4. When preceding the indefinite tense used as a future, it affects it with antithesis, and answers to the Latin *donec* followed by the subjunctive mood. إِمْشِ حَتَّى تُدْرِكَهُمْ *march until you overtake them.*

عَدَا, خَلَا ,حَاشَا, and عَدَا. These are exceptive particles, originally verbs, signifying *to be separated from, to be beyond*; thus قُتِلُوا جَمِيعُهُمْ عَدَا زَيْدٍ literally means the whole of them beyond, or separated from Zaid, have been slain.

عَلَى. *On, above,* is a preposition denoting superiority of place; it may sometimes be rendered by *against*, as خَرَجَ عَلَيْهِ *he went forth against him.*

2. *According to*; as عَلَى عَادَةٍ *according to custom.*

3. Office, or duty, or debt, as عَلَى أَلْفَ دِينَارٍ literally, *upon me a thousand dínárs,* i. e. I owe a thousand dinárs. عَلَيْكَ أَنْ تَفْعَلَ هَذَا *you ought to do that.*

4. عَلَيْكَ. Is used to signify خُذْ *take*, as عَلَيْكَ زَيْدًا *take Zaid.* An ellipsis for عَلَيْكَ أَنْ تَأْخُذَ زَيْدًا *it is your place to take Zaid.*

عَنْ. This usually signifies *separation from*, or the capability of doing without a thing. إِنَّ ٱللَّهَ غَنِيٌّ عَنِ ٱلْعَالَمِينَ *verily God is rich enough without men*. From this is derived another signification, of *leaving behind*, as مَاتَ عَنْ وَلَدٍ *he died leaving a son*.

فِى. This denotes *in*, whether of time or place, and is used to express multiplication or proportion, as ثَلَاثَةٌ فِى خَمْسَةٍ *three multiplied by five*; طُولُهُ خَمْسُونَ ذِرَاعًا فِى ٱثْنَى عَشَرَ ذِرَاعًا عَرْضًا *its length is fifty cubits by twelve cubits broad*. It sometimes answers to the preposition *with*, as *he departed with fifty thousand men*. تَوَجَّهَ فِى خَمْسِينَ أَلْفًا.

لَدَى, لَدَ, لَدُنْ *to, with, nigh*, &c.

مُنْذُ, or مِنْذُ, مُذْ, مِذْ. These denote the commencement of a certain period of time, and are equivalent to *since*; as مَا رَأَيْتُهُ مُنْذُ يَوْمِ ٱلْجُمْعَةِ *I have not seen him since Friday*. When the period is not yet finished, مُذْ or مُنْذُ governs the genitive, as مَا كَلَّمْتُهُ مُذْ شَهْرِنَا هَذَا *I have not spoken to him during this month*.

مِنْ. *From, of, for, than*, as عِنْدَ خُرُوجِ ٱلْأَمِيرِ مِنَ ٱلدَّارِ *when the Amír departed from the palace*.

2. It denotes composition, جَنَّةٌ مِنْ نَخِيلٍ وَأَعْنَابٍ *a garden of palm-trees and vines*.

3. In negative propositions, or interrogative propositions implying negation, it often happens that the subject, or object of the verb, instead of appearing in its proper case, is expressed by the preposition مِنْ governing the genitive; as مَا جَاءَنِى مِنْ رَجُلٍ *no man came to me*; مَا لَكُمْ مِنْ إِلهٍ غَيْرُهُ *you have no God but him.*

Adverbs.

The Adverbs of the Arabic language are few in number, but this deficiency is amply supplied by the means of putting nouns in the accusative case, or adverbially; and as this is applied to all nouns of action, and active participles, there is no noun, adjective, or verb, which cannot form an adverb; thus مَعًا *toge-ther with*; دَاخِلًا *within*; خَارِجًا *without*; كَثِيرًا *much*; قَلِيلًا *little*; مَعًا *toge-ther with*; غَدًا *to-morrow*; يَوْمًا *one day*; لَيْلًا *by night*; نَهَارًا *by day*; إِتِّفَاقًا *by chance*; يَمِينًا *on the right hand*; شِمَالًا *on the left hand*; سَرِيعًا *quickly*; رَغْبَةً *eagerly*; طَوْعًا *willingly*; كَرْهًا *vio-lently*; أَبَدًا *eternally*, &c. These are all substantives, adjec-tives, or nouns of action, which being put in the accusative case become adverbs.

Nouns thus put in the accusative case, are often found in elliptical expressions, where they depend upon a verb under-stood; as سَمْعًا وَ طَاعَةً meaning *I am ready to obey you*; this is literally, *by hearing and obeying.* سَقْيًا *may God water this land*, literally *by watering.* سُبْحَانَهُ *by his praise*, i. e. *may he*

be praised. These are elliptical expressions for سمعت سمعًا و
أطعت اطاعة *I heard by hearing and obeyed with obedience;*
سقاك ٱلله سقيا *may God water thee by watering!*
I praise him with his due praise. These modes of speaking are
very common in Arabic; as تعسًا لك *may you perish!* مرحبًا
و سهلًا *you are welcome,* literally, *at your ease and convenience;*
حبًا و كرامةٌ *all is at your service,* literally, *a pitcher and a
pot-lid,* or, on the contrary, لا و لا كرامة *which is a double ellipsis*
for لا حبًا و لا كرامة *neither pitcher nor pot-lid,* i. e. *expect nothing
from me.*

A List of the most common Adverbs and Adverbial Names.

أجل *yes.*

إنّما ,إذا ,إذاما and إذاما *when.* إذا ,إذاما are conjunctive
adverbs usually employed with a future sense. إن is limited to
the present, and signifies also, *seeing that.*

إن and إذا signify also, *then, behold.*

إنْ ذاك or إنّاك *then, at that time.*

إذا or إنّن *well done!*

ألا or ألّا *unless, otherwise, verily.*

أَمَّ *whether?* this often acts as a conjunction expressing doubt, and then signifies, *or else.*

أَمَا *is it not?*

أَمْسِ *yesterday.*

إِنِ . This when followed by إِلَّا signifies, *not*; as إِنِ ٱلْحُكْمُ إِلَّا لِلَّهِ *there is no judgment but with God.* Sometimes when the word إِلَّا does not follow, this adverb still expresses negation; as وَ إِنْ أَدْرِى لَعَلَّهُ فِتْنَةٌ لَكُمْ *and I know not whether this may be a trial to you.*

إِنَّ *yes, verily.*

إِنَّمَا *because, since, only*; as إِنَّمَا أَجْرِى عَلَى ٱللَّهِ *my reward is only with God.*

أَنَّى *how? wherefore?*

آهًا *alas!*

إِى *yes*; equivalent also to نَعَمْ; it is only used when a form of oath follows; as إِى وَ رَبِّى *yes, by God.*

أَىْ *that is*—as also the exclamation *oh!*

أَيَّانَ and إِيَّانِ *when, whensoever.*

أَيْنَمَا *wheresoever*; إِلَى أَيْنَ *whither*; مِنْ أَيْنَ *whence*; أَيْنَ *where*; أَيْنَ *where*; soever.

إِيهِ, إِيهَ, إِيهِ bravo! well done!

إِيهَاً stop! that is enough!

بَعْدُ after, behind; مِنْ بَعْدُ hereafter. When this word is used as a preposition it ceases to be indeclinable, and appears either in the accusative بَعْدَ, or in the genitive, if preceded by the preposition مِنْ, as مِنْ بَعْدِ. The formula أَمَّا بَعْدُ, is commonly employed in letters, or the prefaces of books, in order to announce the commencement of the real subject, after the praises of God, or the usual expressions of politeness.

بُعَيْدَ the diminutive of the preceding signifies, a little after.

بَلَى yes, certainly.

بَيْنَ between; this is the noun بَيْن—difference, separation; in the accusative.

بَيْنَا whilst; and sometimes like the preceding, between.

بَيْنَما whilst; in the mean time.

تَحْتَ below; to this word what has been said of بَعْدُ, applies also.

تُحَيْتَ a little lower.

ثُمَّ and ثَمَّتْ then, afterwards.

ثَمَّ here.

جَيْرِ yes, certainly.

حَاشَ . حَاشًا *God forbid!* When this word appears with the nunnation, it becomes an adverb, though before described as a preposition.

حَىّ هَلَا , حَىّ *hallo!*

إِلَى حَيْثُ *whither;* مِنْ حَيْثُ *whence;* حَيْثُ *where;* حَيْثُمَا *wheresoever;* it is also written حَيْثُ .

دُونَ *except, under, besides.*

رُبَّمَا *often, sometimes.* This is compounded of the preposition رُبَّ , always governing an indefinite noun in the genitive case, and also signifying *sometimes*, or *often*; and of the particle مَا .

رَيْثَ *until.*

سَفْ , سَى , سَوَ , سَوْفَ . These indicate the future.

لَا سِيَّمَا *above all, principally.*

عَلْ *above.*

لَعَلّ . عَلَّ *perhaps, by chance.* This adverb receives the affixed pronouns.

عَوْضُ and عَوْضَ . This adverb conveys a negation, is only employed with a verb in the future, and signifies *never*.

غَيْرَ *except.* This is the accusative case of the noun غَيْر *difference;* it is also used adverbially, thus لَا غَيْرَ , signifying *not otherwise;* and is then indeclinable, like تَحْتَ , بَعْدَ , &c.

فَضْلًا and فَضْلًا عَنْ *far from, much less*, &c.

14

فَقْطَ *only, solely.*

فَوْق *above.* It is with this word as with بَعْد.

قَبْل *before.* This word is in the same case as the preceding.

قِبَلاً *along with, in the power of.*

قُبَيْل diminutive of قَبْل, *a little before.*

قَد, لَقَد, فَقَد *certainly, sometimes.*

قَط, قَطّ, قَطُّ, قَطِّ, قَطّ, قَطْ, *never.* This adverb is only used with a verb in the preterite; if a future time is spoken of, عوض or اَبَدًا must be used.

كَأَنَّ *as if.*

كَأَيِّن *how much?*

كَذَا *thus.*

كَلاَّ *assuredly not.*

كُلَّمَا *every time that, as often as.*

كَم *how many? how much?*

كَمَا *as if, according to.*

كَيْفَ *wherefore, in the same manner as, how?*

كَيْفَمَا *any how.*

لا *no, not, not at all, is not;* لاَبُدَّ *necessarily;* لاَجَرَم *undoubtedly.*

لَم *unless, no, not;* applied to the past tense.

لَمَّا *not yet, when.*

and لِمَ *why?* This is compounded of the preposition لِ, and of the indeclinable word مَا.

لَنْ *no, not.*

لَوْمَا or لَوْلَا *unless.*

لَيْتَ *would to God!* This admits the affixed pronouns.

مَا, negative adverb of the present tense, and conjunctive noun, meaning *that which*, and as an interrogative particle *what?* or *how?*

مَتَى *when;* مَتَى مَا *in whatever way.*

مَعًا *with, together with.*

مَهْمَا *as often as.*

نَعَمْ *yes.*

وحد. This word always requires an affixed pronoun, thus.

وَحْدَهُ *he alone;* وَحْدَهَا *she alone.*

وَيْكَ and وَى. Adverbs of admiration or reproach.

هَا *behold!* This with the affixed pronoun of the second person, has the signification of خُذْ *take!* The affixed pronoun changes, however, then into *Hamzah,* as هَاءَ, هَاءِ, هَاؤُمَا, هَاؤُمْ, هَاؤُنَّ; according to the variation of gender, and number, for هَاكَ *take thou,* (mas.); هَاكِ *take thou,* (fem.); هَاكُمَا *take you two,* &c.

هَانَذَا *see here! behold!* هَانَذِهِ *fem.*

هَلْ *whether?* An interrogative adverb.

هَلَا and هَلَّا *whether? is it not? well done!*

هَلُمَّ and هَلُمَّ لَكَ ; لَكُمْ , &c. *come on!*

هَنَا and هَنَا *here.* From this adverb other demonstrative adverbs are formed, in the same manner as demonstrative pronouns; as هَنَاكَ, هَنَاكَ *there*, in speaking of things at a distance; هَاهُنَا *here*, in speaking of things at hand.

هُوذَا *see there! behold!*

يَا أَيَّتَهَا, يَا أَيُّهَا, يَا, مَيْتَ, هَيَا ; these five adverbs are used in invocation and speaking to.

Conjunctions.

It is with conjunctions as with adverbs, they must be learned by the Dictionary, but a few of the most common may be here enumerated.

اَلَّا. This is compounded of the conjunction أَن *that*, and the negative adverb لا *not;* with the prefixed particle لِ; it is written thus, لِئَلَّا *that it may—not.*

إِلَّا *if not.*

أَمَّا *but, however, nevertheless.*

إِمَّا *or, or else;* فَأَمَّا *if, but.*

أَنْ , أَنَّ *that.* أَنَّ is used when this conjunction is immediately followed by a noun; it is often written with the affixed pronoun ه. The purpose of this addition of the pronoun, is to remove the influence of the conjunction, which would, but for such addition, require the accusative case.

إِنَّ , and by contraction إِنْ . This conjunction comes before the subject of a proposition, when that subject is placed before the verb, and adds energy to the expression. It is also written إِنَّه , as is done with أَنَّه , and for the same reason; from the inseparable particle فَ , joined to this conjunction, are formed the words فَإِنَّ and فَإِنَّه , signifying *and indeed.*

إِنْ *if;* from the affirmative adverb لَ *certainly;* and this conjunction if formed; لَئِنْ *certainly if.*

أَوْ *or, or else, until.*

كَى *in order that;* لِكَى is used in the same sense and with the negative adverb لا , it becomes كَيْلا and لِكَيْلا *lest not, so as not.*

لَكِنْ and لَكِنَّ *but.* لَكِنَّ is only used before nouns and pronouns.

Interjections.

وَا *ah! alas!* This exclamation may be followed by the nominative case; or the nunnation being dropped, *Alif* preceded by *Fathah,* or أَه , may be added وَا زَيْدٌ , or وَا زَيْدَا ,

or وَا زَيدَاه, when two nouns in construction follow, the syllable اه is added to the last, as وَا غُلَامَ زَيدَاه *alas the boy of Zaid!*

وَيل *alas! woe!* This is sometimes used disjunctively, as يَا وَيلَنِى *woe to him!* or conjoined, وَيلَكَ *woe to thee!* وَيل لَه woe to him! *woe to me!*

SYNTAX.

The concordance of the substantive with the adjective, of the relative with its antecedent, and the nominative with the verb, has but few peculiarities in the Arabic language. The substantive however precedes the adjective, the verb the nominative, and the nominative the genitive.

Syntax of the Noun.

A proper name being definite by its very nature, takes no article; but the epithet, if it have one, always requires it, as إِبْرَاهِيم ٱلْأَمِين *Abraham the faithful.* This is the case also when a substantive is rendered definite by an affixed pronoun, as أَبِى ٱلْمُكْرَم *my honored father.*

The nominative, in the beginning of a sentence, is often found to be, what may be called, the nominative absolute, as ٱللَّه لَهُ مَا فِى ٱلسَّمٰوَاتِ وَ عَلَى ٱلْأَرْضِ *God, to him is what is in heaven and on earth.*

A noun substantive governs another in the genitive, which, as above observed, is always placed after the nominative; as كِتَابُ سُلَيْمَان *a book of Solomon;* خَاتِم نَهَبٍ *a ring of gold.*

The governing substantive sometimes has the effect of an adjective; as طُول ٱلتَّجَارِب *length of experience,* i. e. *long experience;* this is always the construction of the word كُلّ *the whole;*

which is used for *all* or *every*; as كُلّ شَىْءٍ *every thing*; اَلنَّاسِ *all men*. This, and some other substantives, such as نَفْس *the soul, self*; when they have the possessive pronouns annexed, and follow another substantive, with which they agree, become as it were adjectives, and follow their construction, as حَبِيب نَفْسه *a friend his-self, a real friend*. خُبْز كُلّه *the whole of the bread, all the bread*; gen. خُبْز كُلّه *of all the bread*.

It has been observed that the accusative termination conveys an adverbial meaning, which may often be rendered by the Latin Gerund in *do*, as جَاءَ رَاكِبًا *he came riding* (equitando) اُدْخُلُوا اَلْبَابَ سَجَّدًا *enter the gate adoring* (adorando.)

The sense of the Latin *quoad*, *by reason*, or *in respect of*, is conveyed by the accusative, as طَابَ يُوسُفُ نَفْسًا *Joseph is good*, *in respect of his mind*, or *disposition*, i. e. he is well disposed.

The Arabic noun having no vocative case, the nominative and accusative are both used in its place; if the person or object addressed be present, the noun is in the nominative case, without nunnation, as يَا سَمَاءُ *O heaven!* يَا نَبِيُّون *O Prophets!* but in this case the noun must not be followed by a word which it governs, either immediately, or by a preposition; in these cases it appears in the accusative, as يَا عَبْدَ اَللّٰهِ *O Abd-Allah!* (*O Servant of God*) يَا حَسَنًا وَجْهُهُ *O thou whose face is beautiful*. The accusative is also used when the object addressed is indeterminate, that is to say, without an article, and is not considered to be present, as يَا نَبِيًّا *O Prophet!*

The principal use of the passive voice is to consider an action, only with relation to the patient, the agent being left out of sight; if it is only desired to fix the principal, but not exclusive attention on the object or patient, the name of the subject or agent may be added; and it may be said, *the Vazir was killed by the Sultan*, but this form of construction is very rare in Arabic.

The transitive verb, when entering the passive voice, loses its object; which then becomes its subject. Verbs doubly transitive, however, preserve both their objects, the second remaining in its preceding form, and the first becoming the subject of the proposition, thus in the active voice سَقَى ٱلسُّلْطَانُ وَزِيرَهُ مَآءً مَسْمُومًا *the Sultan gave his Vazir poisoned water to drink.* In the passive voice this becomes سُقِىَ ٱلْوَزِيرُ مَآءً مَسْمُومًا *The Vazir received poisoned water to drink.* In the same way it is said أَعْطَى زَيْدٌ عَمْرًا ثَوْبًا مُفْخَرًا *Zaid gave Amru a splendid Vest.* In the passive voice أَعْطِىَ عَمْرُو ثَوْبًا مُفْخَرًا *Amru has been presented with a splendid vest.*

As in other languages, so in Arabic, two nouns meaning the same thing, or as it is termed in Grammar, put in apposition, must agree in gender, number, and case, nor can the second, when one word governs another, be the same thing as its antecedent. Such grammatical anomalies are however sometimes met with; as يَوْمُ ٱلْخَمِيسِ *the day of tuesday* (the fifth) صَلَاةُ

سُحُف عَمَامَة اَلْأُولَى *the prayer of the first*; that is, the first prayer
a worn-out of a turban; that is, a worn-out turban. Many
nouns indicating time, or portions of time, govern complete propositions; the governing noun then loses its nunnation, هَذَا يَوْم

يَنْفَعُ ٱلصَّادِقِينَ صِدْقُهُمْ *That day the justice of just men will aid*

them; اَلسَّلَامُ عَلَىَّ يَوْمَ وُلِدْتُ *Peace was upon me the day when*

I was born; لَهُ ٱلْمُلْكُ يَوْمَ يُنْفَخُ فِى ٱلصُّورِ *To him will be the*
royalty, on the day when the trumpet is sounded.

The subject and object of a transitive verb represented by
the noun of action, being both expressed, the subject may be
put in construction with the noun of action, that is, may re-
ceive the genitive case; as كَانَ قَتْلُ ٱلْخَلِيفَةِ جَعْفَراً فِى هَذِهِ ٱلسَّنَةِ
In this year it was that the Khalíf slew Jáfar; or the object
may be put in the genitive, and the subject in the nominative,
وَمَنَعَ ٱلنَّاسَ كَافَّةً مِنْ مُخَاطَبَتِهِ أَحَدٌ وَمُكَاتَبَتِهِ بِسَيِّدِنَا وَمَوْلَانَا as
He forbade all men in speaking or writing to call him our Lord
and our Master.

The active participle may, like all verbs, except the substantive or abstract verb, express an attribute of a subject, and
as the subject of a verb is always in the nominative whenever
the active participle has a subject, that subject is placed in the
nominative thus عَمْرٌو ٱلْقَاتِلُ أَبُوهُ مَحْمُوداً *Amru whose father has*
killed Mahmúd; زَيْدٌ نَاكِحٌ ٱبْنُهُ غَدًا زُبَيْدَةَ *The son of Zaid will*
to-morrow marry Zubaidah.

If, however, the active participle expresses a quality inherent

in the subject, and unconnected with any circumstance of time,
it may govern its subject in the genitive. It is not therefore
incorrect to say زيد القائم الاب Zaid, whose father stands firmly.
This construction, where the noun, which is really the subject,
is put in the genitive case, and governed by the participle,
seldom takes place but when the participle is of a neuter verb;
it is sometimes found, however, with participles derived from
transitive verbs, when they are used as mere adjectives, as
الرَّاحِم القلب merciful of heart.

The active participle, accompanied by the article, is equivalent to the relative pronoun and a verb; thus هذا القاتل أبوه
عمرًا is the same as هذا الذى قتل ابوه عمرا This is he whose
father killed Amru.

The subject to which the passive participle is attached,
appears also in the nominative case زيد مقتول حالا أبوه Zaid,
whose father is at this moment killed. It may, however, be put
in the genitive, being then governed by the participle, or in
the accusative case; thus it may be written زيد مقتول الاب,
or المقتول أبا.

If the passive participle belongs to a verb doubly transitive,
it preserves in the accusative the second object governed by
the verb; thus زيد معطى عبده درهمًا The slave of Zaid has
been presented with a piece of silver.

The substantive signifying the object to which the adjective
refers, or by which the quantity or quality of that adjective
is defined, is often joined to it; as when we say a man learned

in (quoad) *music; a young man handsome of* (quoad) *counte-nance; a man whose father is just;* the Arabians express such sentences in three ways.

1. The adjective preserves its nunnation, or article, and the following substantive is in the nominative case, as جَاءَنِى رَجُلٌ حَسَنٌ أَبُوهُ or حَسَنُ ٱلْأَبِ *There came to me a man whose father is handsome;* مَرَرْتُ بِرَجُلٍ قَبِيحٍ وَجْهُهُ or قَبِيحِ ٱلْوَجْهِ *I passed by a man whose face was ugly.*

2. They put the adjective with the following substantive in construction, as جَاءَنِى رَجُلٌ حَسَنُ ٱلْوَجْهِ or حَسَنُ وَجْهِهِ *there came to me a man handsome of countenance;* مَرَرْتُ بِرَجُلٍ حَسَنِ ٱلْوَجْهِ or حَسَنِ وَجْهِهِ *I passed by a man handsome of countenance.*

3. The adjective preserves its nunnation, or its article, the following substantive appearing in the accusative, as جَاءَنِى رَجُلٌ حَسَنٌ وَجْهًا or حَسَنُ ٱلْوَجْهِ *There came to me a man handsome in countenance;* مَرَرْتُ بِرَجُلٍ حَسَنٍ وَجْهًا or حَسَنٍ ٱلْوَجْهِ *I passed by a man handsome in countenance.*

In the three ways here indicated, the adjective which precedes the substantive, shewing the object, may have the article or not; the substantive, itself may also be definite or not. It is made definite, first by the article, second by a substantive governed by itself, and which substantive has the article, third by the affixed pronoun, fourth by a substantive governed by itself, and which substantive has an affixed pronoun. From this results a great number of different forms, some disapproved, and others authorized, but more or less elegant.

The adjective, even when taking the article, may receive the affixed pronouns, thus وَ ٱلرَّاسِ ٱلشَّدِيدِ ٱلْمَنْظَرِ ٱلْقَبِيحِ ٱلصَّغِيرَةِ *he who is ugly of countenance, who has a strong head, and a little one.*

The adjective, in the form of construction just before indicated, must agree with the preceding substantive in regard to the use of the article, as رَجُلٌ حَسَنُ ٱلْوَجْهِ *a man handsome of countenance*; and زَيْدٌ ٱلْحَسَنُ ٱلْوَجْهِ *Zaid handsome of countenance.*

If such an adjective have a substantive following, which it governs in the genitive, it must itself agree with its preceding substantive in gender, number, and case, as مَرَرْتُ بِرَجُلٍ حَسَنِ ٱلْوَجْهِ *I passed by a man handsome of countenance*; رَأَيْتُ ٱمْرَأَةً حَسَنَةَ ٱلْوَجْهِ *I saw a woman handsome of countenance*; جَاءَنِي رَجُلَانِ حَسَنَا ٱلْوَجْهِ *there came to me two men handsome of countenance.* This agreement of the adjective with the preceding substantive, is equally observed, though the following substantive may be in the accusative case; as مَرَرْتُ بِرَجُلٍ حَسَنٍ وَجْهًا *I passed by a man handsome in* (quoad) *countenance.*

If however the substantive following the adjective be put in the nominative, the adjective then agrees with the preceding substantive in case, but with the substantive following in gender and number, thus مَرَرْتُ بِرَجُلٍ حَسَنٍ وَجْهُهُ *I passed by a man whose face is handsome;* مَرَرْتُ بِامْرَأَةٍ حَسَنٍ وَجْهُهَا *I passed by a woman whose face is handsome.* If the following substantive be a broken plural, the adjective is usually put in the feminine singular, as مَرَرْتُ بِرَجَالٍ حَسَنَةٍ وُجُوهُهُمْ *I passed by men whose faces are handsome;* فَوَيْلٌ لِلْقَاسِيَةِ قُلُوبُهُمْ *woe be to them whose hearts are hard!*

Before a substantive masculine in the plural number, the adjective usually appears in the masculine singular, as رَأَيْتُ رَجُلًا مَرِيضًا غِلْمَانُهُ *I saw a man whose boys are sick.* The adjective may however appear in the plural, either broken or regular, as رَأَيْتُ رَجُلًا مَرْضَى غِلْمَانُهُ, or مَرِيضِينَ غِلْمَانُهُ.

If after a substantive definite by its nature, by the use of the article, or an affixed pronoun, an indefinite adjective follows, an ellipsis of the abstract verb *to be* must be understood, as أَبِى مَرِيضٌ *my father is sick;* ٱلسُّلْطَانُ مَرِيضٌ *the Sultan is sick;* يُوسُفُ مَرِيضٌ *Joseph is sick.*

If however the adjective be limited by the article, the pronoun personal هُوَ is interposed between it, and the subject, and supplies the place of the verb *to be,* as ٱللهُ هُوَ ٱلْحَىُّ ٱلْقَيُّومُ *God is living and self-subsisting.*

An adjective constituting the predicate of a proposition, agrees with the subject in gender and number, unless that subject be a broken plural, in which case the adjective may be in the feminine singular تَعْمَى ٱلْقُلُوبُ وَٱلْعُيُونُ نَاظِرَةٌ *their hearts are blind though their eyes see.*

If the predicate precede the subject, as takes place in interrogative and negative propositions, and the subject be dual, or plural, the predicate is to be placed in the singular, as أَدَاخِلٌ ٱلرَّجُلَانِ *do the two men enter?* مَا خَارِجٌ ٱلرِّجَالُ *the men do not go out.*

A substantive preceding an adjective, and forming with it a proper name, throws away the article, as عَبْدُ ٱلْمَجِيدِ (Abd-ul-Majíd) *the servant of the glorified* (God).

When two substantives meet in construction, the antecedent is commonly indefinite, and the following noun definite, and the effect of their union is to determine the antecedent, thus غُلَامُ عَمْرٍو *the slave of Amru*; أَمَةُ أُخْتِي *the servant of my sister*; وَزِيرُ ٱلسُّلْطَانِ *the Vazir of the Sultan.* When both terms of the proposition are indefinite, the antecedent so continues to be, as حِمَارُ بَقَّالٍ *a green-seller's ass*; إِمْرَأَةُ رَجُلٍ حَجَّامٍ *a barber's wife*; صَاحِبُ مَالٍ *a possessor of riches.* In this case, though the antecedent do not become a definite noun, it is no longer entirely vague, and it will be perceived that *a Vazir of a Sultan,* and *an ass of a green-seller,* are more definite than a Vazir, and an ass. This case the Arabian grammarians term مُخَصَّص, or *particularized.* The antecedent never takes the article, though some of the principal authors of the last four or five centuries do not observe this rule, and prefix the article to both the antecedent, and the consequent; اَشْبَعَ الْجَمَّ الْغَفِيرَ مِنَ الْقُرْصِ

الشَّعِير *he satisfied a vast multitude with barley bread.*

When the meaning of the construction cannot be resolved into *possession*, or some synonymous interpretation, the nominative is either with or without the article, according as the signification is definite or indefinite, as الضَّارِبُ الْعَبْدِ *the scourger of the servant*; or ضَارِبُ الْعَبْدِ *a scourger of the servant*. Nouns of measure and weight govern the accusative singular, as رِطْلَانِ زَيْتًا *two pounds of oil of olives.*

The cardinal numbers, from three to ten, may be considered either as adjectives, or substantives; as adjectives they agree in gender and case with the name of the thing numbered, as كَانَ لَهُ بَنُونَ ثَلَاثَةٌ وَ بَنَاتٌ خَمْسٌ *he had three sons and five daughters.* As substantives they govern the following word in the genitive plural. The numeral must agree in gender with the name of the thing numbered, as ثَلَاثَةُ رِجَالٍ *three men*; سِتُّ بَنَاتٍ *six girls.*

The numerals, from ten to one hundred, govern the accusative singular. The tens excepted, they not admitting any variation of gender, these numerals agree in their gender with the name of the thing numbered, as أَحَدَ عَشَرَ كَوْكَبًا *eleven stars*; تِسْعٌ وَ تِسْعُونَ نَعْجَةً *ninety-nine sheep.*

In the numbers above twenty, the unities are put before the tens, thus خَمْسَةٌ وَ عِشْرُونَ دِينَارًا *twenty-five pieces of gold.*

After the numerals of hundreds, the name of the thing numbered is in the genitive singular, the numeral antecedent losing
its nunnation, and the dual the termination ون as مِائَةُ رَجُلٍ
a hundred men; مِائَتَا حِمَارٍ *two hundred asses*; خَمْسُ مِائَةِ كَلْبٍ
five hundred dogs.

The numerative أَلْفٌ *one thousand*, is a masculine noun governing the genitive singular.

If the number to be expressed is composed of numerals of
different classes, it is sufficient to put the name of the thing
numbered after all the numerals, and in the number and case
demanded by the last of them : بَيْنَ الْهِجْرَةِ وَ الطُّوفَانِ ثَلاثَةُ
آلَافٍ وَ تِسْعِمَايَةٍ وَ أَرْبَعٍ وَ سَبْعُونَ سَنَةً *between the Hijrah and
the Deluge there are three thousand nine hundred and seventy-four
years.*

In the dates of years the cardinal numbers are employed,
governed by the word سَنَةٌ. This word is then made definite
by the numerals which it governs, and is consequently without
an article; the numerals agree in gender with the word سَنَةٌ,
which is feminine; the units are put first, then the tens, the hundreds, and the thousands, inserting the conjunction وَ between
each numeral. ثُمَّ دَخَلْتُ سَنَةَ سِتٍّ وَ تِسْعِينَ وَ ثَلْنِمَايَةٍ وَ أَلْفٍ
then began the year 1396.

15

Ordinal Numbers.

These are true adjectives, and agree with the nouns which they qualify, in the use of the article, as well as in gender, number, and case.

The ordinal numbers of tens, hundreds, and thousands, being the same as the cardinal numbers, are employed for both genders.

When the ordinal numbers are made definite by the article, they do not appear in construction with the name of the thing numbered, but are joined with it by means of a preposition, thus ٱلثَّالِثُ وَ عِشْرُونَ مِنْ شَهْرِ رَمَضانَ *the twenty-third of the month of Ramadhán.* When the numerals are without an article, they may govern a noun in the genitive, or an affixed pronoun.

وَ سُلِّمَ عَلَيْهِ بِٱلْخِلافَةِ بَعْدَ ٱلظُّهْرِ مِنْ يَوْمِ ٱلثُّلاثَاءِ ثَامِنٍ وَ عِشْرِينَ شَهْرِ رَمَضانَ *he was saluted Khálif after the hour of noon of Wednesday the twenty-eighth of Ramadhán;* and thus with an affixed pronoun, فِى ثَالِثِ عِشْرِينَهُ نُودِىَ بِٱلْقاهِرَةِ *the twenty-third of it (the month) a proclamation was made at Kahirah.* The indeclinable numeratives كَأَىِّ ,or كَأَيِّنْ , كَمْ *how many,* put the noun which follows them in the accusative, as كَمْ دِرْهَمًا أَخَذْتَ *how many Dirhams have you received?* كَأَيِّنْ رَجُلًا قُتِلُوا *how many men have been killed?* It is the same with كَذَا .

If, however, before the indeclinable numerative, or before the thing numbered which follows it, a preposition occurs, the thing numbered is in the genitive, in the first case, as being governed by the indeclinable noun, and in the second as being governed by the preposition, as بِكَمْ دِرْهَمٍ *for how many Dir-hams?* كَايِنْ مِنْ رَجُلٍ *how many men?* If the indeclinable words here spoken of, are not used as interrogatives, the name of the thing numbered, may be in the genitive, either singular or plural, as لَا أَدْرِى كَمْ رِجَالٍ قَتَلْتَ *I know not how many men thou hast killed;* or كَمْ رَجُلٍ.

The comparative adjective, when governing an indefinite word, always remains in the singular number and masculine gender, as هِىَ أَفْضَلُ امْرَءَةٍ *she is an excellent woman;* هُوَ أَفْضَلُ *he is an excellent man;* هُمْ أَعْظَمُ رِجَالٍ *they are great men.*

When the word governed by the comparative adjective is definite, that is, takes the article, the comparative may remain of the singular masculine, or agree with the noun it governs in gender and in number, as هِىَ أَفْضَلُ ٱلنِّسَاءَ *she is the most excellent of women;* or thus, هِىَ فُضْلَى ٱلنِّسَاءَ.

When the comparative adjective is without the article, and does not govern another word, it is always of the masculine singular, and ought to be followed by the preposition مِنْ, as ٱلْفِتْنَةُ أَشَدُّ مِنَ ٱلْقَتْلِ *sedition is worse than murder.*

The comparative adjective of the form أَفْعَلُ, when governing another word, or accompanied by the article, expresses the superlative, as ٱللَّهُ أَرْحَمُ ٱلرَّاحِمِينَ *God is the most merciful of the merciful;* ٱللَّهُ هُوَ ٱلْأَكْبَرُ *God is most great.*

When followed by وَمِنْ, and a word which that preposition governs, it is merely the comparative, as أَحْمَدُ أَصْدَقُ مِنْكَ *Ahmad is more faithful than thou.*

The relative pronoun اَلَّذِى agrees with its antecedent, if it be a rational noun, in gender and number, as has been observed, it knows no variation of case, excepting in the dual. Where the antecedent, however, is an irrational noun in the plural, the relative is put in the feminine singular, as اَلْكُتُبُ اَلَّتِى *the books which.* This also takes place with the personal reciprocal pronouns, as أَخَذْتُ كُتُبًا وَ قَرَأْتُهَا *I took books and read them.* The oblique cases of the relative are likewise supplied by these affixed pronouns, as ضَرَبَنِى اَلرَّجُلُ اَلَّذِى نَصَرْتُهُ *the man whom I assisted beat me.* The relative however is sometimes dropped, and the affixed pronoun used alone, as اَللّٰهُ جَلَّ شَانُهُ *God of whom the condition is glorious.* The relative and the affixed pronouns always require an antecedent in the sentence, either expressed or understood, as اَلَّذِى خَلَقَنَا هُوَ يُدَبِّرُنَا *who created us, he directs us;* the antecedent *he* being understood before the relative pronoun.

These affixed pronouns are generally thrown to the end of the sentence, or followed only by the nominative when a proper name, as ضَرَبَ غُلَامَهُ زَيْدٌ *he beat servant his Zaid,* for *Zaid beat his servant;* فِى اَلدَّارِ صَاحِبُهَا *in house master his,* for *the master is in his house,* but not صَاحِبٌ فِى اَلدَّارِ.

Syntax of the Verb.

When the noun which is the subject of the verb precedes it, the verb must agree in gender and number with the noun, اللهُ يَبْدَأُ الْخَلْقَ ثُمَّ يُعِيدُهُ *God produces creatures, then he gives them life.*

It must be observed, however, that if the subject is an irregular plural, coming from a noun, whether masculine or feminine, or a regular plural feminine, the verb may be, and usually is, in the feminine singular, as أَلَا يَا حَمَامَاتِ الْأَرَاكِ صُبَّ تَحَمَّلِي , رِسَالَةَ صَبٍّ لَا يَفِيقُ مِنَ السُّكْرِ *O doves who rest on the branches of the Arák! bear the message of a lover, who cannot recover from his intoxication.*

If, however, the irregular plural be of rational beings, of the masculine gender, the verb may be in the masculine plural, لِلّٰهِ مَلَائِكَةٌ يَتَعَاقَبُونَ فِيكُمْ مَلَائِكَةٌ بِاللَّيْلِ و مَلَائِكَةٌ بِالنَّهَارِ *God has angels who by turns watch over you; angels in the night, and angels in the day,* إِنَّ الْمُلُوكَ إِذَا دَخَلُوا قَرْيَةً أَفْسَدُوهَا *when kings enter a town, they lay it waste.*

When the verb precedes the subject, if that subject be singular and masculine, their concordance is always preserved. If, however, it be a singular feminine, the verb must agree with its subject in number, but may differ in gender.

If the subject, be a creature, really of the female sex, and that it immediately follows the verb, the verb must then be in the feminine; but if the noun does not immediately follow the verb, the verb may be either masculine or feminine, yet the feminine is to be preferred, as قَالَتِ ٱمْرَأَةُ ٱلْعَزِيزِ *the wife of Azíz said.*

If the subject be merely a grammatical feminine, the verb may be of either gender, whether it precede its subject immediately, or not; in the second case the verb should rather be in the masculine, لِئَلَّا يَكُونَ لِلنَّاسِ عَلَيكُم حُجَّةٌ *in order that men may have no pretence against you.*

If the verb is separated from the feminine subject by إِلَّا, it is put in the masculine مَا زَكَى إِلَّا فَتَاةٌ *there is no one innocent but the servant maid,* the verb may, however, here agree with the noun in gender, the word فَتَاةٌ would then be understood directly after the verb زَكَتْ.

When the subject is a masculine plural, the verb preceding it may be in the singular, as أَنُؤْمِنُ كَمَا آمَنَ ٱلسُّفَهَاءُ *do we believe as fools have believed.*

If the subject be an irregular plural, coming from a singular, whether masculine or feminine, the verb may be put in the singular, and in either gender.

When the subject is a regular masculine plural, the verb must not be in the feminine, but it may be so with بَنُونَ plural of إِبْنٌ *a son,* and with such like words; which, though having the termination of regular masculine plurals, do not keep the forms of their singulars; for these plurals are in fact broken ones, as قَالَتْ بَنُوا إِسْرَائِيلَ *the children of Israel said.*

The verb may also be in the feminine, and even in the plural number, when the noun following is a collective one, as قَوْم *a nation;* or a name of a species, as غَنَم *sheep;* طَيْر *bird.*

The subject, if it be a mere grammatical or conventional feminine, or a broken feminine plural, may have the verb preceding it in the singular feminine, or even masculine, قَالَ نِسْوَةٌ فِى ٱلْمَدِينَةِ *women in the city said.*

The dual follows the same rules of concordance as the plural, دَخَلَ ٱلسِّجْنَ مَعَهُ فَتَيَانِ *two youths entered the prison with him,* قَالَتِ ٱلرِّجْلَانِ *the two feet said.*

Though, as has been said, it is usual when the verb precedes the subject, to put it in the singular, with the subject, dual or plural, yet the verb may agree in number and in gender with its subject. رَأَيْنَ ٱلْغَوَانِى ٱلشَّيْبَ لَاحَ بِعَارِضِى *the girls have seen the grey hairs appear upon my face.*

In the compound tenses expressed by the union of the verb كَانَ and the preterite, or indefinite of another verb, if the subject is put between the two verbs, the verb كَانَ follows the rules of concordance of the verb preceding its subject, and the second verb follows those of the verb placed after its subject.

When the subject is a collective noun, preceding the verb, the verb is commonly placed in the plural وَلَٰكِنَّ أَكْثَرَ ٱلنَّاسِ لَا يَشْكُرُونَ *but the greater part of men are not grateful.*

If the same verb have several subjects of different persons, it agrees with that subject which, in the language of grammarians, is of the best person; the first person being better

than the second, and the second better than the third, أَنَا وَ
ٱلْغَلَم نَمْضِى إِلَى ثَمّ وَ نَسْجُد *I and the young man will go thither, and we will worship.*

When the same noun is the subject of one verb, and the
object of another, it is necessary to attend to the way in
which the two verbs are placed. If the verb which governs
the noun as its object, is placed first, and then the verb to
which that noun is the subject, the objective case is understood, and the noun appears only in the nominative, as ضَرَبْت
وَ ضَرَبَنِى زَيْد مَرَرْت وَ مَرّ *I struck Zaid and Zaid struck me;*
بِى عَمْرُو *I passed by Amru, and Amru passed by me.* It is
permitted, however, to give an affixed pronoun as its object
to the first verb, ضَرَبْتُه وَ ضَرَبَنِى زَيْد.

If the verb to which the noun acts as subject, comes first,
and then that which governs the noun or object, the object
is equally suppressed, and the usual rules are observed in the
agreement of the first verb with the subject, ضَرَبَنِى وَ ضَرَبْت
زَيْدَان *the two Zaids struck me, and I struck them.*

The noun may also be expressed in the objective or accusative case; giving to the first verb the termination which
indicates its agreement with the latent, or understood pronoun, which represents that noun in the nominative case, as
ٱلْزَيْدُون ضَرَبُونِى وَ ضَرَبْت ٱلْزَيْدِين for ضَرَبُونِى وَ ضَرَبْت ٱلْزَيْدِين
the Zaids struck me and I struck them. If a verb be used
which requires a subject and a predicate, such as كَان *to be;*

صَار *to become*; and that the predicate be common to two propositions; as *I was ill, and Zaid was ill*; the predicate may be given only once, or may be represented by a separate compound pronoun, as كُنْتُ وَكَانَ زَيْدٌ مَرِيضًا *I was, and Zaid was, ill*, or كُنْتُ إِيَّاهُ وَكَانَ زَيْدٌ مَرِيضًا *I was so, and Zaid was ill*, or كُنْتُ وَكَانَ زَيْدٌ مَرِيضًا إِيَّاهُ *I was and Zaid was ill, it*; that is, *Zaid was ill, and I was so*. The first of these three methods is the one most in use. All this requires that the two subjects should be of the same gender and number, otherwise the predicate must be repeated.

The same rule takes place with verbs, such as ظَنَّ *to believe*; حَسِبَ *to suppose*, when governing a complete proposition, formed from a subject and predicate both in the accusative, as ظَنَنْتُ زَيْدًا عَالِمًا *I believed Zaid was learned*. The predicate may be common to two propositions, and, of course, to two different subjects; and the noun, which in one of the propositions is the subject of the verb *to believe*, may, in the other, be the subject of the proposition which is governed by that verb, thus, *Zaid has believed me learned, and I have believed Zaid learned*. ظَنَّنِي وَظَنَنْتُ زَيْدًا عَالِمًا *he has believed me, and I have believed Zaid learned*; or ظَنَّنِي إِيَّاهُ وَظَنَنْتُ زَيْدًا عَالِمًا *he has believed me it, and I have believed Zaid learned*; or وَظَنَّنِي ظَنَنْتُ زَيْدًا عَالِمًا إِيَّاهُ *he has believed me and I have believed Zaid learned it*; that is, *I have believed Zaid to be learned, and he has believed me to be so*. The first is the method most approved. If the subjects be of different gender and number, the predicate must be repeated; اَظُنُّ وَ يَظُنَّانِى اَخَا زَيْدًا وَ عَمْرًا اَخَوَيْنِ *I regard Zaid and Amru as my two brothers, and they two regard me as a brother.*

In treating of the tenses of the verb, an enumeration has been made of the various particles which affect the indefinite tense, with apocope, antithesis and paragoge. The indefinite tense, as has been observed, (page 64,) is by the Arabians denominated مُضَارِع, or *resembling*, because, in some of its accidents, it resembles the noun. As the noun has various cases, so the verb, in the indefinite tense, has various terminations; these, by some European grammarians, are considered as moods of the verb.

The first, which is the natural and proper state of the indefinite يَكْتُبُ, is by them called the indicative mood; by the Arabians رَفْع, *elevation*, i. e. of the final vowel *o* or *u*. The second, which is when the indefinite tense receives antithesis يَكْتُبَ, the same European authors call the subjunctive mood; by the Arabians themselves it is denominated نَصْب, or *erection*. These epithets, which belong also to the noun, when applied to that, designate respectively what we call the nominative and accusative cases, distinguished by the final vowels *o* or *u*, and *a*. The third state of the indefinite tense is when it receives *Jazmah* يَكْتُبْ, or *apocope*; this the same authors call the conditional mood; while the fourth, which is when the indefinite tense receives, what the Arabians call the ن *of confirmation*, and which Erpenius has distinguished by the term *paragoge*, is denominated the indefinite tense energetic.

The more simple distinctions, as they appear to be, of Erpenius, have been followed in this grammar.

1. The indefinite, having a future sense, is subjoined to the preceding verb in the preterite, in order to denote the immediate and consequential succession of the action which itself indicates; a meaning conveyed in English by the future of the conditional mood, as أَتَى إِلَى عَيْنِ مَآءٍ يَشْرَبُ *he came to a fountain of water* THAT HE MIGHT DRINK ; ثُمَّ اسْتَوَى عَلَى الْعَرْشِ يُدَبِّرُ الْأَمْرَ *then he ascended the throne, that he* MIGHT ADMINISTER *justice* ; إِذْ غَدَوْتَ مِنْ أَهْلِكَ تُبَوِّى الْمُؤْمِنِينَ مَقَاعِدَ *when thou wentest out in the morning that thou might lead the faithful into the camp.*

2. The indefinite is subjoined, in the manner of a simple complement, to some verbs, the sense of which remains imperfect without the addition of another verb. In such cases the indefinite usually receives أَنْ before it, but the interposition of this particle is frequently dispensed with :

1. It is seldom used with verbs denoting inclination or tendency to action. The verbs اسْتَطَاعَ and قَدَرَ *to be able*, are usually joined immediately to the indefinite شَآءَ and أَرَادَ *to wish* or *desire*, more rarely so, as أُرِيدُ أَنْظُرُ *I wish to see* (that I could see) ; أَرَادَ أَنْ, is however more correct, and in more general use. With some verbs the common forms of speech

seek brevity more than grammatical purity; as عَرِفَ يَسْبَحُ *he knew how to swim.* This verb عَرِفَ *to know*, should receive أَنْ after it, as عَرِفَ أَنْ يَفْعَلَ.

2. Verbs indicating an action about to be immediately. Among these the most frequent is كَادَ *to be nearly*, or *almost.* (Lat. parum abfuit quin,) which is almost always immediately joined to its indefinite; as كَادَتِ ٱلنَّفْسُ تَزْهَقُ *the spirit was nearly departing.*

يَكَادُ ٱلْبَرْقُ يَخْتَفُ أَبْصَارَهُمْ *the lightning nearly took away their sight.* More rare, but of the same tendency, and of the same species of connection, are أَلَمَّ, كَرَبَ, and أَوْشَكَ *to be near to.* All these very seldom require the interposition of أَنْ; but عَسَى expressing apprehension of any thing, and which may be considered as an impersonal verb, requires the conjunction أَنْ; as عَسَى أَنْ تَكْرَهُوا شَيْئًا وَ هُوَ خَيْرٌ لَكُمْ *it may perhaps be that you may hate a thing, and it may be good for you.* Even this verb عَسَى, however, among the poets is found without أَنْ preceding the indefinite, as عَسَى يَرَى نَارَكَ مَنْ يَمُرُّ *perhaps he who is travelling may see your fire.* When a negation takes place, it must be put before the first verb, as مَا عَسِيتُمْ أَنْ *he is hardly able to speak plainly;* لَا يَكَادُ يُبِينُ تَفْعَلُوا *perhaps you will not do it.* It is to be observed that عَسَى, and كَرَبَ are only in use in the preterite, where they

assume the meaning of adverbs, as is probably the case with
لَعَلَّ, which, if so, has entirely lost its verbal sense.

3. The indefinite expressing a present sense, is often in
apposition with another verb; this indefinite holding the place
of a participle, is in very common use, and is subjoined to the
first verb to explain the mode of its action, as أَرْسَلَ يَعْلِمُهُ بِذَلِكَ
he sent announcing this to him, مَنْ مَاتَ يَشْهَدُ أَنَّ لَا إِلَهَ إِلَّا ٱللَّهَ
دَخَلَ ٱلْجَنَّةَ *he who dies testifying that there is no God but God
will enter paradise.*

There are several classes of verbs taking the indefinite immediately after them. As 1, *verbs of beginning*, which, when
thus joined to another verb, always point out the commencement of some situation, or action; although the spaces of time
occupied by that situation or action, may be very different.

The most frequent of this description is the verb جَعَلَ as
جَعَلَ قَارُونُ جَعَلَا يَتَشَاجَرَانِ *they two began to dispute together*,
يَقُولُ يَا مُوسَى أَرْحَمْنِي وَ مُوسَى يَقُولُ يَا أَرْضُ خُذِيهِمْ
*Kárún began to say, O Moses pity me! and Moses to say, O earth
swallow them up!* Such are the verbs اِقْبَلَ, شَرَعَ, أَخَذَ, بَدَأَ,
ذَهَبَ and طَفِقَ, طَبَقَ, أَنْشَأَ, عَلِقَ.

2. *Verbs expressing duration* of any state, or continued, and repeated action; as بَقِيَ, *to continue, to remain*,
or *to persist*, بَقِيَ زَيْدٌ يُرَاسِلُ اِبْنَ بُوَيْهِ وَ يَسْتَدْعِيهِ وَ ٱبْنُ بُوَيْهِ
يَعْتَذِرُ وَ لَا يَحْضُرُ إِلَيْهِ *Zaid continued to send to Ibn Buwaih in-*

viting him to come, and Ibn Buwaih to excuse himself and not to appear. To this class belong also the verbs اِسْتَمَر *to continue, or persist;* أَقَام *to remain, to persevere;* رَسَا *to be firm, or unmoved;* عَاد *to be accustomed;* ظَلَّ *to continue, not to cease;* (during the day) بَات *to continue;* (during the night) as well as these; and مَا اِنْفَكَّ; مَا زَال ,مَا بَرِح ,مَا فَتِئَ ,مَا زَال *not to cease;* *not to fail;* i. e. to continue to do until the end of the period mentioned.

3. Of the same description are all verbs denoting *to be, to exist.* The most frequent of this class is كَان, and those whose meaning is derived from a particular point of time; as أَسْفَر *to travel in the morning,* أَصْبَح *to be in the morning, &c.*

That state of the indefinite which the Arabians call مَنْصُوب, *nasbated,* or bearing *Fathah* for its final vowel, and which Erpenius denominates *antithesis,* is subjected to some particle always conveying the sense of *that.* Its most frequent use is after the conjunction أَن *that;* if a verb of will precede, as طَلَبُوا مِنْهُ أُرِيد أَن تُحْسِن إِلَيْه *I wish that you would favor him* أَن يَبْعَثَهُم *they sought from him that he would send them.* In like manner, after أَن رَضِيَ فِي أَن ;عَزَم عَلَى أَن *he labored that;* (or رَضِيَ أَن) *he was pleased that.* There are many verbs of this description, as well as others indicating the reverse, as مَنَع أَبَى ,كَرِه *to be unwilling,* حَاذَر ;خَشِيَ ,خَاف *to fear;* and *to hinder, to prevent.* It is the same after all verbs of *com-*

manding, and *forbidding*; as حَرَّم , أَوْصَى , أَمَرَ أَنْ ; of *pardoning*,
swearing, *testifying*, and *vowing*; as حَلَفَ , تَعَاهَدَ , نَذَرَ . Verbs
of *efficiency*, or of *power*, constitute another class of this description, as أَلْزَمَ *to compel*. In the same way إِسْتَحَقَّ أَنْ يَكُونَ
he is deserving that he be, يَنْبَغِي , يَجِبُ أَنْ *it is necessary that*;
يَجُوزُ أَنْ *it is permitted that*, (licet ut.) Hence after the word
عَادَةٌ *custom*, as كَانَ عَادَةَ ٱلْخُلَفَاءِ أَنْ يَحْبِسُوا أَوْلَادَهُمْ *it was a
custom of the Khalifs that they should confine their sons*. Nei-
ther is it necessary that a verb, or verbal noun, should always
precede, as إِمَّا أَنْ يَكُونَ وَ إِمَّا أَنْ لَا يَكُونَ *whether that it be, or
whether that it be not.*

The indefinite, however, does not always bear antithesis after
أَنْ , for if it have the meaning of the simple present tense,
and أَنْ points out nothing more than a certain event, contem-
porary with the preceding verb, it remains in its first state, and
does not take antithesis; أَعْلَمُ أَنْ يَنُومُ *I know that he sleeps*;
though in such a case, to avoid all ambiguity, the use of أَنَّهُ
is to be preferred. After verbs of *doubting* or *thinking*, as
ظَنَّ , خَالَ , and such like, the antithesis is not necessary, but
it is sometimes found.

لَنْ . This is a more emphatic denial of the future, and
being composed of لَا and أَنْ , always requires antithesis, as لَنْ
يَفْعَلْ *he will not do it* (I do not believe that he will do it.)

لِ . This preposition, placed before the verb, becomes a
conjunction, denoting the *end* or *purpose* of the action (Gr. ἵνα,)

whence it always requires the antithesis, as indicative of a subjunctive sense; as يَأْتُونَكَ لِيَشْهَدُوا *they come to you that they may testify;* مَدَّ يَدَهُ لِيَصْفَعَهُ *he stretched out his hand that he might strike him.* Observe particularly this form of speech, مَا كُنْتُ لِأَفْعَلَهُ *I am not he that I can do it,* that is, I do not wish to do this. لَمْ تَكُنْ لِتَسْتَزِلَّهُمْ *thou wert not he who wished to lead them astray.* If however a negation occurs, the particle لِ does not immediately join, أَنْ being always interposed, whence comes the negative لِئَلَّا (لِ أَنْ لَا).

Of the same meaning is the conjunction كَيْ *that* (Gr. ὅπως) and its compounds لِكَيْلَا , كَيْلَا , لِكَيْ.

The verb bearing antithesis is subjoined to certain other particles, when, from the whole tendency and connection of the discourse, the action which that verb expresses, stands as if depending on the first. The particles are then placed immediately preceding, and the meaning of the verb subjected to them, points out the peculiar idea belonging to the whole sentence.

حَتَّى. This conjunction signifying, *that, in order to,* denotes the end or continuation of the action, until that which is wished is obtained, as أَجِرْهُ حَتَّى يَسْمَعَ كَلَامَ ٱللَّهِ *protect him until he hears the word of God,* (in order that he may hear). It may also indicate the deferring of an action, not to be done until something preceding is accomplished; لَا تَدْخُلُوا بُيُوتًا غَيْرَ

بِيُوتِكُمْ حَتَّى تَسْتَأْنِسُوا و تَسْلِمُوا عَلَى أَهْلِهِ *do not enter houses,*
except your houses, until you ask permission, and salute its in-
habitants; مَنَعَ دُخُولَ امْرَأَةٍ صُوَ إِلَى دَارِ ٱلْخِلَافَةِ حَتَّى يَعْرِفَ مَنْ
هِيَ *he forbade any woman entering the palace of the Khalíf*
until he knew who she was.

ف. This conjunction usually joins two propositions, indicating, in the second, an immediate dependance on the first,
of which it is a consequence, and requires to be followed by
antithesis; as إِغْفِرْلِى يَا رَبِى فَادْخُلَ ٱلْجَنَّةَ *pardon me, O Lord!*
that I may enter paradise; هَلْ زَيْدٌ فِى ٱلدَّارِ فَأَمْضِىَ إِلَيْهِ *is*
Zaid in his house, that I may go to him? After a negative
imperative, it answers to the Latin *ne,* and the English *lest,*
as لَا تُوَاخِذْنِى فَأَهْلِكَ *punish me not, lest I perish.*

From a similar connection of ideas, the antithetical form
of the indefinite follows the particle إِذًا or إِذَنْ, if it describes
a consequence immediately following the antecedent, as in the
case of any movement or intention of the mind; as if any one
were to say, *I will visit you to-morrow,* the answer might be,
then I will honor you, that is, *I will receive you with honor.*
The difference between فَ and إِذَنْ is, that فَ denotes a closer
connection, and إِذَنْ a connection less immediate.

و. The difference between this conjunction and فَ is, that
the latter, besides the simple connection, expresses also the
order of things which و does not, but merely an intention, sub-

16

ordinate to the first, and something to be done at the same

time; as لَا تَنْهَ عَنِ الخُلُقِ فَتَأْتِىَ مِثْلَهُ *do not condemn a temper

and then shew the same;* هَلْ تَأْكُلُ السَّمَكَ وَ تَشْرَبَ اللَّبَنَ *do

you eat fish and at the same time drink milk?*

أَوْ. This conjunction, which properly signifies *or, or else,*

receives also the meaning of, *in order that, until that, unless

that;* نُحَاوِلُ مُلْكًا أَوْ نَمُوتَ *we will regain the empire unless we

die.* In such cases it always requires the antithesis of the inde-

finite. This conjunction has the same effect on the indefinite,

when it is repeated, then signifying *whether,* as لَا أَتَكَلَّمَ أَوْ أَظْفَرَ

أَوْ أُقْتَلَ *I will not speak, whether I conquer, or am killed.*

From what has been said, it will appear that, properly

speaking, it is only the conjunctions أَنْ and كَىْ, either ex-

pressed, or understood, which affect the indefinite tense with

antithesis; for the other words, such as حَتَّى, لِ, فَ, &c.

more or less, contain the same signification as those two par-

ticles, and are equivalent to the word *that.*

The jazmated form of the indefinite, or apocope, takes place

when two propositions are conditionally connected, whether this

connection be pointed out by the conjunction إِنْ *if;* or by one

of these words; مَنْ *whoever;* مَا *that which,* and its compounds,

كُلَّمَا *all that;* كُلَّمَا *every time that;* مَهْمَا *whatever it be that;*

إِذَامَا *when;* and أَيَّانَ *wherever it be;* حَيْثُمَا, أَيْنَمَا, أَيْنَ, أَنَّى

كَيْفَمَا and كَيْفَ when, at whatever time that; مَتَىمَا and مَتَى in whatever way that; أَيْمَنَ and أَىٰ whoever.

It is the same if one of the two propositions be in the imperative, and that the other depend conditionally upon it; as, *if you do well you will be rewarded.*

The particle لَمْ also requires apocope, but when there are several indefinite tenses depending on each other, that which immediately follows the particle لَمْ is the only one affected by it; as لَمْ يَكُنْ يَعْرِفُ يَسْبَحُ *he did not know how to swim.* It is the same with the particle لَمَّا *not yet.*

After the prepositions لَا or لِ, giving to the indefinite an *imperative* meaning, apocope also takes place; as لَا يَفْعَلْ *let him not do it!* لِيَفْعَلْ *let him do it!*

The indefinite takes the same shape after the negative adverb لَا, when it carries *deprecative* meaning, as لَا تَسْتَطِلْ مِنِّى بِقَاءَى وَ مُدَّتِى وَ لَكِنْ يَكُنْ لِلْخَيْرِ مِنْكَ نَصِيب *lengthen not my life and my days, but let me have a portion of thy felicity!*

The use of the two forms of paragoge is subjected to no fixed rule; they are employed to add force to the expression, whether in interrogating, in affirming with or without an oath, or when the indefinite carries an imperative or prohibitive sense.

Syntax of Particles.

All those relations of the subjoined noun, which cannot be expressed by the genitive, governed by the antecedent noun,

16—2

nor by the accusative, are pointed out by prepositions. This is their first, and most frequent use; there is, however, another; for as the Arabic language has no compound words, nor verbs compounded with prepositions, many prepositions, which in European languages coalesce with the verbs, whose meaning they complete and define, are in Arabic only found in apposition.

Active verbs for the most part govern the accusative, thus رمَى حَجَرًا, *he threw a stone*. Yet such verbs often take the genitive with a preposition, as رمَى بِحَجَرٍ *he threw with a stone;* this happens frequently, when the verb, by common use, indicates the object upon which it acts; as بعَث *to send*, which in common use means to send an ambassador, to delegate, this always takes بِ of the thing with which the legate or messenger is sent; another cause of such anomalies may be found in the new meaning which a verb may acquire; thus أَشَادَ in its first and original meaning, signifies *to construct with clay*, as a wall, a cottage, &c.; from this is derived the metaphorical meaning, *to build up a name, to raise to renown*, which requires the preposition بِ, as أَشَادَ بِذِكْرِهِ *he exalted his fame*. So the verb وضَعَ, whose original meaning is *to put*, passes on to the kindred signification, *to put down*, and with the use of the preposition مِن, takes the meaning of *to detract, to render contemptible*, ideas synonymous with the *diminishing of praise* or *detracting from*.

The brevity of speech to which the use of prepositions so much contributes may be particularly observed in verbs, which,

though intransitive, become transitive verbs by their assistance;
thus قَامَ إِلَيْهِ, *rising, he proceeded to him.* The poets take great
freedoms with such modes of construction.

It happens frequently, however, that after an intransitive
verb, the preposition which should point out the relation between that verb and the word which it governs, is suppressed;
and the word governed by the verb appears in the accusative,
as if the verb were a transitive one.

When the intransitive verb governs a complete proposition,
whether verbal or nominal, beginning by the conjunction أَنْ,
or أَنَّ, the preposition which ought to connect the intransitive
verb with the following proposition may be dropped; thus لَمْ
يَقْدِرْ أَنْ يَفْعَلَ ذٰلِكَ instead of لَمْ يَقْدِرْ عَلَى أَنْ يَفْعَلَ ذٰلِكَ

he could not do that; تَقَدَّمَ إِلَيْهِ أَلَّا يَأْذَنَ لِأَحَدٍ *he ordered him*

to grant permission to no one; instead of بِأَلَّا يَأْذَنَ the last example is particularly remarkable, as it is only by means of the
preposition بِ that تَقَدَّمَ signifies *to order.*

In no case, however, must the preposition be omitted, if
a doubtful meaning would result; thus it cannot be said رَغِبْتُ
أَنْ تَفْعَلَ ذٰلِكَ instead of رَغِبْتُ فِى أَنْ تَفْعَلَ ذٰلِكَ *I desire*
that you would do that; for if the preposition were left out,
it might be supposed that the sense was رَغِبْتُ عَنْ أَنْ تَفْعَلَ
ذٰلِكَ *I am averse from your doing that.*

On the one hand, however, as there are verbs having an unrestricted power in this respect, so there are others with which the suppression of the preposition is a mere poetical licence to be used only in cases of necessity.

What has been just said of intransitive, applies equally to transitive verbs, with regard to their government of words requiring the interposition of a particle; this particle is often left out, and the noun, or rather the pronoun which represents it, subjoined immediately to the verb, which then governs it virtually in the accusative case; as شكرته *I thanked him*, for شكرت له *I gave thanks to him*; نصحته *I gave him good advice*, for نصحت له *I gave good advice to him*.

It sometimes happens, though but rarely, that the preposition being suppressed, the word which it governs remains yet in the genitive case. This is a pure ellipsis:

$$ إِذَا قِيلَ أَىُّ ٱلنَّاسِ شَرُّ قَبِيلَةٍ $$

$$ أَشَارَتْ كُلَيْبٍ بِٱلْأَكُفِّ ٱلْأَصَابِعُ. $$

When it is asked which among men is a wicked tribe? The fingers of the hand point to Kulaib.

It will be observed that the word كُلَيْبٍ is an ellipsis for إِلَى كُلَيْبٍ.

The particle ما is sometimes used between a preposition, ‸and the word which it governs, without changing the influence of the preposition on that word. This particle ما is then merely expletive رَحْمَةٌ, and بِمَا رَحْمَةٌ, instead of عَمَّا قَلِيلٍ and عَنْ قَلِيلٍ.

The preposition عَنْ sometimes follows immediately the preposition مِنْ, as مِنْ عَنْ يَمِينٍ *from the right side*.

The prepositions ب and مِنْ are sometimes employed pleonastically, or seemingly so; but they always preserve their grammatical influence over the word which they govern.

The words employed by the Arabians as exceptives, are إِلَّا *if not*; composed of the conjunction إِنْ *if*, and of the negative adverb لَا *not*; غَيْرَ, بَيْدَ, سِوَى, سَوَى and سَوَآءٌ which are all properly nouns, signifying *difference*; حَاشَا, خَلَا, and عَدَا *except*; words, which, though considered as prepositions, were originally verbs, and لَا سِيَّمَا an expression signifying *above all*.

The noun expressing the thing excepted, appears in Arabic, sometimes in the nominative and sometimes in the accusative, or genitive.

1. إِلَّا. The general subject from which a thing is excepted being expressed, if the proposition be negative, the noun expressing the thing excepted may agree with the noun expressing the general subject; or may be put in the accusative, as مَا كَلَّمَنِي أَحَدٌ إِلَّا زَيْدًا or إِلَّا زَيْدٌ *no one has spoken to me except Zaid*, مَا أَتَيْتُ بِٱلْكُتُبِ إِلَّا ٱلتَّوْرِيَةَ or إِلَّا ٱلتَّوْرِيَةُ *I have not brought the books except the Pentateuch*.

If the proposition be affirmative, the noun expressing the thing excepted must be in the accusative, as جَاءَنِى ٱلنَّاسُ إِلَّا زَيْدًا *the men came to me except Zaid.*

If the general subject from which the exception is made, be not expressed, but understood, the noun of the thing excepted must be in the same case as would have been the subject understood. The principal proposition is then always negative. As مَا جَاءَنِى إِلَّا جَعْفَرٌ *no one came to me but Jâfar;* مَا مَرَرْتُ إِلَّا بِجَعْفَرٍ *I passed by no one but Jâfar;* لَمْ أَضْرِبْ إِلَّا جَعْفَرًا *I have struck no one but Jâfar.*

In the first of these examples Jâfar is in the nominative in agreement with أَحَدٌ *one,* understood, in the second the word understood is بِأَحَدٍ, and in the third أَحَدًا.

If the word preceding إِلَّا, be the subject, and that which follows it the predicate of a proposition, the two words must be in the nominative, as مَا جَعْفَرٌ إِلَّا كَاذِبٌ *Jâfar is not but a liar* (Jâfar is nothing but a liar) إِنَّ ٱلْكَافِرُونَ إِلَّا مَلْعُونُونَ *verily the unbelievers are but cursed.*

If the thing expected be not of the nature of that comprised in the general subject, the noun following إِلَّا must be in the accusative مَا جَاءَنِى أَحَدٌ إِلَّا فَرَسًا *no one came to me except a horse.*

Among negative propositions, must be comprised those which

are so in their sense, though not by their form; such are prohibitive propositions, or interrogatives expressing negation.

The words غَيْر , بَيْد , سَوَاءٌ , سِوًى and سُوَى , which are also exceptives, govern the noun of the thing excepted, in the genitive; and are themselves always in the same case in which the noun of the thing excepted would be, if the particle إِلَّا were used; thus غَيْرُ زَيْدٍ *no one*, or مَا كَلَّمَنِى أَحَدٌ غَيْرُ زَيْدٍ *has spoken to me except Zaid*; مَا أَتَيْتُ بِالْكُتُبِ غَيْرَ التَّوْرِيَةِ *I have not brought the books except the Pentateuch*; or غَيْرِ التَّوْرِيَةِ ; مَا جَاءَنِى النَّاسُ غَيْرَ زَيْدٍ *the men came to me except Zaid*; مَا مَرَرْتُ جَاءَنِى غَيْرَ جَعْفَرٍ *no one came to me except Jafar*; لَمْ أَضْرِبْ بِغَيْرِ جَعْفَرٍ *I have passed by no one except Jafar*; مَا جَاءَنِى أَحَدٌ غَيْرَ جَعْفَرٍ *I have struck no one except Jafar*; غَيْرَ فَرَسٍ *no one came to me except a horse*.

The two words سِوًى and سُوَى, being among those whose three cases are alike, they only follow the preceding rule virtually.

After the words عَدَا, خَلَا, حَاشَا and عَدَا, the noun of the thing excepted, may be either in the genitive, accusative, or even nominative. When, however, مَا خَلَا or مَا عَدَا is used, the noun of the thing excepted must be in the accusative, because خَلَا and عَدَا then preserve the nature of verbs.

لَا سِيَّمَا. This literally signifies, *not equal to*, but is used in the sense, *above all, principally*. The noun following may be either in the nominative or genitive, as أَعْجَبَنِي ٱلنَّاسُ لَا سِيَّمَا or لَا سِيَّمَا زَيْدٍ زَيْدٌ *the men have enchanted me, above all Zaid.* The genitive is then viewed as being governed by سِيّ , synonymous with مِثْلُ , and مَا as a mere expletive without influence.

If on the contrary the nominative is used, مَا is considered as the conjunctive noun, signifying *that which,* and an ellipsis is supposed of the pronoun هُوَ , between مَا and the following noun. It results from this, that the case of the noun following لَا سِيَّمَا , and which noun expresses the thing excepted, depends in no manner upon the case of the noun expressing the general subject, from which the thing excepted is subtracted.

After إِلَّا , غَيْرِ , and بَيْدَ , a complete proposition may follow; إِلَّا has then no influence over the proposition, and after غَيْرِ and بَيْدَ , which are adverbially put in the accusative, the conjunction أَنَّ is used.

When إِلَّا is repeated, forming fresh exceptions, and not merely used for the purpose of greater energy, the general subject being understood, and not expressed, the noun shewing the first thing excepted, takes the nominative case, and the others the accusative; مَا قَامَ إِلَّا جَعْفَرٌ إِلَّا سَعِيدًا إِلَّا مُحَمَّدًا *no one stood up except Jafar, except Said, except Muhammad.*

If the general idea be expressed, and the proposition an affirmative, all the exceptions are in the accusative; قُتِلَ ٱلْقَوْمُ

إِلَّا زَيْدًا إِلَّا عُمَرَ إِلَّا عَمْرًا *all the people were killed except Zaid, except Omar, except Amru.* If the general idea is expressed, and the proposition negative, and that there be an inversion, it is the same; مَا نَجَا إِلَّا جَعْفَرًا إِلَّا احمدَ أحد *no one escaped except Jafar, except Ahmad.*

If there be not an inversion, one of the nouns will be in the case in which would be the noun following إِلَّا, if there were but one exception, and all the others will be in the accusative; لَمْ يَنْجُ أحد إِلَّا زيد إِلَّا عَمْرًا *no one has escaped except Zaid, except Amru.*

لَا يَكُون, or the negative verb لَيْسَ, is sometimes used to convey exception, the noun of the thing excepted is then in the accusative, لَيْسَ زَيْدًا or قتلوا لَا يَكُون زَيْدًا *they have been killed except Zaid.*

It has been before observed, that the negative adverbs لا and ما govern, in certain circumstances, the predicate of a proposition in the accusative case, and that لا, when used to deny the very existence of a thing, governs the noun in the accusative case, but without nunnation.

To give these negative adverbs the power of governing in the accusative, as when we say مَا هٰذَا بَشَرًا *this is not a man,* it is necessary, first, that the attribute, or predicate, should follow the subject.

2nd. That the particle of exception إِلَّا, do not come between the subject and its attribute.

3rd. That if the negation مَا be used, the negative particle إِنْ must not be added to it.

4th. That if the negative لَا is used, the subject must be an appellative noun indefinite; in all other cases these negative adverbs lose their influence on the predicate, which must then be in the nominative, according to the general rule; thus مَا قَائِمٌ زَيْدٌ *Zaid is* مَا زَيْدٌ إِلَّا كَاذِبٌ *Zaid is not standing up;* *nothing but a liar;* مَا إِنْ مُحَمَّدٌ نَائِمٌ *Muhammad does not sleep;* لَا مُسْتَوْدَعُ ٱلسِّرِّ ذَائِعٌ لَدَيْهِمْ *the secret trusted to them is not betrayed;* لَا زَيْدٌ مَرِيضٌ *Zaid is not ill.* With an indefinite noun, thus, لَا إِنْسَانٌ بَاقِيًا *there is no man immortal.*

After مَا, as well as after لَيْسَ, and لَا, the predicate of a nominal proposition often takes the preposition بِ, as مَا ٱللَّهُ بِغَافِلٍ *God is not negligent.*

When the negative adverb لَا denies existence, the noun ends in *Fathah* without nunnation, as لَا إِنْسَانَ فِى ٱلدَّارِ *there is no man in the house.*

In order to have this effect the noun must be wholly indefinite, and must immediately follow the negation.

If after this particle there are two nouns joined by a conjunction, and to each of which the negation equally belongs, the second noun may either be in the nominative, or in the same state as the first, as لَا رَجُلَ و لَا امْرَأَةَ فِى ٱلدَّارِ or لَا رَجُلَ

وَ ٱمْرَاةٌ *there is not man or woman in the house.* The negation however is usually repeated.

If the negative adverb be repeated, it may operate upon the two nouns, or only upon either of them.

لَا حَوْلَ وَ لَا قُوَّةَ إِلَّا بِٱللَّهِ

لَا حَوْلَ وَ لَا قُوَّةَ إِلَّا بِٱللَّهِ

لَا حَوْلَ وَ لَا قُوَّةَ إِلَّا بِٱللَّهِ

لَا حَوْلَ وَ لَا قُوَّةَ إِلَّا بِٱللَّهِ

there is no strength nor power but in God.

If the subject of which the existence is denied, be qualified by an adjective, the adjective may be pronounced in three different ways; as

لَا رَجُلَ نَائِمٌ فِى ٱلدَّارِ

لَا رَجُلَ نَائِمًا فِى ٱلدَّارِ

لَا رَجُلَ نَائِمَ فِى الدَّارِ

there is no man sleeping in the house.

If after the negative adverb لا denying existence, there be a noun definite, it appears in the nominative, لَا زَيْدٌ فِى ٱلدَّارِ *Zaid is not in the house.*

The negative and conditional particle لَوْلَا has no grammatical influence on the subject of the proposition which follows it. This proposition in general wants its predicate, or attribute; thus لَوْلَا زَيْدٌ لَزُرْتُكَ *if it were not Zaid, I would visit you,* that is, *if Zaid did not exist,* or *made no obstacle.*

The subject of the proposition following this particle, may be represented by an affixed pronoun, as لَوْلَاهُ لَمْ تَخْرُجِ ٱلدُّنْيَا مِنَ ٱلْعَدَمْ *if it had not been for him the world would not have come out of nothing.* The detached personal pronoun may also be employed, as لَوْلَا أَنْتُمْ لَكُنَّا مُؤْمِنِينَ *if it had not been for you we should have been believers.*

The various emotions of the mind are interjectionally expressed, sometimes by nouns in their simple state, as سَلَامٌ عَلَيْكَ *peace be to thee!* or لِلَّهِ دَرُّكَ *may your abundance be with God!* a form of benediction; نَاهِيكَ بِهِ *may you be contented!* (*may it suffice you*) نَاهِيكَ بِهَا سُبَّةً *may this disgrace be sufficient to you!*

If, however, the interjection is expressed by a single word, abruptly uttered, it appears in the accusative, elliptically, as سَلَامًا *peace;* سُحْقًا لَهُ *distance be to him!* that is, *let him be gone!* لَا مِسَاسَ *touch not!*

The same word is often repeated interjectionally, expressing alarm, and to give warning; ٱلْأَسَدَ ٱلْأَسَدَ *the lion! the lion!* that is, *beware of the lion!* ٱلْجِدَّ ٱلْجِدَّ وَ ٱلنَّجَاءَ ٱلنَّجَاءَ *diligence, diligence, safety, safety,* (*be diligent and you will succeed*) ٱلنَّجَاءَ ٱلْهَرَبَ *flight! flight!*

In a similar way an urgent address, or warning to another, is conveyed by the use of the affixed pronoun of the second

person, and the accusative case of the thing to be avoided;
a conjunction coming between the two words, as اِيَّاكَ وَ عِزَّةَ
اَلْغَضَبِ *thee, and vehemence of anger!* that is, *beware thou of
great anger!* اِيَّاكُمْ اَنْ تَكُونُوا اَمْثَالَهُمْ *beware that you be not the
same!* اِيَّاكَ اِيَّاكَ وَ الْقُرَانِ وَ الدِّينِ *beware! beware! that you
injure not the Kurán and the faith.*

Among the particles of affirmation, and of answering, نَعَمْ
yes, well done! be it so! is of very common use; بَجَلْ is sometimes used among ancient authors in the same sense as the
preceding; it properly means *enough.* اَجَلْ simply affirms, and
is generally used in assenting to a preceding proposition whe-
ther affirmative or negative, as اَظُنُّهُ يُحَدِّثُكُمْ اَنَّهُ كَانَ بَرَّا قَالُوا
اَجَلْ *I think he tells you that he is innocent, they answered yes.*
جِيرِ *certainly!* this is much like the preceding. اِي this is
only used before a form of swearing.

—————

PROVERBS

SELECTED FROM THE COLLECTION OF

ABU' L FADL AHMAD IBNU MUHAMMAD AL MAIDÁNI.

---

1. إِنَّكَ لَا تَجْنِى مِنَ ٱلشَّوْكِ ٱلْعنب .

Thou canst not gather grapes from thorns.

2. أَوَّلُ ٱلْحَزمِ ٱلمَشُورَةِ .

The beginning of determination is deliberation.

3. إِيَّاكَ وَ أَنْ يَضْرِب لِسَانَكَ عُنْقَكَ .

Beware that thy tongue does not cut thy neck.

4. إِنَّ ٱلْحَسَنَ شَقْوَةٌ .

Verily beauty is a misery.

5. إِنَّمَا تَغُرُّ مَنْ تَرَى وَ يَغُرَّكَ مَنْ لَا تَرَى .

If thou deceivest him whom thou seest, he whom thou dost not see, will deceive thee.

6. إِذَا كُنْتَ كَذُوبًا فَكُنْ ذَكُورًا .

If thou art a liar be of good memory.

17

7. ‏إِنَّ الْهَوَى شَرِيكُ الْعَمَى‏

Love is the companion of blindness.

8. ‏أَخَذَنِي بِأَطِيرِ غَيْرِي .‏

He punished me for the fault of another.

9. ‏إِنَّ لِلْحِيطَانِ آذَانًا .‏

Verily walls have ears.

10. ‏إِذَا قَالَ الْمَجْنُونُ سَوْفَ أَرْمِيكَ فَاعِدَّ لَهُ رِفَادَةً .‏

When the madman says I will throw at thee, prepare a plaister.

11. ‏إِذَا افْتَقَرَ الْيَهُودِيُّ نَظَرَ فِى حِسَابِهِ الْعَتِيقِ .‏

When the Jew grows poor he looks into his old accounts.

12. ‏بَعْضُ الشَّرِّ أَهْوَنُ مِنْ بَعْضٍ .‏

Some misfortunes are lighter than others.

13. ‏بِعِلَّةِ الدَّايَةِ يُقَبَّلُ الصَّبِىُّ .‏

The child is kissed for the sake of its nurse.

14. ‏تَقِيسُ الْمَلَايِكَةَ إِلَى الْحَدَّادِينَ .‏

Thou comparest angels with jailers.

15. ‏تَحْتَ جِلْدِ الضَّانِ قَلْبُ الْأَذْوُبِ .‏

The heart of a wolf under the skin of a sheep.

16. تَقَارَبُوا بِالْمَوَدَّةِ وَ لَا تَتَّكِلُوا عَلَى ٱلْقَرَابَةِ .

Be kindred by love and put no trust in kin.

17. ٱلتَّدْبِيرُ نِصْفُ ٱلْمَعِيشَةِ .

Good management is the half of a livelihood.

18. ثَمَرَةُ ٱلْعُجْبِ ٱلْمَقْتُ .

The fruit of self-love is hatred.

19. ثَمَرَةُ ٱلْجُبْنِ لَا رِبْحٌ وَ لَا خُسْرٌ .

The fruit of timidity is neither gain nor loss.

20. حَافِظْ عَلَى ٱلصَّدِيقِ وَ لَوْ فِى ٱلْحَرِيقِ .

Adhere to your friend though he be in the flames.

21. ٱلْحُرُّ حُرٌّ وَ إِنْ مَسَّهُ ٱلضُّرُّ .

The freeman is free though misfortune assail him.

22. حَرُّ ٱلشَّمْسِ يَلْجِىءُ إِلَى مَجْلِسِ سَوْءٍ .

The heat of the sun makes us sit down in a bad place.

23. ٱلْحَيَاءُ مِنَ ٱلْإِيمَانِ .

Modesty is a part of religion.

24. ٱلْحِرْصُ قَايِدُ ٱلْحِرْمَانِ .

Avarice is the leader of disappointment.

25.

الْحَكِيمُ يَقْنَعُ ٱلنَّفْسَ بِٱلْكَفَافِ .

The wise man contents himself with a sufficiency.

26.

الْحُرُّ عَبْدٌ إِذَا طَمِعَ وَ ٱلْعَبْدُ حُرٌّ إِذَا قَنِعَ .

The freeman when desirous of any thing is a slave, and the slave when contented is free.

27.

الْحَقُّ خَيْرُ مَا قِيلَ .

Truth is the best that can ever be said.

28.

الْحَسَدُ دَاءٌ لَا يَبْرَأُ .

Envy is a disease that can never be cured.

29.

خِيَارُكُمْ خَيْرُكُمْ لِأَهْلِهِ .

The best among you is he who is best to his family.

30.

خَيْرُ ٱلنَّاسِ مَنْ فَرِعَ لِلنَّاسِ بِٱلْخَيْرِ .

The best of men is he who rejoices in the good of others.

31.

خَالِفْ هَوَاكَ تَرْشُدْ .

Constrain your inclinations, and you will be conducted well.

32.

الْخَيْرُ فِيمَا يَصْنَعُ ٱللَّهُ .

Good is in that which God does.

33.

الْخُضُوعُ عِنْدَ ٱلْحَاجَةِ رَجُولِيَّةٌ .

Submission to necessity is the duty of man.

34. دِمَاءُ ٱلْمُلُوكِ أَشْفَى مِنَ ٱلْكَلَبِ .

The blood of kings cures the madness of dogs.

35. ٱلدَّهْرُ أَرْوَدُ مُسْتَبِدٌّ .

Time goes softly and finishes all things.

36. رُبَّ أَخٍ لَكَ لَمْ تَلِدْهُ أُمُّكَ .

Sometimes he is your brother whom your mother did not bear.

37. رَأْىُ ٱلشَّيْخِ خَيْرٌ مِنْ مَشْهَدِ ٱلْغُلَامِ .

The counsel of an old man is better than the presence of a young one.

38. رُبَّ عَجَلَةٍ تَهَبُ رَيْثًا .

Speed sometimes makes delay.

39. رُبَّ نَعْلٍ شَرٌّ مِنَ ٱلْحَفَا .

A slipper is sometimes worse than a naked foot.

40. رُبَّمَا كَانَ ٱلسُّكُوتُ جَوَابًا .

Silence is often an answer.

41. أَرْسِلْ حَكِيمًا وَ لَا تُوصِهِ .

Send a wise messenger and give him no orders.

42. أَرَى خَالًا وَ لَا مَطَرَ .

I see a heavy cloud but there is no rain.

43.

رُبَّ كَلِمَةٍ سَلَبَت نِعْمَةً .

A single word sometimes destroys favor.

44.

رُبَّ طَرْفٍ أَفْصَحَ مِن لِسَانٍ .

A glance of the eye sometimes says more than the tongue.

45.

رُبَّ طَمَعٍ يَهْدِى إِلَى طَبْعٍ .

Avarice sometimes leads to disgrace.

46.

رُبَّمَا أَرَادَ الأَحْمَقُ نَفْعَكَ فَضَرَّكَ .

The fool who wishes to serve you often injures you.

47.

رُبَّ زَارِعٍ لِنَفْسِهِ حَاسِدٌ سِوَاهُ .

He often sows for himself while another reaps.

48.

رِزْقُ اللهِ لَا كَدُّكَ .

The goodness of God not your labour.

49.

رَأْسُ الدِّينِ المَعْرِفَةُ .

Knowledge is the head of religion.

50.

رُبَّ حَرْبٍ شَبَّت مِن لَفْظَةٍ .

War is often kindled by a single word.

51.

رُبَّ عَطَبٍ تَحْتَ طَلَبٍ .

There is sometimes ruin under what we seek.

52.

زَيْن فِى عَيْنِ وَالِدٍ وَلَدُّه .

In the eye of his father the son is always handsome.

53.

زُرْ غِبًّا تَزْدَدْ حُبًّا .

Visit seldom you will increase love.

54.

ٱلسَّعِيد مَنْ وُعِظَ بِغَيْرِهِ .

He is happy who is taught by the example of another.

55.

أَسْرِعْ فِقْدَانًا تُسْرِعْ وِجْدَانًا .

Quickly seek you will quickly find.

56.

سَائِل ٱللَّه لَا يَخِيب .

He who asks of God will not be deceived.

57.

ٱلسِّنَّوْر ٱلصَّيَّاح لَا يَصْطَاد شَيًّا .

A noisy cat catches no mice.

58.

ٱلشُّبْهَة أُخْت ٱلْحَرَامِ .

Doubt is sister of the unlawful.

59.

سَاوِرْ فِى أَمْرِكَ ٱلَّذِين يَخْشَوْن ٱللَّه .

Consult in your affairs those who fear God.

60.

شَرّ ٱلنَّاس مَنْ لَا يُبَالِى أَنْ يَرَاه ٱلنَّاس مُسِيئًا .

The worst of men is he who does not heed men seeing his wickedness.

61.

اَلشَّبَاب جُنُون بَرْوَة ٱلْكِبَر.

Youth is a madness, old age is its cure.

62.

اَلشَّيْطَان لَا يُخَرِّب كَرْمَهُ.

The devil does not destroy his own vineyard.

63.

اَلصَّمْت يَكْسِب أَهْلَهُ ٱلْمَحَبَّة.

Silence procures love for those who keep it.

64.

اَلصِّدْق عِزّ وَ الكَذُوب خُضُوع.

Truth is honor and falsehood vileness.

65.

اَلصَّبْر مِفْتَاح ٱلْفَرَح.

Patience is the key of pleasure.

66.

اَلصِّنَاعَة فِى ٱلْكَفّ أَمَان مِنَ ٱلْفَقْر.

Art in the hand is safety from poverty.

67.

طُول اللِّسَان يَقْصِر ٱلْأَجَل.

The length of the tongue shortens life.

68.

اَلْعَادَة طَبِيعَة خَامِسَة.

Custom is a fifth nature.

69.

غَضَب ٱلْعُشَّاق كَمَطَر ٱلرَّبِيع.

The anger of lovers is like a spring rain.

70. غَضَبُ ٱلْجَاهِلِ فِى قَوْلِهِ وَ غَضَبُ ٱلْعَاقِلِ فِى فِعْلِهِ .

The wrath of the fool in words, and the anger of the wise
in deeds.

71. غُبَارُ ٱلْعَمَلِ خَيْرٌ مِنْ زَعْفَرَانِ ٱلْعَطْلَةِ .

The dust of labour is better than the saffron of idleness.

72. كُلُّ كَلْبٍ بِبَابِهِ نَبَّاحٌ .

Every dog barks at his own door.

73. كُلُّ ٱمْرِىءٍ فِيهِ مَا يُرمَى بِهِ .

In every man there is what may be attacked.

74. كَمَا تَدِينُ تُدَانُ .

As you pay so you shall be paid.

75. ٱلْكَلْبُ لَا يَنْبَحُ مَنْ فِى دَارِهِ .

The dog does not bark at one in his house.

76. لِكُلِّ مَقَامٍ مَقَالٌ .

Every place has its speech.

77. لَيْسَ عَلَى ٱلشَّرْقِ طَخَآءٌ يَحْجُب .

No cloud hides the light of the sun.

78. لَا يَضُرُّ ٱلسَّحَابَ نَبَّاحُ ٱلْكِلَابِ .

The barking of dogs does not injure the clouds.

79.

لَا تَهْرِفْ بِمَا لَا تَعْرِفْ .

Praise not that which you know not.

80.

لَا أَفْعَلُ كَذَا حَتَّى يَلِجَ ٱلْجَمَلُ فِى سَمِّ ٱلْخِيَاطِ .

I will not do this till a camel goes through the eye of a needle.

81.

لَا قَرَارَ عَلَى زَارٍ مِنَ ٱلْأَسَدِ .

There is no rest when the lion roars.

82.

لَا يَجْمَعُ سَيْفَانِ فِى غَمْدٍ .

Two swords cannot be in one sheath.

83.

لَا يَقُلُّ ٱلْحَدِيدَ إِلَّا ٱلْحَدِيدُ .

Iron is only cut by iron.

84.

لَا تَأْمَنِ ٱلْأَحْمَقَ وَ بِيَدِهِ ٱلسَّيْفُ .

*Do not think you are safe from a fool while he has a sword
in his hand.*

85.

لَا تَسْأَلِ ٱلصَّارِخَ وَ ٱنْظُرْ مَا لَهُ .

Do not question one who wants help, but look to his condition.

86.

لَا يَنْفَعُ حَذَرٌ مِنْ قَدَرٍ .

Caution is vain against the decree of God.

87.

لَا تَكْذِبَنَّ وَ لَا تَشَبَّهَنَّ .

Neither lie nor be like one who lies.

88.

لَا تَذْهَبُ ٱلْعُرْفُ بَيْنَ ٱللَّهِ وَ ٱلنَّاسِ .

Benevolence passes not away between God and man.

89.

لَا تَأْمَنِ ٱلْأَمِيرَ إِذَا غَشَّكَ ٱلْوَزِيرُ .

Do not think you are safe from the prince when the Vazir hates you.

90.

مَنْ لَمْ يَأْسَ عَلَى مَا فَاتَهُ أَرَاحَ نَفْسَهُ .

He who is not afflicted by what he loses keeps his mind tranquil.

91.

مَنْ حَفَرَ مُغْوَاةً وَقَعَ فِيهَا .

He who digs a pit falls into it.

92.

مَنْ يُطِلْ ذَيْلَهُ يَطَأْ فِيهِ .

He who wears a long skirt treads upon it.

93.

مَنْ خَشِيَ ٱلذِّئْبَ أَعَدَّ كَلْبًا .

He who fears the wolf procures a dog.

94.

مَنْ سَلَّ سَيْفَ ٱلْبَغْيِ قُتِلَ بِهِ .

He who draws the sword of injustice shall be killed by it.

95.

مَنْ أُعْجِبَ بِرَأْيِهِ ضَلَّ .

He who admires his own council errs.

96.

مَنِ ٱسْتَغْنَى بِعِلْمِهِ زَلَّ .

He who is content with his own knowledge falls.

97.

مَنْ تَسَمَّعَ سَمِعَ مَا يَكْرَهُ .

He who listens hears what displeases him.

98.

مَنْ أَنْفَقَ وَلَمْ يَحْسُبْ هَلَكَ وَلَمْ يَدْرِ.

He who spends and does not reckon, loses and does not know.

99.

مَنْ نَامَ رَأَى الْأَحْلَامَ .

He who sleeps sees dreams.

100.

مَنْ زَرَعَ الْمَعْرُوفَ حَصَدَ الشُّكْرَ.

He who sows benevolence reaps thanks.

THE following Extracts have been chosen as Examples of the plain and simple style, in which the Arabian Chronicles are usually written, and are printed without the vowel-points, to supply which will be a useful exercise to the learner.

و فيها اعنى سنة ثمانين و ماية و قيل سنة سبع و سبعين
و ماية توفى سيبويه النحوى يقرية يقال لها البيضاء من قرى
شيراز، واسم سيبويه عمرو بن عثمان بن قنبر كان اعلم
المتقدمين و المتاخّرين بالنحو و جميع كتب الناس فى النحو
عيلة الى كتاب سيبويه، و اشتغل على الخليل بن احمد، و
كان عمره لما مات نيفًا و اربعين سنة، و قيل توفى بالبصرة
سنة احدى و ستين و ماية، قال ابو الفرج الجوزى توفى سيبويه
فى سنة اربع و تسعين و ماية و عمره اثنتان و ثلثون سنة و
انه توفى بمدينة ساوه، و ذكر خطيب بغداد عن ابن دريد
ان سيبويه مات بشيراز و قبره بها، و سيبويه لقبه و هو لفظ
فارسى و معناه بالعربية رَائِحَة التفاح و قيل انما لقب سيبويه
لأَنَّه كان جميل الصورة وجنتاه كَأَنَّهما تفاحتان، و جرى له
مع الكساى البحث المشهور فى قولِكَ كنتُ أَظنّ لسعة العقرب

اشد من لسعة الزنبور، قال سيبويه فاذا هو هى و قال الكساى

فاذا هو ايّاها، و انتصر الخليفة للّكساى، فحمل سيبويه من

ذلك، همّا و ترك العراق و سافر الى جهة شيراز و توفى هناك،

و فيها (سنة) قدم رسل ملك الروم الى بغداد، فلما

استحضروا عَبِىَ لهم العسكر و صَفّت الدار بالاسلحة و انواع الزينة و

كان جملة العسكر المصفوف، حينئذ ماية الف و ستين الف ما

بين راكب و واقف، و وقف الغلمان الحجرية بالزينة و المناطق

المحيّلات و وقف الخدام الخصيان كذلك و كانوا سبعة الاف

خادم اربعة الاف خادم ابيض و ثلاثة الاف اسود، و وقف

الحجاب كذلك وهم حينئذ سبعماية حاجب، و القيت

المراكب و الزيارق فى الدجلة باعظم زينة و زُيِّنَت دار الخلافة و

كانت الستور المعلّقة عليها ثمانية و ثلثين الفا ستر منها ديباج

مذهبة اثنى عسر الفا و خمسماية و كانت البسطا اثنين و عشرين

الفا، و كان هناك ماية سَبُع مع ماية سَبّاعٍ، و كان من جملة

الزينة شجرة من ذهب و فضة تَشْتَمَل على ثمانية عشر غصنا و

على الاغصان و القضبان الطيور و العصافير من الذهب و الفضة و كذلك الوراق من الذهب و الفضة و الاغصان تتمايل بحركاتٍ موضوعةٍ و الطيور تصفر بحركات مرتّبة و شهد الرسول من العظمة ما يطول شرحه و احضر بين يدى المقتدر و صار الوزير يُبَلِّغ كلامد الى الخليفة و يرد الجواب عن الخليفة ،

و فيها توفى ابو العلا احمد بن سليمان المعرّى الاعمى و له نحو ست و ثمانين سنة، و اختلف فى عماه و الصحيح انه عَمِى فى صغره من الجدرى و هو ابن ثلاث سنين، و قيل ولد اعمى، و كان عالما لغويا شاعرا، و دخل بغداد سنة تسع و تسعين و ثلثمائة و اقام بها سنة و سبعة اشهر و استفاد من علمايها و لم يَتَلَمَّذْ ابو العلا لاحد اصلا، ثم عاد الى المعرّة و لزم بيته و طبت الارض ذكره و نقلت عنه اشعار و اقوال علم بها فساد عقيدته و نسب الى التمذهب بمذهب الهنود لتركه اكل اللحم خمسا و اربعين سنة و كذلك البيض و اللبن، و كان يحَرِّم إِيلام الحيوان، و له مصنّفات كثيرة، و كان يظهر الكفر و يزعم ان لقوله باطنا و انه مسلم فى الباطن،

و فيها توفى الشيخ الرييس ابو على الحسين بن عبد الله

بن سينا البخارى و كان والده من اهل بلخ و انتقل منها الى

بخارا فى ايّام الامير نوح بن منصور السامانى ثم تزوّج امراة بقرية

افشنة و قطن بها و وُلِدَ له الشيخ الرييس و اخوه بها و ختم

الرييس القران و هو ابن عشر سنين و قرأَ الحكمة على ابن عبد

الله الناتلى و حلّ اقليدس و المجسطى و اشتغل فى الطب و

اتقن ذلك كله و هو ابن ثمانيه عشر سنه و كان ببخارا ثم انتقل

منها الى كركنج و هى بالعربى الجرجانية ثم انتقل الى اماكن

شتّى حتّى اتى الى جورجان فاتصل به ابو عبد الله الجورجانى

اكبر اصحاب الشيخ الرييس المذكور، ثم انتقل الى الرى و

اتصل بخدمة مجد الدولة بن فخر الدولة ابى الحسين على بن

ركن الدولة بن بويه ، ثم خدم شمس المعالى قابوس بن وشمكير،

ثم فارقه و قصد علاَّ الدولة بن كاويه باصفهان و خدمه و تقدّم

عنده ، ثم ان الرييس المذكور مرض بالصرع و القولنج و ترك الحمية

ومضى الى همدان و هو مريض و مات بهمدان ، و كان عمره

ثمانيا و خمسين سنة و مصنّفاته و فضايله مشهورة ، و قد كفّر

الغزالى ابنَ سين المذكور و صرّح بذلك فى كتابه الموسوم بالمنّقِذ

من الضلال ، و كذلك كفّر ابا نصر الفارابى ، و من الناس مَن

يرى رجوع ابن سينا الى الشرايع و اعتقادها ، و حكى الريس

ابو على المذكور فى المقالة الاولى من الفن الخامس من طَبيعيّات

الشفاء قال و قد صحّ عندى بالتواتر ما كان ببلاد جورجان فى

زماننا من امر لعلّه يزن ماية و خمسين منّا نزل من الهوا فنشب

فى الارض ثم نبا نبوةَ الكُرةِ التى يّرمى بها الحايطَ ثم عاد فنشب

فى الارض فسمع الناس لذلك صوتا عظيما هايلا ، فلما تفقدوا

حاله ظفروا به و حملوه الى والى جورجان ، ثم كاتبه سلطان

خراسان محمود بن سبكتكين يرسم بانفاذه او انفاذ قطعة منه فتعذّر

نقله لثقله فحاولوا كسر قطعة منه فما كانت إلَّتُ تعمل فيه الّا

بجهد و كانت كل آلةٍ تعمل فيه تنكسر ، لكنهم فصلوا منه آخِرَ

الامرِ شيا فانفذوه اليه و رام ان يطبع منه سيفا فتعذر عليَه ، و

حكَى ان جملة ذلك الجوهر كان ملتيما *من اجزاء جاورسية

صغار مستديرة التصفف بعضها ببعض ، قال و هذا الفقيه عبد

الواحد الجورجانى صاحبى شاهد ذلك كله ،

-----

* From—لَأَمَ

ذكر ظهور التتر، فى هذه السنة كان ظهور التتر و فتكهم بالمسلمين، و لم ينكب المسلمون باعظم مما نكبوا فى هذه السنة، فمن ذلك ما كان من تمكن الفرنج بملكهم دمياط و قتلهم اهلها و أُسرهم، و منه المصيبة الكبرى و هو ظهور التتر و تملكهم فى المدة القريبة اكثر بلاد السلام و سَفَك دمايهم و سَبَّى حريمهم و ذراريهم، و لم يفجع المسلمون مذ ظهر السلام مثل هذه الفجيعة ؛،

و فيها خرجوا على علاء الدين محمد خوارزمساه بن تكش و عبروا نهر سيحون و معهم ملكهم جنكزخان لعنه الله تعالى فاستولوا على بخارا رابع ذى الحجة من هذه السنة بالأمان و عصت عليهم القلعة، فحاصروها و ملكوها و قتلوا كل مَن بها، ثم قتلوا اهل البلاد عن آخرهم ؛،

من تاريخ ظهور التتر تأليف محمد بن احمد بن على المنشى النَسَوِى كاتب انشاء جلال الدين، قال ان مملكة الصين متسعة دورها ستة اشهر، و قد انقسمت من قديم الزمان ستة اجزاء كل جزو منها مسيرة شهر يتولى امره خان (و هو بلغتهم الملك) نيابة عن خانهم الاعظم، و كان خانهم الكبير الذى عاصر

خوارزمشاه محمد بن تكش يقال له الطون خان و قد توارث
الخانية كابرا عن كابر (بل كافرا بعد كافر)، و من عادة خانهم
الاقامة بطوغاج و هى واسطة الصين، و كان من زمرتهم فى عصر
المذكور شخص يسمى دوشى خان و هو احد الخانات المتولى احد
اجزاء الستة، و كان مزوّجا بعمة جنكزخان اللعين، و قبيلة
جنكزخان اللعين المعروفة بقبيلة التَّمَرْخى سكّان البرارى و مشتاهم
موضع يُسَمَّى ارغون، و هم المشهورون بين التتر بالشر و الغدر،
و لم تر ملوك الصين ارخاء عنانهم لطغيانهم، فاتفق ان دوشى
خان زوج عمة جنكزخان مات، فحضر جنكزخان الى عمة
زايرا و معزّيا، و كان الخانان المجاوران لعمل دوشى خان المذكور
المتوفى من الجهتين، فارسلت امراة دوشى خان الى كشلى
خان و الخان الاخر تنعى اليهما زوجها دوشى خان و انه لم
يخلف ولدا و انه كان حسن جوار لهما و ان ابن اخيها جنكزخان
ان اقيم مقامه يحذو حذو المتوفى فى معاضدتهما، فاجابها
الخانان المذكوران، فلما انهى الامر الى الخان الاعظم الطون
خان انكر تولية جنكزخان و استحقره و انكر على خانين اللذين
فعلا ذلك، فلما جرى ذلك خلعوا طاعة الطون خان و انضمّ
اليهم كل من هو من عشايرهم ثم اقتتلوا مع الطون خان، فولى

منهزما ، فتمكّنوا من بلاده ، ثم ارسل الطون خان و طلب منهم

الصلح و ان يبقوه على بعض البلاد ، فاجابوه الى ذلك ، و

بقى جنكزخان و خانان الاخران مشتركين فى الامر، فاتّفف موت

الخان الاحد و استقلّ بالامر جنكزخان و كشلو خان ثم مات كشلو

خان و قام ابنه (و لقب بكشلوخان ايضا) مقامه ، فاستضعف

جنكزخان خانت كشلوخان بن كشلوخان لصغره و حداثة سنّه و اخلّ

بالقواعيد التى كانت مقرّرة بينه و بين ابيه ، فانفرد كشلو خان

عنى جنكز خان ، فاخرج جنكزخان جيشا مع ابنه دوشى خان بن

جنكزخان و انهزم كشلو خان و تبعه دوشى خان و قتله و عاد

الى جنكزخان· براسه ، فانفرد جنكزخان بالمملكة ، ثم ان جنكزخان

راسل خوارزمشاه محمد بن تكش ، فلم ينتظم ، فجمع جنكزخان

عساكره و التقى مع خوارزمشاه محمد ، فانهزم خوارزمشاه ،

فاستولى جنكرخان على بلاد ما وراء النهر ثم تبع خوارزمشاه

محمد و هو هارب بين يديه حتى دخل بحر طبرستان ، ثم

استولى جنكزخان على بلاد ، ثم كان من خوارزمشاه و من

جنكزخان ما سنذكره ان شاء تعالى ،

ذكر قتل جلال الدين .

و لما تمكّن التتر من بلاد اذربيجان سار جلال الدين يريد

يريد دياربكر ليسير الى الخليفة و يلتجى اليه و يَعْتَضدَ بملوك
الاطراف على التتر و بتخوّفهم عاقبة امرهم ، فنزل بالقرب من امد
و لم يشعر الّا و التتر قد كبسوه ليلا و خالطوا مخيمه ، فهرب
جلال الدين ،، و من تاريخ ظهور التتر تصنيف كاتب انشاء
جلال الدين النسوى المنشى المقدم الذكر فى سنة ست عشرة و
ستماية ما اخترناه و اثبتناه من اخبار خوارزمشاه محمد و ابنه
جلال الدين و المنشى المذكور كان معه ،

فلذلك كان أَخْبَرَ بأَحْوال جلال الدين و والده من غيره ، قال
محمد المنشى المذكور ان خوارزمشاه محمد بن تكش عظّم شانه
و اتّسع ملكه ، و كان له اربعة اولاد قسم البلاد بينهم ، اكبرهم
جلال الدين منكبرنى و فوّض اليه ملك غزنة و باميان و الغور
و بست و تكاباد و زميرداور و ما يليها من الهند ، و فوّض
خوارزم و خراسان و مازندران الى ولده قطب الدين أُزلاغ شاه و
جعله ولّى عهده ، ثم فى اخر وقت عزله عن ولاية العهد و فوّضها
الى جلال الدين منكبرنى ، و فوّض كرمان و كيش و مكران الى
ولده غياث الدين تترشاه و قد تقدّمت اخباره ، و فوّض العراق
الى ولده ركن الدين غورشاه بحيى ، و كان احسن اولاده خَلقا

و خُلقا ، و قتل المذكور التتر بعد موت ابيه ، و ضرب لكل
واحد منهم النوب الخمس فى اوقات الصلوات على عادة الملوك
السلجوقية و انفرد ابوهم خوارزمشاه محمد بنوبة ذى القرنين و انها
تضرب وقتى طلوع الشمس و غروبها و كانت سبعا و عشرين دبدبة
من الذهب قد رصعت بانواع الجوهر ، و كذا باقى الآلات النوبتية ،
و جعل سبعة و عشرين ملكا يضربونها فى أول يوم قرعت ، و
كانوا من اكابر الملوك اولاد السلاطين ، منهم طغريل بن ارسلن
السلجوقى و اولاد غياث الدين صاحب الغور و الملك علاء الدين
صاحب باميان و الملك تلج الدين صاحب البلخ و ولده الملك
الاعظم صاحب ترمذ و الملك سنجر صاحب بخارا و اشباههم ،
و كانت ام خوارزمشاه محمد تركان خاتون من قبيلة بباووت و
هى فرع من فروع يمسك ، و كانت بنت ملك من ملوكهم
تزوّج بها تكش بن ارسلن بن اطسز بن محمد بن انوشتكينى
غرشه ، فلما صار الملك الى ولده محمد بن تكش قدم الى
والدته تركان خاتون قبايل يمسك من الترك ، فعظم شان ابنها
السلطان محمد بهم ، فلم يملك ابنها اقليما آلا و افرد لخاصّها
منه ناحية جليلة ، و كانت ذات مَهَابة و رأى و كانت تنتصف
للمظلوم من الظالم و كانت جسورة على القتل و عظم شانها

بحيث ان ورد توقيعان عنها و عن ابنها السلطان محمد ينظر
الى تاريخهما فيعمل بالاخير منهما ، و كان طغر توقيعها عصمة
الدنيا و الدين الخ تركان ملكة نساء العالمين ، و علامتها اعتصمت
بالله وَحْدَهُ ، قال المُؤَلِّف المذكور ثم ان خوارزمشاه محمدا لما
هرب من التتر بماوراء النهر و عبر جيحون ثم سار الى خراسان
و التتر تتبعه ثم هرب من خراسان و وصل الى عراق العجم و نزل
عند بسطام احضر عشرة صناديق ثم قال انها كلها جواهر لا يعلم
قيمتها ، ثم اشار الى صندوقين منها و قال ان فيهما ما يساوي
خراج الارض بجملتها ، ثم امر بحملها الى قلعة ازدهن ، و هي
من امنع قلاع الارض ، و اخذ خط النايب بها بوصول الصناديق
المذكورة بختومها ، ثم ان التتر ادركت السلطان محمد المذكور،
فهرب و ركب في المركب و لحقه التتر و رموه بالنشاب و نجى
السلطان منهم و قد حصل له مرض ذات الجنب ، قال و قد
وصل الى جزيرة في البحر و اقام بها فريدا طريدا لا يملك طارفا
ولا تليدا و المرض يزداد ، و كان في اهل مازندران اناس يتقربون
اليه بالماكول و ما يشتهيه ، فقال في بعض الايام اشتهى ان
يكون عندى فرس يرعى حول خَيْمتى ، و قد ضربت له خيمة
صغيرة ، فأهْدى له فرس اصفر ، و كان للسلطان محمد المذكور

ثلثون الف جشار من الخيل ، و كان اهدى اليه شى و هو على
تلك الحالة من ماكول و غيره يطلق لذلك الشخص شيا ، و
لم يكن من يكتب التواقيع ، فيتولى ذلك الرجل كتابة توقيعه
بنفسه و كان يعطى مثل السكين و المنديل علامة باطلاق البلاد و
الاموال ، فلما تولى ابنه جلال الدين امضى جميع ما اطلقه ابوه
بالتواقيع و العلام ، ادركت السلطان المنية و هو بالجزيرة على
تلك الحالة و غسله شمس الدين محمود بن بلاغ الجاويش و
مقرّب الدين مَقَّدَّم الفرّاشين ، و لم تكن عنده ما يكفن به ،
فكفن بقميصه و دفن بالجزيرة فى سنة سبع عشرة و ستماية بعد ان
كان بابّة مباصَ مباصَ ملوك الارض و عظماؤها يشتدّون بجنابه و
يتفاخرون بلثم ترابه و رقى الى درجة الملوكية جماعة من مماليكه
و حاشيته ،

ثم سار جلال الدين بعد موت ابيه السلطان محمد من الجزيرة
الى خوارزم ثم هرب من التتر و لحق بغزنة فهرب جلال الدين
من غزنة الى الهند ، فلحقه جنكزخان على ماء السند ، فتصافافا
صبيحةَ يوم الأَرْبَعَاء لثمان من شَوّال سنة ثمانى عشرة و
ستماية، و كانت الكرة آولا على جنكزخان ثم عاودت على جلال

الدين و حال بينها الليل و ولى جلال الدين مُنهَزِمًا و اسر ولد

جلال الدين (و هو ابن سبع او ثمان سنين) و قتل بين يدى

جنكزخان صبرا، و لما عاد جلال الدين الى حافة ماء السند

كسيرا راى والدته و لم ولده و جماعة من حريمه يَصِحَّنَ بالله بالله

عليك اقتلنا او خلّصنا من الاسر، فامر بهِنَّ نَغَرِقنَ، و هذه من

عجايب البلايا و نوادر المصايب و الزرايا، ثم اقتحم جلال الدين

و عسكره ذلك النهر العظيم فنجى منهم الى البَرّ تقدير اربعة

الاف رجل حَفَاة عَرَاة و رمى الموج جلال الدين مع ثلثة من

خواصّه الى موضع بعيد و فقده اصحابه ثلثة ايام و بقى اصحابه

لفقده حايرين و فى تيه الفكر سايرين الى ان اتصل بهم جلال

الدين، ثم جرى جلال الدين و بينه و بين اهل تلك البلاد

وقايع انتصر فيها جلال الدين و وصل الى لهاور من الهند، و

لما عزم جلال الدين على العَود الى جهة العراق استناب بهلوان

ازبك على ما كان يملكه من بلاد الهند و استناب معه حسن

قراق و لقبه وفا الملك، و فى سنة سبع و عشرين و ستمائة

طرن وفا ملك بهلوان ازبك و استولى وفا ملك على ما كان

يليه البهلوان من بلاد الهند، ثم ان جلال الدين عاد من الهند

و وصل الى كرمان فى سنة احدى و عشرين و ستماية و قاسى و

عسكره فى البَرَارى القاطعة بين كرمان و الهند شدايد و وصل معه

اربعة الاف رجل بعضهم ركاب ابقار و بعضهم ركاب حمير، ثم

سار جلال الدين الى خوزستان و استولى عليها ، ثم استولى على

ساير بلاد اران ، ثم ان جلال الدين نقل اباه من الجزيرة الى قلعة

ازدهن و دفنه بها ، و لما استولى التتر على قلعة المذكورة

نبشوه و احرقوه ، و هذا كان فعلهم بمن عرفوا قبره ، فانهم

نبشوا محمود بن سبكتكين من غزنة و احرقوا عِظَامَهُ ؛؛

ثم ذكر ما تقدمت الاشارة اليه من استيلاء جلال الدين على

خلاط و غيره ، ثم ذكر نزوله على جسر قريب امد و ارساله

يَسْتَجِدَّ الملك الاشرف بن الملك العادل، فلم ينجده ، فعزم

جلال الدين على المسير الى اصفهان ثم انثنى عزمه عنه و بات

بنزلة و شرب تلك الليلة و سكر سكرا خمارُه دوارُ الراس و تقطّع

الانفاس ، و احاط التتر به و بعسكر مصبحين

فمساهم و بسطهم حرير و صبحهم و سطهم تراب ،

و من فى كفّه منهم قناة كمن فى كفّه منهم خضاب ،

و احاطت اطلاب بخركاه جلال الدين و هو نايم سكران ،

فحمل بعض عسكره و هو ارخان و كشف التتر عن الخركاه

و دخل بعض الخواص و اخذ بيد جلال الدين و ايقظه و عليه
طاقية بيضا و اركبه الفرس ، و ساق ارخان مع التتر و تبعه
التتر ، و قال جلال الدين لارخان انفرد عنّى بحيث يشتغل
التتر بتبع سوادك ، و كان ذلك خطاء منه ، فان ارخان تبعه
جماعة من العسكر و صاروا تقدير اربعة الاف فارس و قصد
اصفهان و استولى عليها مدة ، و لما انفرد جلال الدين عن
ارخان ساق الى امد ، فلم يَمّكِن من الدخول الى امد ،
فسار الى قرية من قرى .ميفارقين طالبا شهاب الدين غازى بن
الملك العادل صاحب ميفارقين ، ثم لحقه التتر فى تلك
القرية ، فهرب جلال الدين الى جبل هناك و به اكراد
يتحفظون الناس ، فاخذوه و سلخوه و ارادوا قتله ، فقال جلال
الدين لاحدهم انى انا السلطان ، فاستبقنى ، اجعلك ملكا ، فاخذه
الكردى و اتى به الى امراته و جعله عندها و مضى الكردى
الى الجبل لاحضار ما له هناك ، فحضر شخص كردى و معه حربة
و قال للامراة لِمَ لا تقتلون هذا الخوارزمى ، فقالت الامراة لا
سبيل الى ذلك فقد آمنه زوجى ، فقال الكردى انه السلطان و
قد قتل لى اخا بخلاط خيرا منه ، و ضربه بالحربة فقتله ، و كان
جلال الدين اسمر قصيرا تركى الشارة و العبارة ، و كان يتكلّم
بالفارسية ايضا ، و كان يكاتب الخليفة بمبتداء الامر على ما كان

يكاتبه ابوه خوارزمشاه محمد فكان يكتب خادمه المِطوَّاع منكبرنى

ثم بعد اخذ خلاط كاتبه بعبده، و كان يكتب الى ملك الروم

و ملوك مصر و الشام اسمه و اسم ابيه و لم يرض ان يكتب

لاحد منهم خادمه او اخوه و غير ذلك، و كانت علامته على

تواقيعه النصرة من الله وَحْدَه، و كان اذا كاتب صاحب الموصل

او شبهه يكتب له هذه العلامة تعظيما عن ذكر اسمه، و كان

يكتب العلامة بقلم غليظ، و كان جلال الدين يخاطب بخذاوند

عالم أى ماحب العالم، و كان مقتله فى منتصف شَوَّال من

هذه السنة (اعنى سنة ثمان و عشرين و ستماية) و هذا ما

نقلناه من تاريخ محمد المنشى و هو ممن كان فى خدمة جلال

الدين الى ان قتل و كان كاتب الانشاء الذى له و كان محظيا

متقدّما عنده،

Extracts from the Chronicle of the Sultán Al Malik As Sálih Imád ud dín Abú 'l Fadá Ismáíl.

AND in this, I mean the year 180, and it is said the year 177, died Sibúyah the grammarian, in a village called Baidhá, one of the villages near Shíráz. And his name was Sibúyah Amrú ibn Othmán ibn Kunbar; he was more learned in grammar than any who have preceded, or followed him, and all the books of men upon grammar, are nothing to the book of Síbúyah. He studied in the school of Khalíl ibn Ahmad. And when he died his age was more than 40 years. It is also said that he died at Basrah in the year 161. Abu'l Faraj al Júzí however relates that Sibúyah died in the year 194, and that he was 32 years old; and that he died in the city of Sáwah. Khálib Baghdád relates, on the authority of Ibn Duraid, that Sibúyah died at Shíráz, and that his tomb is there. Sibúyah was his cognomen; this is a Persian word, and its meaning in Arabic is, "the odour of apples;" and it is said, that he was so called, because he was handsome of countenance, and as if his two cheeks were two apples. Between him and Kasáí was the well-known dispute on the words, "I thought the sting of a scorpion worse than the sting of a wasp." Sibúyah maintained that this (the word sting) was in the nominative (هى), and Kasáí maintained that it was in the accusative (إِيَّاهَا), and the Khalif decided in favor of Kasáí, and Sibúyah bore great distress from this, and he left Irák, and travelled to the neighbourhood of Shíráz, and died there.

And in this (year) came ambassadors from the King of Rúm
to Baghdád; and when they were presented, the army was drawn
out, and the palace was decorated with armour, and arms, and
various ornaments; and the whole army was drawn up in the
order of battle.   There were then 160,000 cavalry and infantry;
and the pages of the palace were drawn out, splendidly dressed,
and wearing costly girdles; and the eunuchs were drawn up in
the same way, and of these there were 7000; 4000 white and
3000 black, and the chamberlains in attendance were 700; and
there were vessels and boats on the Tigris, splendidly decorated;
and the palace of the Khalíf was richly ornamented.   There were
38,000 veils (or pieces of tapestry) suspended; 12,600 of these
were interwoven with gold; and there were 22,000 rich carpets
laid down.   And there were there 100 lions, with their 100 keepers.
But among the ornaments there was a tree of gold and silver,
containing 18 branches, and on the branches and twigs, were birds
of various sorts of gold and silver; the leaves were also of gold
and silver; and the branches waved by certain springs, and the birds
sang by springs disposed there also; and the ambassador testified
his astonishment at the magnificence that was displayed; and he was
presented to the (Khalíf) Muktadir, and the vazir interpreted his
words to the Khalíf, and returned him the Khalíf's answer.

And in this (year) died Abu'l Olá Ahmad ibn Sulaiman al
Moarri the blind.   He was about 86 years old.   There is a difference about his blindness; but the truth is, that he became
blind in his childhood from the small pox; he was then a child
of three years old.   The other report is, that he was born blind.
He was most learned in philology and poetry.   And he entered
Baghdád in the year 399; and resided there one year and seven

months; and he associated with the learned, but Abu'l Olá did not become the disciple of any one in particular. Then he returned to Moarra, and resided in his own house, while the world proclaimed his glory, and his poems and sayings were repeated everywhere; by these is known the corruption of his faith; and his perversion to the sect of the Hindús is known by his abstaining for 45 years from the eating of meat or eggs, and the drinking of milk; he held it unlawful to injure any living thing; his writings were very numerous, and his infidelity appears in them; but he pretended that there was a secret sense in his writings, and that he was spiritually a Muslim.

And in this (year) died the Shaikh ar Raíís ibn Áli Alhusain ibn Abdallah ibn Sína al Bukhárí. His father was a native of Balkh, who removed from thence to Bukhárá in the time of the Amír Núh ibn Mansúr as-Sámání; he then married a woman of the village of Afsanah, and resided there, and the Shaikh Ar Raíís was born there, as well as his brother, and the Raíís read through the Korán when he was a boy of 10 years old. And he studied the philosophy of Alí ibn Abdallah an-Nátulí, and he went through Euclid, and the Almagest, and applied himself to medicine, and completed all these studies when he was a youth of 18, and was still at Bukhárá; then he removed from thence to Kurkanj, and this in Arabic is Jurjániyah; then he journeyed hither and thither, till he came to Júrján; then Ibn Abdallah Al Júrjání attached himself to him, and was the greatest of the companions of the said Shaikh ar Raíís. Then he removed to Rai and entered the service of Majd ad daulah ibn Fahkr ad daulah ibn 'lhusain Ali ibn Rukn ad daulah ibn Buyah. Then he was in the service of Shams al Mââlí Kábús ibn Washmagír.

He then left him, and went to Âlá ad daulah ibn Káwíh at
Isfahán, and was much preferred by him. Then the said Raíís
became ill with the epilepsy and cholic, and he neglected medicine, and he went to Hamadán, and became ill and died there.
He was 58 years old; his writings and great accomplishments
are well known. Al Ghazálí accuses Ibn Síná of infidelity, and
openly charges him with it in his book called *The Deliverer
from Error*. In the same way he charges with infidelity Abú
Nasr al Fárábí; some however believe, that Ibn Síná returned
to the true faith. The Raíís Abú Ali aforesaid, in the first part
of the fifth section of his book *Of the Nature of Medicines*,
writes thus. Among the events that came to my knowledge, in
the country of Júrján in our time, was that of a substance weigh-
ing perhaps 150 mina, which fell from the air, and struck into
the ground, then rebounded like a ball repelled by a wall; it
then returned and fixed in the ground. Some people on the spot
hearing at the same time a loud and terrible sound, and when
they sought to find out its nature they were unable to do so,
and they carried it to the Governor of Júrján, and the Sultán
of Khurásán Mahmúd ibn Sabaktagín wrote to him, that he
should send it to him, or should send a portion of it; and he
excused himself from sending it on account of its weight; and
they sought the breaking of a portion from it, and there was no
diminution made in it but with great labor, and all the imple-
ments that were used upon it were broken; but they divided, at
last, a piece from it, and sent it to him, and he desired that a
sword should be made of it, which was done with great difficulty;
and it is related that the whole of this substance was composed
of little round particles like millet, adhering together; and Al
Fakíh Abd al Wáhid al Júrjání, my companion, was the witness of this.

History of the Invasion of the Tatars.

In this year the Tatar invasion occurred, and their attack of the Muslims, who never indured greater distress than what they suffered this year; for at that time it was that the Franks accomplished the conquest of Damietta, with the slaughter and captivity of its inhabitants.

But the greatest affliction was the invasion of the Tatars, and their conquest in a short space of time, of the greatest portion of the territories of the Muslims, the spilling of their blood, and the taking captive their females and their children. The Muslims never suffered from the first rise of Islam such dreadful adversity.

It was in this year that they marched against Âlá ad dín Muhammad * Khwárizmsháh ibn Takash, and they crossed the river Sihún, and with them was their king Jangizkhán, May the most high God curse him! and they took Bukhara by capitulation, on the 4th of Dzú'l hijjah of this year, but the citadel held out, and they besieged and took it, and they slew every one that was in it. Then they butchered the people of the surrounding territories, unto the very last of them.

Extract from the History of the Invasion of the Tatars; the work of Muhammad ibn Ahmad ibn Áli al Munshí, an Nasawí Secretary of Jalál ad dín. He says thus.

The kingdom of China is of vast extent; its circumference a six month's journey. From ancient times it has been divided into

---

* Pronounce "Kárizm," as in the Persian word "Khwájah," commonly written "Coja," *a merchant.*

19

six parts, each part a month's journey in extent, and each is
governed by a Khán (which in their language means a king,) in
turn governed by the great Khan. And the great Khan, with
whom Khwárizmsháh Muhammad ibn Takash was cotemporary,
was called Altún Khán, he had inherited the power of Khan by
hereditary right, great prince after great prince; (verily infidel
after infidel) and the usual abode of the Khán was at Túgháj,
which is in the centre of China. And among them (the Kháns)
at the time aforesaid, was a person named Túshí Khán; and he
was one of the Kháns, ruler of one of the six divisions. And
he had married the aunt of Jangizkhán the accursed. And the
tribe of Jangizkhán, the accursed, was the well known tribe
Tamargai, inhabiting the deserts, and their winter quarters were
a place called Arghún. And they were well known among the
Tatars for their wickedness and perfidy. And the kings of China
did not relax the reins of their bridle on account of their perver-
sity. And it happened that Túshí Khán who had married the
aunt of Jangizkhán died, and Jangizkhán went to his aunt visiting,
and consoling. And there were two Kháns residing near the province of the aforesaid Túshí Khán deceased on either side. And
the widow of Túshí Khán sent an ambassador to Kashlú Khán
and the other Khán, announcing the death of her husband Túshí
Khán, and that he had left no son, reminding them how good a
neighbour he had been to them, and that she wished to put her
brother's son Jangizkhán in his place, that he might occupy the
seat of the deceased by their assistance. And the two Kháns
aforesaid agreed to this; and when this news came to the great
Khán Altún Khán, he disapproved the appointment of Jangizkhán
to the government, and despised him, and disapproved the con-
duct of the two Kháns; and when that news came to them, they
threw off obedience to Altún Khán, and every member of their

tribes was collected around them, and they fought with Altún
Khán. And he turned his back and fled, and they took possession of his territories. Then Altún Khán sent an ambassador
and requested peace, and that they would leave him a portion of
his territories, and they consented to that; and Jangizkhán, and
the two other Kháns, remained associated together in alliance.
And the death of one Khán happened; and Jangizkhán and
Kashlú Khán remained in greater power. Then Kashlú Khán
died, and his son (and he was also named Kashlú Khán) occupied his place, and Jangizkhán conceived that the government
of Kashlú Khán ibn Kashlú Khán was weak on account of his
childhood, and the youth of his age, and he violated the treaties
which had been established between him and the father of Kashlú
Khán. And Kashlú Khán was left alone to oppose Jangizkhán.
And Jangizkhán, with his son Tushí Khán ibn Jangizkhan drew
out his army, and Kashlú Khán fled, and Túshí Khán pursued
him, and slew him, and returned to Jangizkhán with his head.
And Jangizkhán was now alone in power. Then he sent an
ambassador to Khwárizmsháh Muhammad ibn Takash, but they
disagreed, and Jangizkhán collected his armies, and marched
against Khwárizmsháh Muhammad, and Khwárizmsháh was de-
feated, and Jangizkhán conquered the countries of Máwará annahr;
then he pursued Khwárizmsháh, who fled from before him, until
he embarked upon the sea of Tabaristán (the Caspian sea,) and
Jangizkhán subdued all those countries. Then happened between
Khwárizmsháh and Jangizkhán that which we will relate, if it
please the most high God.

Account of the slaying of Jalál ad dín.

AND when the Tatars had subdued Azarbíján Jalál ad dín went to Diyár bakr, that he might journey to the Khalíf, that he might take refuge with him, and might implore help against the Tatars from the kings of those parts, and that he might alarm them with the probable termination of their command. And he encamped in the neighbourhood of Amid; but he made no alliance*, and the Tatars attacked him by night, and penetrated his camp, and Jalál ad dín fled. And all this is extracted from the history of the invasion of the Tatars, the work of An Nasawí, the secretary of Jalál ad din, under the date of the year 616. Whatever we have selected and have learned of the history of Khwárizm sháh Muhammad, and his son Jalál ad dín (is from that work,) and the said secretary was with him, and on this account no one was better informed than he, on all concerning the affairs of Jalál ad dín. And the aforesaid Muhammad al Munshí says, that Khwárizmsháh Muhammad ibn Takash, was of great power, and his kingdom of vast extent; and he had four sons, among whom he divided his territories. The eldest of them was Jalál ad dín Mankbarní, and he gave to him the kingdom

---

* This line ولم يشعر الاّ و التتر كبسوه ليلا و خالطوا مخيمه appears to be corrupted; I hesitate, however, to change a text which has passed under the eye of so great a scholar, and acute a critic, as Reiske; those who are acquainted with his editions of the "Oratores Græci," and "Dionysius Halicarnassensis," are aware, that he was by no means timid in his emendations; his translation here, of what appears to me to be somewhat obscure, is this. "Interea vero dum hæc consiliis versat et molitur, opprimebant ipsum Tatari de nocte derepente in castra penetrantes."

of Ghaznah, and Bámián, and Ghúr, and Bost, and Takábád, and Zamírdáwir, and the adjoining parts of India; and he gave Khwárizm, and Khurásán, and Mázandarán, to his son Kutb ad dín Uzlágh sháh, and appointed him the heir of his empire; then at a later time he removed him from the succession to the empire, and gave it to Jalál ad dín Mankbarní; and he gave Karmán, and Kísh, and Makrán, to his son Ghayát ad dín Tatarsháh, whose history has been given before; and he gave Irák to his son Rukn ad dín Ghúrsháh Yáhya, and he was the fairest of all his sons, both in person and disposition; and the Tatars slew him after the death of his father. And the *Naubat was beaten for each of them at the five hours of prayer, according to the custom of the Saljúkian kings; and their father Khwárizmsháh Muhammad reserved for himself, as his Naubat, the march of Dzú 'l karnain (†Alexander the Great) which was played twice, that is, at sunrise and sun-set, and there were twenty-seven drums of gold set with jewels. Such was the order of the Naubat. And twenty-seven kings played in the band, when the Naubat was beaten at the beginning of the day; and they were great kings, sons of Sultáns, among them was Tughríl ibn Arslán the Saljúkain; and the sons of Ghayát ad dín, the prince of Ghúr; and Al Malik Alá ad dín, the prince of Bámián; and Al Malik Táj ad dín, the prince of Balkh, and his son Al Malik al Âazim, the prince of Tarmad; and Al Malik Sanjar, prince of Bukhárá, and others like them. And the mother of Khwárizmsháh Muhammad was Turkán Khátún,

---

* The "Naubat" is the music played at the five hours of prayer, at the gates of the palaces of Eastern Princes.

† Dzú 'l Karnain, or "*with the two horns*", is the title given to Alexander the Great: no doubt from his effigies upon the Greek medals appearing with the horns of Jupiter Ammon.

of the tribe of Babáwut, which is one of the tribes of Yamsak;
she was the daughter of one of their kings, and Takash ibn Arslán
ibn Atsiz ibn Muhammad ibn Anúshtagíní Ghúrsháh married her;
and when the kingdom came to her son Muhammad ibn Takash,
the tribes of Yamsak among the Turks obeyed Turkán Khátún,
and the state of her son Sultán Muhammad was much increased
in power by them, and her son never conquered any territory without
setting apart a fair portion of it as her private estate; and she
was much revered and of great wisdom; and she dealt out strict
justice to the injured against the unjust, and was very severe;
and her power was so great, that wherever two letters came, one
from her, and one from her son the Sultán Muhammad, their date
was examined, and the orders in the last of the two were performed.
And the superscription of her letters was " *The refuge of the World
and of the Faith, Olagh Turkán, the Queen of created women,*"
and her motto was " *My refuge is in God alone.*"   And the aforesaid author says, that then Khwárizmsháh Muhammad fled from
the Tatars to Má wará annahr, and crossed the Jaihún, and went
to Khurásán; and the Tatars pursued him, and he fled from thence
to Irák al Âjam, and he stopped at Bistam; he brought with him
ten chests, which he said were filled with jewels, whose value was
unknown; and he pointed to two of them, which he said contained
what was equal to a year's income of the whole world.   He commanded that they should be carried to the castle of Azdahan, which
is among the most impregnable castles of the world, and that a
receipt should be taken from the governor of it, for the arrival
of the said chests, with their seals unbroken.   The Tatars however followed the Sultan Muhammad, and he went on board a
boat (on the Caspian sea,) and the Tatars came up, and shot
their arrows after him; and he escaped from them, but sickness
came on him, and he was attacked with the pleurisy.   And he

came to an island in that sea, and remained there a solitary exile destitute of all; and his illness increased, and some of the people of Mázandarán brought him provisions, and what he was in want of. And one day he said, " I wish that I had a horse which could feed round my tent," for they had pitched a small tent for him; and they brought him a bay horse. And this Sultan Muhammad had once had thirty thousand studs of horses. And while in this state, for whatever was brought to him of provisions or such like, he gave something in return, but he had no one with him who could write for him, and he made the man who brought him any thing write a deed of gift, and he gave, as if things of no consequence, his signature to the gift of countries and great wealth; and when his son Jalál ad dín obtained power, he confirmed all that his father had given by deeds or by seals. While in this condition in the island, death seized the Sultán, and the Chaush Shams ad dín Mahmúd ibn Balágh, and Mukarrab ad dín, the chief of the servants of the bedchamber, washed the corpse; and they had no winding sheet; and its place was supplied by his shirt; and he was buried in the island in the year 617. He whose gate had been the refuge of the kings of the earth, the great ones of which had served in his palace courts, and had been proud to kiss the ground before him; and many who had been his servants or attendants arrived at royal dignity.

THEN Jalál ad dín, after the death of his father the Sultan Muhammad, in the island, went to Khwárizm still fleeing from the Tatars; he went to Ghaznah, and from thence to India, and Jangizkhán overtook him at the river Indus; and a battle was fought on Wednesday morning the 8th of the month of Shawwál of the year 618: and at first the battle went against Jangizkhán, but then turned against Jalál ad dín, and night came over them; and Jalál ad dín fled, and his son, a child of seven or eight years old, was taken captive, and he was murdered in cold blood in the presence of Jangizkhán. And when Jalál ad dín fled to the banks of the river Indus, he saw his mother but not his son. And all the females of his haram cried out, "*In the name of God! In the name of God! kill us, or save us from captivity.*" And he commanded, and they were drowned. This was one of the wonders of affliction, and one of the most overwhelming of misfortunes and sorrows! And Jalál ad dín and his army plunged into this great river, and about four thousand escaped to the other side, naked and shoeless. And the waves threw Jalál ad dín, together with three of his private attendants, on a distant spot; and his friends sought him for three days, and continued wandering in search of him, and straying in the desert of anxiety, till Jalál ad dín joined them: then he went forth and there were battles between him and the people of those countries, and Jalál ad dín conquered, and reached Lahor in India. And when he proposed to return to Irák, he appointed Pahlawán Uzbak to govern his territories in India; and along with him he appointed Hasan Karak, and gave him the title of Wafá al Mulk. And in the year 627 Wafá al Mulk expelled Pahlawán Uzbak, and made himself master of all those parts of India that Pahlawán governed. Jalál ad dín went to Karmán in the year 621, and he and his army suffered great distress in the deserts lying between Karmán and India, and there were with him four thousand men, some mounted upon oxen, and some upon asses; then he marched to Khúzistan, and conquered it, as well as the neighbouring districts of Irán. He then removed the body of his father from the island to the castle of Azdahan, and buried him there; and when the Tatars took that castle, they dug up the body and burnt it; this was what they did to every hostile prince whose grave they knew; and in the same way they dug up the body of Mahmúd ibn Sabaktagín at Ghazna, and burnt his bones.

Then is related what has preceded, and to which I refer for an account of the conquest by Jalál ad dín of Khalát, and other places, and his encamping near a bridge in the neighbourhood of Amid; and of his sending to request assistance from Al Malik ibn Al Malik al Âadil; but he did not assist him; then Jalál ad dín meditated a journey to Isfahán, but changed his design, and he passed a night in a certain place, and he drank the whole of that night and became intoxicated, and the sickness of drunkenness is the swimming of the head, and weakening of the mind; and the Tatars surrounded him and his army in the morning.

'Tis evening, and their bed is of silk, and when morning comes their bed is the earth,

And he in whose hand is the lance, is like him in whose hand is the paint for the face.

And they who were in pursuit of him surrounded the tent* of Jalál ad dín, who was sleeping intoxicated; and one of his army, whose name was Urkhán, made an attack upon, and repulsed the Tatars from the tent; and some of his servants entered and took Jalál ad din by the hand, and wakened him; and he had on nothing but a white vest; and they placed him on a horse, and Urkhán fought with the Tatars who pursued him; and Jalál ad dín said to Urkhán, separate yourself from me, so that the Tatars may be occupied in following your troops; but this was an error of his, for Urkhán who was followed by all the soldiers, being about four thousand cavalry, reached Isfahán, and remained

---

* Khargáh, Turkish and Persian for a tent, or pavilion.

master of it for some time. And when Jalál ad dín was alone,
he rode to Amid but could not obtain entrance, and he went to
one of the Villages of Mífárikín seeking Shaháb ud dín Ghází
ibn al Malik al Âadil prince of Mífárikín, and the Tatars overtook him in this village, and he fled to a mountain which was
there, and which was inhabited by Kurds, and they took and
plundered him, and were about to kill him, and he said to one
of them, " *I am the Sultan; preserve my life and I will make
thee a king;*" and the Kurd took him to his wife, and then went
away to the mountain, to his companions who were there. And
there came a certain Kurd holding a short spear, and he said to
the woman, " *Why do you not kill this Khwárizmian?*" and she
said, " *That would not be right, my husband has taken him under
protection.*" And the Kurd replied, " *This is the Sultán who
when at Khalát, killed a brother of mine who was a better man
than he.*" And he struck the Sultán with the spear, and killed
him. And Jalál ad dín was of dark complexion, short of stature,
and Turkish, both in appearance and speech ; though he spoke
Persian also. In the beginning of his reign, when he wrote to
the Khalif, he subscribed himself " *his most humble servant Mank-
barni;*" but after he had taken Khalát, he subscribed himself
only " *his servant;*" when writing to the kings of Rúm, or to
the kings of Egypt or Syria, he wrote merely his name and the
name of his Father; and never chose to write to any one of
them with the epithet of *servant*, or *brother*, or any thing of that
kind; and the inscription upon his letters was this, " *Help is
from God alone;*" and when he wrote to the prince of Mausel,
or such as he, he used this inscription, not condescending to
make use of his name ; and he wrote this with a large reed ;
and he was himself styled *Khudáwand i Âalam;* that is, *Lord
of the World;* and the time of his death was the middle of

Shawwál of this year; I mean 628. And this is what I have extracted from the chronicle of Muhammad al Munshí, who was in the service of Jalál ad dín, until he was killed; he was his private secretary, and was much favoured and preferred by him.

———————

It will be observed in these extracts, that the final vowels are always discarded, thus Jalál ad dín for Jalálu 'l, or ud dini. This is in conformity to constant practice; those vowels never being pronounced in conversation. It has even been questioned whether they were ever any thing more than a grammatical refinement; but there is sufficient evidence, that anciently, they were in common use, though now only employed in poetry, and books of elevated style.

THE chief attention of the student of Arabic Grammar should be given to the rules of Permutation, upon which depend all the irregularities of the Verb: and it will be seen, that they require only a little application, presenting in themselves no difficulty whatever. The many forms which the Plural assumes, will prove but a slight obstacle, as those in most common use are but few, and practice in reading will soon render them familiar. In the Syntax, ·it will also be found that the forms of speech which are most opposed to what may be considered the natural construction of a sentence, are of rare occurrence, so much so, that although the examples given in the preceding Grammar, of such inversions, are not numerous; some of these even, are but seldom met with. The many quotations of such examples which are to be found in more voluminous Grammars, are chiefly taken from Arabian Lexicographers and Grammarians, and it may perhaps be doubted whether like constructions are always to be considered as authorized by the genius of the language.

I subjoin a list of a few of the most useful books, in the order in which I think they may be read to most advantage by the student. If I may be allowed, in such a case, to follow the example of the late Mr Cobbett in recommending my own writings, I would say that the learner should first make himself a thorough master of this book, and if disposed to study the Arabian Commentators and Grammarians, he should preface that study by the careful and repeated perusal of the Grammar of M. de Sacy. For him, however, who has no such intention, the perusal of the " Chrestomathie," followed by the " Kalilah wa Dimnah," will be sufficient, and enable him to read with ease the life of Tímúr.

The Mákamát of Haríri, with the Commentary of M. de Sacy, are adapted only to the use of those who desire to become profound Arabic scholars.

I have not taken any notice of the prosody and metre of the Arabs; M. de Sacy and M. Ewald have each, though upon different principles, given a short treatise upon these subjects, it is my own intention, should I meet any encouragement, to publish a Translation of the "*Darstellung der Arabischen Verskunst*" of M. Freytag, where they are discussed in the most complete manner.

THE END.

GOLII, Lexicon Arabico–Latinum, folio, *Lugd. Bat.* 1653.

Freytag, Lexicon Arabico–Latinum, 4 vols. 4to. *Halæ,* 1830.

This, which is the best Arabic Dictionary, will very well admit of being bound in two vols., which will render it more convenient for constant use.

De Sacy, Grammaire Arabe, 2nd edit. 2 vols. 8vo. *Paris,* 1831.

.... Chrestomathie Arabe, 2nd edit. 3 vols. 8vo. *Paris,* 1827.

.... Anthologie Grammaticale Arabe, 8vo.

.... Calila et Dimna en Arabe, 4to. *Paris,* 1816.

Of this there is an English translation by the Rev. E. Knatchbull.

Ahmadis Arabsiadis Vita Timuri a Manger, 3 vols. 4to. *Leovard,* 1767.

Of this work there is an edition by Golius, but it is the Arabic text only; of which there is an edition also printed at Calcutta.

De Sacy, Les Seances de Hariri en Arabe avec un Commentaire, folio, *Paris,* 1821.

The peculiar style of this work, in which all the eloquence of the Arabic Language is displayed, makes it almost incapable of being translated; should the student, however, wish to have the aid of a translation, he may use a Latin version which was published by M. Peiper, in 4to. at Hirschberg in 1832.

————

The following books will also be found of great use.

Arabum Proverbia, a G. G. Freytag, 2 vols. 8vo. *Bonnæ,* 1838.

Fákihat al Khulafá, a Freytag, 4to. *Bonnæ,* 1832.

Alf Lailah wa Lailah, or the Thousand and One Nights. Arabic text by W. H. Macnaghten, Esq. 4 vols. 8vo. *Calcutta.*